A Survey of Choral Music

A Survey of Choral Music

Homer Ulrich

University of Maryland

THE HARBRACE HISTORY OF MUSICAL FORMS
Under the General Editorship of Karl Geiringer
University of California, Santa Barbara

 Harcourt Brace Jovanovich, Inc.
New York   Chicago   San Francisco   Atlanta

© 1973 by Harcourt Brace Jovanovich, Inc.

ISBN: 0-15-584863-1

Library of Congress Catalog Card Number: 72-92359

Printed in the United States of America

COVER Caricature of Berlioz by Gustave Doré, 1850, from the Music Division—The New York Public Library at Lincoln Center, Astor, Lenox, and Tilden Foundations.

PHOTO CREDITS Page 18, The New York Public Library Picture Collection; page 36, G.D. Hackett Photography; pages 51 and 64, Frederic Lewis, Inc.; pages 75 and 91, The Bettmann Archive; page 114, The New York Public Library Picture Collection; page 133, Austrian National Library; page 153, Culver Pictures; page 171, The New York Public Library Picture Collection; page 189, G.D. Hackett Photography; page 199, Copyright © 1967 by Moeck Verlag, and used by permission; page 209, D.P.A.

Preface

Choral music constitutes one of the oldest genres of music literature. Well established about a century before opera was invented, it reached a high point of development well before chamber music and symphonic music emerged as independent genres, and during its long history it has occupied the attention of countless composers, the great majority of them in the service of the Church.

Since no single book can possibly account for every work in this vast field, the choice of works to be examined and discussed has had to be highly selective. Works that represent historical or stylistic turning points have therefore been emphasized, even when this has meant discussing certain forgotten compositions in detail. On occasion it has been necessary to resort to large general statements covering the music of individual composers or even of extended time spans. An attempt has been made to do justice to the monuments of the literature, within the limits of a small volume. And above all, the main purpose has been to write a connected account embracing the historical evolution and stylistic characteristics of the principal forms of choral music.

The discussion of the various works is partly historical, partly analytical, but always descriptive. Musical structure, text sources and treatment, and kinds of texture loom large in the account. Certain sacred texts are referred to often, and for that reason the principal texts employed in choral music—Mass, Requiem, Magnificat, and the like—are given in the Appendices. In the interest of avoiding ambiguity, the word "choir" has been used consistently in referring to a performing group and "chorus" when speaking of a musical form or setting.

This book was begun during a sabbatical-year leave of absence, spent mainly in Italy. I am grateful to the administrative officers of the University of Maryland who made that leave possible—particularly to Dr. Charles Manning and Dr. R. Lee Hornbake. And to Miriam, who holds the most difficult of all jobs—that of an author's wife—I owe more than a word of thanks; in fact, I owe her this book.

Homer Ulrich

Table of Contents

1

Introduction

Choral music may be defined as music written in parts designed to be performed with several voices on each part. It is a product of the mid-fifteenth century; during its long history the number of parts for which it was written has varied from two to a dozen or more, and the number of voices required for each part has been similarly unstandardized. Many works in the choral literature can be performed adequately with eight to twelve voices, while others may require two hundred or more to make their fullest effect. Music has been written for choirs of women's, boys', and men's voices, and for choirs of mixed voices. Further, works for several choirs exist; in such cases each choir may perform individually at times and become part of the total ensemble at others. In many works the music is meant to be heard only with voices; others require instrumental accompaniment—sometimes as elaborate as a large orchestra; in still others, accompaniment is optional.

Much of the choral literature is sacred in function, written to be sung in a service of worship. Many other works are secular (that is, "worldly") in text and function and may be considered purely concert music. And a few, sacred in intent, go so far beyond the practicable limitations of a church service that perforce they can be heard only in concert. Among the secular works are many that lie on the border between choral music and vocal chamber music—that is, music with one, or at the most two, singers on each part; yet many of these works are suitable for performance with small groups and hence may be considered choral music. Such works, especially madrigals, will therefore be included in this book.

A large number of choral works are cast in forms that originated even before choral music itself came into being—notably the Mass and the motet. These forms owe their texts and, in part, their function to the body of liturgical music that has served the Roman Catholic Church for almost two thousand years, the monophonic plainsong called Gregorian chant. The structures and the techniques of composition that underlie the Mass and motet are in turn outgrowths of the polyphonic elaborations of Gregorian chant that occupied composers from about the eleventh century to the fifteenth. Thus, while a discussion of choral music itself can be carried back scarcely more than four hundred years, its roots in the history of western music are ancient indeed.

We shall offer here, therefore, a brief survey of the state of music in the centuries just before 1450, a date that may be taken as roughly marking the beginning of both polyphonic choral singing and the Renaissance period in music history. The emergence of the principal forms of choral music; a survey of prominent pre-Renaissance composers writing in these forms; the chief techniques of composition they employed; the way in which choral performance came about—these topics are the chief items in the following survey.

The Mass

The repertoire of Gregorian chant consists of thousands of unmetrical monophonic melodies set to sacred texts and divided into classes according to their place and function in the liturgy. The chants of the Mass constitute one such class and the chants of the Offices (Matins, Lauds, Prime, Vespers, etc.) another. The chants are further distinguished according to method of performance: responsorial or antiphonal (see page 9). This book, however, concerns itself primarily with the chants of the Mass and to a small extent with those of the Office of Vespers.

The Mass, the central service of the Catholic worship, celebrates the Eucharist, in which the elements of bread and wine are mystically transformed into the Body and Blood of Jesus Christ. The chants of the Mass comprise two groups. One group consists of texts proper to (assigned to) a particular season of the Church year, or a particular Sunday or festival; thus these texts are variable. This group includes the Introit, Gradual, Offertory, and Communion; together these chants are embraced in the term "Proper of the Mass." The other group consists of chants that are unchanging and are sung throughout large portions of the Church year—a notable exception being that during Lent the joyful Gloria is omitted; this unvarying group of chants constitutes the "Ordinary of the Mass." Other items of the Mass, including the various Collects, Prayers, Epistle, and Gospel, similarly divided into Proper and Ordinary, are spoken and play no part in a consideration of the Mass as a musical service.

Before the fifteenth century, single chants of the Ordinary were often set in polyphonic style for an ensemble of vocal soloists; since that time composers have often turned to the same chants and composed settings for choir. It is to this group of texts of the Ordinary—Kyrie, Gloria, Credo, Sanctus with Benedictus, and Agnus Dei—that we refer when speaking of the Mass in a musical context. The Mass in this restricted sense is one of the principal forms we shall consider in this book (see Appendix 2a for the texts).

Requiem Mass

A special form of the Mass, represented by many outstanding settings from the sixteenth century on, is the *Missa pro defunctis* (Mass for the Dead). In this form certain chants of the Proper are made invariable, and are grouped with selected chants of the Ordinary in the following order: Introit, Kyrie, Gradual, Sequence, Offertory, Sanctus with Benedictus, Agnus Dei, and Communion (see Appendix 2b). The generally used name of the form is derived from the first words of the Introit: *Requiem aeternam* ("Eternal rest").

Techniques

Isorhythm

The most available sourcebook of Gregorian plainsong is the *Liber usualis*. In that book the chants of the Ordinary are grouped by texts: a number of Kyries, a number of Glorias, and so on. Those responsible for selecting the music for a particular service were free to choose from a variety of melodies for each part of the Ordinary. Given this latitude, and given the variety of melodic types available, any musical unity in the Ordinary is not to be looked for. Beginning in the late fourteenth century, composers sought to bring about a higher level of unity in their polyphonic settings of the chants. One of the techniques they developed to achieve this unity was later called *isorhythm* (Greek *iso:* "same").

Composers in the twelfth and thirteenth centuries had made considerable use of rhythmic patterns, especially in the short compositions called *clausulae*. A clausula consisted of a phrase or more of plainsong above which one or two untexted voices had been added. Usually the plainsong melody was modified and became a series of long-drawn-out tones, each tone held beyond normal length; hence this voice was called the *tenor* (compare "tenant," "tenure," "*tenuto*," etc.). The rhythmic patterns of the upper voices consisted of various combinations of long and short tones; often one such combination, called a rhythmic mode, would prevail throughout a composition. During the course of the fourteenth century an extension of that principle applied mainly to the tenor resulted in the isorhythmic technique.

The effect of isorhythm was to impart a degree of organization and unity to the somewhat amorphous compositions employing borrowed tenors. Many Mass movements of the early fourteenth century employed the device of isorhythm, and occasionally it was applied to other voices than the tenor. Isorhythm remained a potent means of unifying compositions until about the middle of the fifteenth century, after which it became virtually obsolete.

Cantus firmus

Another technique for unifying an extended composition developed under the name *cantus firmus* ("fixed melody"). The unifying element is a fragment of plainsong that typically appears, in whole or in part, in one of the voices—usually the tenor—in each of the movements of the Mass; the other voices are composed in free counterpoint above it. Sometimes the cantus firmus appears throughout each movement (often set in long note values); sometimes it is quoted only intermittently.

Plainsong was not the only source of cantus firmi, however; at later stages in the development of the technique, any preexisting melody could be used, or an abstract melodic pattern was composed for the occasion. A Mass was often named for the source of its cantus firmus. For example, one of the fifteenth-century Masses attributed to both Leonel Power and John Dunstable in various manuscripts is the *Missa Rex saeculorum*, for it is based on the plainsong beginning with that text. Many Masses by various Flemish composers are based on secular chansons, songs, and the like; a notable example is the *Missa L'Homme armé*, after a popular song of the time, set by a number of composers, including Palestrina, Josquin (with two settings), and many more. And a few Masses whose cantus firmi are abstract melodic patterns are often identified by the appropriate solmization syllables, for example, Palestrina's *Missa Ut re mi*. Cantus firmus techniques were also employed in many motets of the time, as we shall see below.

Composers

Machaut

Composers in the eleventh century through the fourteenth were occupied principally in developing the arts of counterpoint and enlarging the resources of rhythm and rhythmic notation. Independence of the voices in a polyphonic context, a notation that permitted both duple and triple meter with proportional divisions of the basic beat, imaginative and free settings of a wide range of texts in both secular and sacred contexts—these were among their accomplishments. Most of these composers worked in virtual anonymity; before about 1325—with the exception of Leonin and Perotin, both active in Paris toward the end of the twelfth century—little is known about any of them.

During the *ars nova*, however, composers began to emerge from their anonymity, and names and careers can be identified. (*Ars nova*, "the new art," refers to the music of the fourteenth century as contrasted to the *ars antiqua*, "the ancient art," of the thirteenth. *Ars nova* is the name of a theoretical treatise written by Philippe de Vitry around 1325.) Among the earliest-known prominent composers was Guillaume de Machaut (c. 1300–1377). Cleric, poet and musician, Machaut served in a number of positions in his long and active life. He traveled as far as Russia as secretary to King John of Bohemia, he was a member of the court of Charles V of France, and from 1340 to his death he served as canon at Rheims. A composer of both secular and sacred music, Machaut is of great historical importance for his polyphonic setting of the entire Mass, the first known to have been composed by one individual.

Machaut's Mass, to which the date 1364 is usually assigned, contains the five chants of the Ordinary plus the concluding *Ite, missa est,* and is set for four voices. Machaut used the isorhythmic technique in all movements except the Gloria, but he handled it differently in each movement. For example, in the Kyrie and Credo it appears in two voices, tenor and contratenor; it is used throughout in the Kyrie, but confined to the final Amen in the Credo. In the Agnus Dei it appears only in the two upper voices, and in the *Ite, missa est* in all four. Machaut was one of the earliest composers to reflect the expressiveness of the text in the music. In the Credo, for example, the section which speaks of the incarnation and crucifixion of Christ is set off in a broad and impressive style that contrasts with the music surrounding the passage, thereby establishing a tradition followed by later composers into the nineteenth century (see Example 1).

Dufay

Machaut's unified Mass remained unusual for almost a century. Settings of single Mass movements in a variety of styles (cantus firmus, chordal style, and *ballata* style; in the latter, one or two voice parts were accompanied by one or two instruments) continued to be composed well into the fifteenth century. Among the composers who wrote in these styles was Guillaume Dufay (c. 1400–1474), one of the most highly esteemed members of the Burgundian school.

Dufay received his early education at Cambrai, after which he lived in Italy for a decade or longer. He was a member of the Papal Chapel at Rome in the years about 1430, lived in Savoy and traveled extensively, and in 1436 was appointed canon of the Cathedral of Cambrai. Ordained as a priest and trained in canon law, he was regarded as much for his learning as his music, and became known as one of the foremost composers of the fifteenth century.

EXAMPLE 1   Machaut, *Mass*, Credo

He composed about 25 single Mass movements or pairs of movements in the styles described above, but beginning about 1430 he also composed complete Masses. Eight or more settings of the complete Ordinary are attributed to him, some in the prevailing three-voice setting, others in four voices. The four-voice setting became standard with him, and was generally adopted through much of the Renaissance period. The tenor became the next-to-the-bottom voice; the former contratenor part was now split into two—one high (*altus*) above the tenor, and one low (*bassus*) below the tenor. The top voice, formerly called *discantus*, was now often called *superius* (highest), from which the word "soprano" evolved (see table below). The modern disposition of the vocal quartet is virtually present in these Masses as well as in the motets of Dufay, although the development of the modern voice *ranges* (especially the development of a true bass range) was an accomplishment of the Renaissance period.

c. 1350	c. 1450	c. 1600
discantus	*superius*	soprano
contratenor	*contratenor altus*	contralto ("alto")
tenor	*tenor*	tenor
	contratenor bassus	bass

Motet

The chants of the Proper were mentioned above as comprising a group of chants with texts assigned to a particular season or festival of the Church year. Since the thirteenth century, texts drawn from the Proper or from other portions of the Gregorian chant repertoire have also been set polyphonically. One type of setting, originating probably in France, employed a phrase of chant above which one or two (occasionally three) newly composed voices were added. The lowest voice, the tenor, retained its original text, but the text supplied to the upper voices was freely chosen from sacred or secular poems, sometimes in the vernacular (as opposed to the Latin of the tenor phrase). Later each of the added voices sometimes had a different text. The original chant phrase, with its sacred text in the tenor and with one or two untexted added voices above, had been called a clausula (the rhythmic aspects of the clausula were mentioned on page 3). When words were supplied to the added voices (called *duplum* and *triplum*, respectively), the whole became known as a *motet* (French *mot:* "word"). From the early thirteenth century to about the fifteenth, motets were performed by solo singers—either in connection with or separate from the Church service. Thereafter, however, the form of the motet was available to composers writing for choral groups.

Machaut

About 23 motets by Machaut have survived, and they too generally employ the isorhythmic principle. He usually adhered to the prevailing setting of the time: three-voice, with the tenor taken from a liturgical chant and designed to be performed instrumentally, and with different texts in the upper voices. Machaut went far on the road toward lyric melody: the upper voices are generally lighter and freer in rhythm than any composer's before him. And a noteworthy feature of his harmonic style is the relatively frequent use of cadential° consonances provided by thirds and sixths. Dissonances of the type common in the thirteenth century are still present, along with many empty octaves and fifths (that is, lacking the interval of the third), but the tendency to employ triadic° harmonies at cadences, a characteristic of later *ars nova* music, is especially prominent in the music of Machaut.

Dufay

The majority of Dufay's motets are built on derived tenors and are composed isorhythmically. They are most often written for three, four, or five voices, with the tenor of the four-voice settings in the next-to-bottom voice; when a derived tenor is not used, the main melody is generally in the top voice. The textures are varied, in that often an extended passage is set for the two upper voices or even for a single voice; such effects together with other passages in chordal style give Dufay's motets an expressive quality and a high degree of charm.

English Discant and Fauxbourdon

Among the methods of composition available to composers about the beginning of the fifteenth century were two, one English and one Burgundian, that had many points in common although their origins were quite different. The English method arose possibly out of the practice of adding two improvised parts to a cantus firmus, one a third above it, the other a sixth above it. Thus a series of chords in the first inversion or a series of sixth chords,° to use modern terminology, resulted in those passages where parallelism was strictly observed. This method, called *English discant,* found its way to Burgundy and France early in the fifteenth century and became the model for a corresponding continental style (see Example 2). Opinions differ among the authorities as to the origin and scope of English discant. According to some theories, the cantus firmus was the middle voice, with one voice added above and one below. (See Ulrich-Pisk, *A History of Music and Musical Style,* p. 103, fn. 2.)

EXAMPLE 2   Anon., *In te Domine Speravi*

°Terms defined or discussed in the Glossary are marked by an asterisk at their first appearance in the text.

The continental version, called *fauxbourdon*, was applied to two-voice compositions moving in parallel sixths; between these two voices a third (unwritten) voice was improvised at an interval of a fourth below the top or principal voice. Again a series of sixth chords resulted; thus the sonorities and harmonic appeal of the two versions were similar. In the English discant the point of departure was the bottom voice; in fauxbourdon it was the top voice. In both cases, however, the chordal effects were identical, and the sixth-chord style, as it may be called, permeated virtually all forms of composition later in the fifteenth century. The interest in vertical tonal combinations undoubtedly had an effect in lessening the independence of the several voices and hastening the adoption of a harmonically motivated homophonic texture.

Dunstable

The early fifteenth century in England was marked by the work of John Dunstable (c. 1370–1453) and the spread of English musical style to France. Dunstable combined the melodic grace of the chanson (see page 9) with the technique of English discant. The result was a high degree of mellifluous sonority presented in clear designs. Many of his works were copied in other manuscripts, especially in France, an unmistakable indication of the regard in which his music was held. Among his works are about a dozen motets, settings of single movements of the Ordinary (but no complete Masses), a few secular songs, and several miscellaneous settings for three voices of various liturgical texts.

The chief styles and forms of the time are represented in Dunstable's compositions. The isorhythmic technique, prominent in the motets and in several of the Mass movements, is often embodied in the sonorities of English discant to bring about a fusion of old and new. Among the miscellaneous three-voice pieces on sacred texts are some in cantus firmus style with liturgical tenors, and others freely composed with independent melodies. An outstanding characteristic of virtually all Dunstable's works is the lightly flowing and expressive melodic line. The melody often outlines triads; larger leaps are used to enhance the expressiveness of the texts, and dissonances are employed largely as passing notes on weak beats (see Example 3). The several melodies are equal in importance and constitute a smooth polyphonic texture in which the natural rhythm of the text to a large extent controls the rhythm of the melodies.

EXAMPLE 3   Dunstable, *Veni Sancte Spiritus*

Per te sci - a - mus___   da Pa-trem nos-ca - mus___   at - que Fi - li   -   um

Binchois

The style of Dunstable is reflected most strongly in the works of the Franco-Flemish composer Gilles Binchois (c. 1400–1460). Binchois was born in Mons and served the Burgundian court at Dijon in various offices for about thirty years.

He was highly respected both in his own time and later; his works were copied in many manuscripts, and many of his melodies were employed by later composers as cantus firmi in their own works. A number of single Mass movements, four settings of the Magnificat, and 22 motets are among the sacred compositions that have survived; his secular compositions will be discussed below. The cantus firmus style, one of the standard methods of composition in Binchois's time, plays no part in his works; isorhythm, fauxbourdon, and occasionally imitative techniques served Binchois adequately in setting the sacred texts.

Chanson

The principal French secular form of the Medieval period was the *chanson*. In a general sense, the term can refer to any song with a French text, but more specialized meanings of "chanson" occur in music history as far back as the thirteenth century. The music of the troubadours and trouvères had included a large number of secular monophonic songs in fixed forms, including *ballades*, *lais*, and *rondeaux.*° Late in the thirteenth century, polyphonic equivalents of these forms had appeared, generally composed for two or three voices. The term "chanson" is applied specifically to these works. In the fourteenth century, Machaut composed almost a hundred polyphonic chansons, constituting one of the largest and most important groups of early secular compositions.

Binchois

The sacred works of Gilles Binchois were mentioned briefly above, but his major contribution was to further the development of the chanson. About fifty of his chansons have survived; the great majority are in fixed forms, the rondeau being the most numerous, and are set in three-part polyphony. The principal melody, generally set as the highest part, is usually the only one supplied with a text. Presumably the lower textless parts were performed instrumentally; indeed, the contratenor part is often angular in contour and serves mainly to fill out the chords outlined by the tenor and soprano. A noteworthy feature of these chansons, as of other works by Binchois and his contemporary, Dufay, is a regularization of cadence structures in the direction of dominant-tonic patterns.

The Emergence of Choral Performance

The emergence of choral performance in the mid-fifteenth century, as opposed to performance by a group of soloists, is closely linked with the principle of contrasting performing forces, as we shall see below. And this principle, in turn, is related to two methods of chant singing that can be traced back to at least the third century, a time when the Roman Catholic liturgy was still being formulated. In that early liturgy, psalm singing in unison played an important role, the psalm texts being set to plainchants. In one method of performance, the *responsorial*, the leader sang or chanted one section of the text, and the choir (which often meant the congregation) "answered" with another. In the second method, the *antiphonal,* successive verses were sung alternately by the two halves of the choir. In both cases, the principle of employing contrasting vocal forces is evident, even though the chants were of course entirely monophonic.

During the time that composers were chiefly concerned with the polyphonic elaboration of Gregorian chant, from the eleventh through the fourteenth century, they kept the principle of contrasting forces. They began to set only certain portions of the chant in polyphonic style, leaving other sections in the original monophony. A soloist was then assigned to each of the two (or occasionally three) parts of the polyphonic sections, and the monophonic sections were given to a larger group singing in unison. Generally the polyphonic and monophonic sections alternated, enhancing the textural contrast. Many manuscripts of thirteenth-century clausulae and motets contain written-out passages only in the sections given to the soloists; sometimes just the beginnings of the sections designed for the unison choir are notated, and sometimes even these are omitted. Since both the clausula and the motet were based on preexisting chants and were presumably known to the members of the unison choir, this economy in notation can have offered little difficulty to the singers of the time.

At first glance, many of the three-part works of the fourteenth century, both secular and sacred, seem to be vocal polyphony; the *ballate* of Francesco Landini (1325–1397) and the ballads and motets of Machaut are of this class. Yet it was generally understood that in these works the upper part was sung by a soloist and the lower part or parts were performed instrumentally, for often the absence of texts in the lower voices and the nature of the melodic lines clearly implied instrumental performance. And in compositions in which a text was applied to each voice, performance by a group of soloists was understood; in other words, such compositions were in the field of vocal chamber music.

Early in the fifteenth century, then, we find the first compositions in which there is a clear distinction between sections for soloists and sections for multi-voiced choir; the first are marked *unus* or *dui,* the second *chorus.* (Details of this development are found in Bukofzer, "The Beginnings of Choral Polyphony," in his *Studies in Medieval and Renaissance Music,* pp. 176–89.) These compositions, in Italian manuscripts from the period 1430–40, are found in Bologna, Cambrai, Munich, and Oxford, but the composers are mainly Franco-Flemish— Binchois and Dufay among them. These works still represent a transitional stage, however; while the solo sections still carry texts in both parts, the three-voice sections marked "chorus" contain a text in only the upper voice and the lower voices are clearly meant for instruments. Thus the "chorus" is still a unison group, even if an accompanied one, and there is as yet no stylistic distinction between the solo and group-unison parts.

We come finally to a work that is of particular historical importance in this development, for it may be characterized as the first-known composition employing *choral* polyphony: a Gloria and Credo by Guillaume Legrant, dated 1426, containing alternate sections set for two soloists and a three-voice choir. Texts are placed under all three voices of the choral sections, thus ruling out the possibility that instrumental performance was intended (although, in keeping with the practices of the time, instruments may have doubled and supported the choral parts). And while the Gloria reveals no significant differences in style between the sections for choir and soloists, the Credo does show such differences. The sections for soloists are more florid and rhythmically more complex than the predominantly chordal sections for the choir. And assuming that solo singers were (and are) more highly trained and had better voices than choristers, we can understand why even in the first-known work of choral polyphony a stylistic difference should exist (see Example 4).

EXAMPLE 4   Legrant, *Credo*

From Davison-Apel, *Historical Anthology of Music,* Vol. I. Used by permission of Harvard University Press.

Title page from Gafurius, *Practica Musicae Utriusque Cantus,* published in Venice in 1512, showing a choir singing from a single large choir-book.

This new style of performance also brought with it a major change in the very appearance of the printed page. Singers of the time had performed from manuscripts of normal page size and multiple copies of these manuscripts were virtually nonexistent. Probably no more than two to four singers could crowd around a manuscript of this size. With the introduction of choral polyphony, requiring several singers on each part, a corresponding change in the means of reading the music was needed. And this change was provided by the introduction of large-size manuscripts—the largest of them about 19 by 28 inches—placed on a lectern, around which members of the choir grouped themselves. These giant choirbooks were introduced about the middle of the fifteenth century and from that point on, choral polyphony developed rapidly and soon replaced the centuries-old tradition of choral unison.

It is likely, however, that certain compositions bearing all the distinguishing marks of *choral* music continued to be performed by groups of soloists. A work whose text implied intimate expression, for example, or a work of small scope, was just as suitable for a small ensemble as for a large choir. Few facts are available and opinions are divided; we may nevertheless assume that Renaissance musicians took advantage of both possibilities and performed their works accordingly—a practice that is sometimes followed in present-day recordings and concerts.

2

Music in the North
1450–1525

In the late fourteenth and early fifteenth centuries the area now comprising the Netherlands, Belgium, and northeastern France was under the control of successive dukes of Burgundy, all of whom were dedicated patrons of the arts. Music flourished especially under Philip the Good (1396–1467), Duke of Burgundy from 1419, and the chapel and court of Philip rose to a preeminent position. A truly international culture took root there, with musicians recruited from France, Flanders, the German states, Italy, and Holland. The majority of the composers associated with the Burgundian court, and the most prominent ones, were representatives of either Gallic or Germanic culture, and their influence spread to all parts of Europe. To this group of fifteenth-century composers the term Franco-Flemish is applied; Binchois and Dufay, mentioned in Chapter 1, were members of this group and contributed greatly to the standards of excellence achieved by later composers. And even after the duchy of Burgundy was seized by France in 1477 and the Netherlands was occupied by Austrian and Spanish branches of the Hapsburg family (in 1477 and 1507, respectively), the historical importance of the Franco-Flemish composers and the quality of their music were maintained.

The Renaissance

The late fifteenth century brought into being a series of developments in all the arts and in cultural life generally that marks that period as one of the turning points in the history of civilization. Many of the innovations and changes in

13

outlook represented in the music of the time are a part of these developments, for they are expressions of a new movement called humanism that arose among literary circles in Italy. The humanists believed that life on earth was equal in importance to life in the hereafter; that each man—as opposed to Man, the abstraction—had strengths and spiritual integrity as a human being that were worthy of attention.

To humanists, the pursuit of personal happiness, in which the quest for beauty played a part, was the legitimate expression of an individual's feelings, his spiritual attributes, and his ability to adapt to change. To Medieval artists and musicians, on the other hand, the concepts of personal pleasure and beauty for their own sake—not just as another means of glorifying God—were largely foreign.

Northerners, in their version of humanism, stressed the virtues of love, reverence, and selflessness as ingredients of personal happiness. Religion, based largely on the cultivation of such human attributes, could thus become a satisfying personal experience. Eventually, in all parts of western Europe the idea of man as an individual took hold. But since the fifteenth century knew that in the ancient world of Greece and Rome man had enjoyed such individuality, the concept of a *rebirth*, a renaissance, was developed. Thus the term Renaissance was eventually adopted by later writers, who applied it to the entire period, which in music extends roughly from the middle of the fifteenth century to the end of the sixteenth.

The humanists gave renewed attention to the literature of the ancient world, especially to the meanings and implications of the texts. This concern with textual significance soon spread to musicians, who became increasingly sensitive to proper declamation, accentuation, and interpretation of subtleties in the texts they were setting. The proper relationship between textual and musical accents, often ignored by Medieval composers, soon became a matter of general concern to Renaissance composers.

Mass

Johannes Okeghem and, a generation later, Jacob Obrecht and Josquin des Prez became the principal figures among later members of the Franco-Flemish school. They differed considerably, however, in their approach to the elements comprising the new style of the Renaissance.

Okeghem

The chief contributions of Johannes Okeghem (c. 1430–1495) are in the field of sacred music. Beginning his career as a choir singer in Antwerp, he served later in Cambrai and Paris. Later, as chaplain and composer at the royal court of France, he became widely known as a teacher as well as a musician. Among his surviving works are about a dozen Masses, a few single Mass movements, nine motets, and a Requiem Mass—the latter being the earliest polyphonic setting of the Requiem that has yet been found. Okeghem's style departs widely from that of his presumed teacher, Dufay. Many of the latter's works, single Mass movements as well as complete Masses and motets, are cast in the *ballata* style and are written for one or two voices and one or two instruments. Okeghem, on the other hand, composed most often for four voices, adding a true bass voice below the tenor. He was probably the first composer to do so consistently, and thus is among the earliest representatives of the new Renaissance style.

Okeghem composed most often in a thick and sonorous texture with long, unbroken contrapuntal lines equally spaced throughout the four-voice setting; the music is noticeably devoid of internal cadences or breathing places. Only occasionally did he depart from the solid four-voice texture and, for the sake of contrast, write passages for two or three voices. At other times he abandoned counterpoint temporarily by composing passages in which all voices are set to the same rhythms, thus creating a chordal style. In so doing he was able to give to the text a degree of emphasis that was unavoidably absent in contrapuntal passages, in which several phrases of the text might be set simultaneously.

It is understandable that the device of imitation,° which reached its highest peak in the sixteenth century, does not play an important role in the sacred works of Okeghem, for he was essentially a conservative composer. Most often each voice in the contrapuntal texture is independently conceived and may even have its own rhythmic scheme (see Example 5).

EXAMPLE 5   Okeghem, *Missa Mi-mi*, Gloria

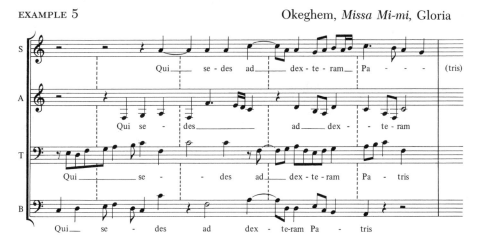

From Friedrich Blume, *Das Chorwerk*, Vol. 4, edited by Heinrich Besseler. Used by permission of Möseler Verlag, Wolfenbüttel and Zurich.

Yet one special aspect of imitative writing, the device of canon,° does appear frequently in Okeghem's works, as it did in the works of his contemporaries. A noteworthy example of canonic writing is seen in his *Missa prolationum*. In this four-voice Mass, the second voice progresses in canon with the first at intervals ranging from the unison to the octave, and each tone is half again as long as the corresponding tone of the first voice. In similar fashion, the fourth voice is designed to form a canon with the third, again with proportionately longer tonal lengths (see Example 6). Since the second and fourth voices move in longer steps than the first and third, the distance between the voices of each pair of canons constantly increases. Periodically, therefore, Okeghem employs other note values and other types of canon in later sections of each movement.

EXAMPLE 6   Okeghem, *Missa Prolationum*, Sanctus

Used by permission of the American Musicological Society.

Only the first and third voices are notated in the manuscript of this work, and cryptic directions are given for working out the second and fourth voices; hence the *Missa prolationum* represents a class of works called "puzzle canons." Such works are found with relative frequency in fifteenth-century manuscripts and give evidence that composers of the time were interested in mastering, even exploiting, the possibilities inherent in contrapuntal writing. Their intellectual play (much of which necessarily escapes listeners who are not properly prepared for the intricacies of the music) adds an extra element of interest to the beauty and flow of the music.

Obrecht

The kind of continuous, nonimitative, overlapping counterpoint with few internal cadences that had served composers of Okeghem's generation gradually fell into disfavor among progressive composers in the second half of the fifteenth century. The latter preferred such forward-looking stylistic devices as the general use of imitative counterpoint; a sectional structure marked by well-defined cadence points; the introduction of extended two- and three-voice passages, for variety, into the four-voice texture; and the alternation of high and low vocal ranges for expressive purposes. Inevitably, the decades around 1450 are a transitional time between the Medieval and Renaissance periods.

Jacob Obrecht (c. 1450–1505) was chief among the composers of the transitional time. Like many other members of the Franco-Flemish school, he divided his time between several cities—Cambrai, Bruges, and various places in Holland among them—and he traveled in Italy. His known works include about two dozen Masses, as many motets, and a number of secular compositions. (According to the latest authorities, a setting of the St. Matthew Passion, still ascribed to him in many reference works, is probably not by him, but by Antoine de Longueval.) Obrecht's works excel in their technical excellence, musical quality, and sensitive approach to the nuances of their texts.

During the course of the fifteenth century the cantus firmus technique became a major means of unifying extended compositions; as an offshoot of that technique, the device of *parody* became important. In a cantus firmus Mass, it will be recalled, a fragment of plainsong or other melody is employed in whole or in part, continuously or intermittently, in at least one of the voices in each movement. In the parody Mass, on the other hand, an extended polyphonic section or an entire composition may be borrowed from another source. The borrowed material may be quoted exactly or it may be modified considerably. It should be pointed out that composers took pains to alter or conceal the borrowed material, probably as a challenge to their technical skill, and that in no sense does this use of the term "parody" have any derogatory connotations.

The majority of Obrecht's Masses are of the cantus firmus type. Usually dividing the borrowed melody into sections, he used the sections in systematic fashion in the successive Mass movements. In a typical Mass, as for example his *Missa super Maria zart*, the first two sections of the borrowed melody appear in the Kyrie, the next four in the Gloria, and so on. Sometimes more than one cantus firmus is employed. In his parody Masses, on the other hand, Obrecht worked more tentatively. Most often he employed the borrowed melodies singly, as in the cantus firmus technique; but at least once in each movement all the voices of the borrowed material appear together. His *Missa Rosa playant*, based on a three-voice chanson, is constructed in that fashion. The parody technique was widely used by later generations of composers; its scarcity in the music of Obrecht calls renewed attention to his position in the transitional stage between two style periods.

Josquin

The forms, styles, and techniques inherited and developed by composers of the fifteenth century found their greatest champion in Josquin des Prez (c. 1450–1521). To this heritage, Josquin applied a boundless imagination, consummate technical skill, an ability to summarize and refine, and the power of a great musical personality. The result was a body of music that served as a model for generations of later composers and established in effect an international style.

Born near the present French-Belgian border, Josquin traveled widely. He served at the court of the Sforzas in Milan, was a member of the Papal Chapel for about ten years, and was active variously in Florence, Modena, Ferrara, and at the court of Louis XII of France. Later he returned to the Flemish provinces, where he spent the remainder of his life. These meager biographical details give little evidence of the great esteem in which he was held. His contemporaries recognized him as the greatest among them; his music was among the earliest to be printed, and was reprinted in many editions through the entire sixteenth century. His reputation as a teacher was equally great and his influence on the entire course of sixteenth-century music was profound.

Josquin's works include about two dozen Masses and almost two hundred works in other forms. One group of compositions, presumably his earlier ones, reveal first of all how thoroughly he had mastered the styles of the time. These works are similar in style to Okeghem's. The texture is sonorous, composed of long contrapuntal lines, and canonic devices appear frequently. Notable in this group are the six-voice settings of *Et ecce terrae motus* (*And behold, there was a great earthquake*) and *In nomine Jesu* (*In Jesus' name*). Even after Josquin developed his individual style he retained his interest in canon and used the device in secular as well as sacred compositions. Other aspects of the earlier Franco-Flemish style—notably the cantus firmus and parody techniques—appear frequently in his later works also.

In the late fifteenth century imitative techniques became potent means of unifying a composition, for in a texture in which a melody or motive° imposes its general contour and style on every succeeding melody, the relationship between all voices and sections of a composition becomes exceedingly close. Thus imitative writing too plays an important part in Josquin's music.

A new style became characteristic in other compositions of Josquin's, however,

Josquin des Prez, from a contemporary woodcut.

IOSQVINVS PRATENSIS.

resulting probably from his many years of activity in Italy. The long phrases and solid polyphony of the older northern music precluded the lightness of texture of much Italian music, which was well articulated in form, with an attractive melodious style. These are the characteristics that Josquin incorporated into his music, and he did so without minimizing the quality of his contrapuntal writing. The result was a fusion of Franco-Flemish and Italian styles, which provided a foundation for a true international style.

Josquin revealed a great interest in varieties of vocal color, perhaps greater than any earlier composer; this characteristic is seen in the majority of his works. For example, although his Masses are all written for four voices, extended passages for two or three voices are common. The top two voices often stand alone, for one vocal color; the bottom two are similarly set alone, for another; occasionally the tenor is omitted, occasionally the bass. The voice parts, whose individual ranges are often extended beyond earlier ranges, are set farther apart to eliminate the need for voice crossings. Yet Josquin never hesitated to cross voices if his expressive requirements so dictated. In every case where the standard four-voice setting or normal distribution of voices is modified, we can assume—and usually find—an expressive reason.

The cantus firmus plays a role in Josquin's Masses also. Plainsong, phrases from motets by his predecessors, and contemporary tunes from the field of popular song all appear in them. On occasion Josquin introduced the technique of paraphrase, in which he most often placed the borrowed material in the upper voice (as opposed to the tenor in a cantus firmus Mass), and altered it as necessary with ornamentation and elaboration. In a famous example of a cantus firmus Mass, his *Missa Pange lingua,* Josquin used the borrowed chant in all voices at one time or another and treated it imitatively as well. Josquin's wealth of devices in this Mass deserves close attention.

The chant itself, beginning *Pange lingua* ("Approach, O tongue"), is essentially stepwise in its contour and contains only two or three small leaps (see Example 7a). Josquin retains mainly the *incipit* (the first four or five tones) of the chant, after which he paraphrases freely (Examples 7b to 7g). Virtually every section of the Mass begins with those tones, among the exceptions being *Christe eleison,* the second Kyrie, and portions of the Sanctus. The incipit itself is often rhythmically modified in its various appearances. Thereafter the nature of the imitations that follow differs in every passage.

For example, the majority of the movements and sections of the Mass begin with one voice, often Tenor II; this is usually followed by the adjoining voice (most often Bass) at a fifth below after one measure. Imitation is likely to be strict for several measures—even to the extent of being canonic—after which both voices dissolve into free counterpoint or further paraphrases of the chant fragments. But before this point has been reached, the other pair of voices has usually entered with an imitation of the passage heard in the first pair (Example 7h). In many cases, however, the sequence of voices differs from the usual pattern. Thus at the words *Christe eleison* the pairs enter as Bass and Tenor I, Tenor II and Soprano, Tenor I and Bass, and Soprano and Tenor II. At *Qui tollis* the entrances are Soprano, Tenor I, Tenor II, and Bass; now the voices are not paired, each voice entering a fifth below its predecessor. The *Crucifixus* begins with Tenor I followed closely by Soprano; in the Sanctus that order is reversed.

EXAMPLE 7   Josquin, *Missa Pange lingua*

(i)

From *Pleni sunt coeli* through *Gloria tua* in the Sanctus only Tenor I and Soprano are employed, and the interval and time of imitation vary throughout: at first in octaves after two measures, then in unison after one measure, and later in fifths after one measure. Likewise, the Benedictus is sung entirely by Bass and Tenor II, but in a series of short phrases imitated at the fifth above after one measure. The first Agnus Dei begins with Tenor I, Bass, Tenor II, and Soprano at varying times but all at the unison or the octave. And in the second Agnus Dei the order of entrances is Soprano, Tenor I, Bass, and Tenor II.

In many of the above passages and in others that reveal still other patterns of imitation, the melody being imitated is not drawn from the paraphrased chant, but is freely composed. And often a pair of voices in close imitation is accompanied by one or two other voices in free counterpoint. Occasionally, as in the Gloria, short motives are distributed among two or three of the voices and freely imitated in constantly shifting vocal combinations (Example 7i). And finally, a few passages are set entirely or largely in chordal texture, notably the *Crucifixus* and a number of the cadential passages at the end of the various movements.

Josquin's treatment of imitation (with entrances greatly varied as to intervals and distance in time), his textures, and his melodic contours gives evidence of the power of his imagination and technical prowess. The constant play of vocal color, shifting degrees of sonority, and sensitivity to the significance of the text combine to give the *Missa Pange lingua* its high position among the works of Josquin.

A noteworthy feature of all Josquin's compositions is the care with which the text is placed under the notes. Before his time, manuscripts and printed editions alike (the latter usually in partbooks, since scores were seldom printed until the end of the century) gave only cursory attention to the matter. A word or syllable was often placed near the note or group of notes to which it referred, and it was left to the singers to determine the proper correspondence of tone and syllable. The composers of the fifteenth century and the printers of the early sixteenth were not much concerned with such matters as correct declamation and accentuation—or even providing any music for short words; they no doubt assumed that the singers trained in the style would place the words correctly.

In the works of Josquin, however, as well as in those of his contemporaries, that casual attitude toward the text disappeared. The meaning of words was, after all, a central humanistic concern. Virtually every syllable is properly related to the notes—in imitative and chordal passages, and in long melismatic° passages as well. Josquin was thus able not only to give proper musical accentuation to the texts but also to bring to light their subtleties of meaning and phrasing (see Example 8).

Other composers

The downward extension of the bass voice, begun by Okeghem and carried further by succeeding composers, was virtually completed by Pierre de la Rue (c. 1460–1518), another of the Franco-Flemish contemporaries of Obrecht and Josquin. Active at the Burgundian court, La Rue composed about 35 motets and as many Masses, one of the latter for six voices—perhaps the earliest to employ this combination. Of particular importance among his works is a setting of the Requiem Mass, set for four voices generally but containing passages for two to five voices. The bass line frequently descends to low B flat, and low ranges in the other voices contribute to the dark coloration characteristic of several of the movements. In contrast, the prevailing colors of the Psalm, *Sicut servus,* and the Communion, *Luceat eis,* are unusually bright.

EXAMPLE 8   Josquin, *Missa da Beata Virgine,* Credo

Nicolas Gombert (c. 1490–1556), a pupil of Josquin, was active as a singer at the court of Charles V; his official duties took him to Spain, Germany, and Austria early in his career, but later he was associated primarily with Brussels and Tournai. His surviving works include ten Masses and almost two hundred motets, which were often performed in many of the musical capital cities of the time, where they served as representatives of the Franco-Flemish style and were widely imitated.

The parody technique, which composers of the previous generation had used sparingly, appears in eight of Gombert's ten Masses; in the early sixteenth century this technique was tending to replace the use of cantus firmi and devices of canon. Settings for five or six voices were favored by many composers as the century ran its course, with four-voice settings representing a conservative trend that paralleled the new. Here too Gombert took a middle course: Masses for four as well as for five or six voices are included in his works.

In his Masses, as well as in many of his motets, Gombert inclined toward the use of long and continuous contrapuntal lines rather than the short, well-separated phrases characteristic of Josquin, but imitation is used even more frequently. Successions of notes of different lengths and a number of syncopations provide rhythmic vitality, and frequently the rhythmic pattern of a phrase being imitated appears in a different form than it had at the beginning of the imitated section (for an example of this treatment in a motet, see Example 9).

Jacobus Clemens (c. 1510–c. 1556) is generally referred to as Clemens non Papa, to distinguish him from a contemporaneous cleric, Father Clemens— Clemens Papa in Italian. He was active in Paris as well as his native Netherlands; his surviving works include fifteen Masses (one of them a Requiem) and well over two hundred motets. His fourteen settings of the Ordinary are all parody Masses for five voices—indicating the extent to which modern practices had permeated his style. Other modern devices include an increase in the amount of chordal, as opposed to contrapuntal, writing, and the frequent use of short motives, which often invade the entire texture of some passages (see Example 12, page 28).

Motet

From its origin in the thirteenth century as a clausula to which texts had been set, the motet rose to a dominant position in the three following centuries. Gradually the isorhythmic principle was abandoned, multiple texts fell into disfavor, there was little overlapping of the words, and the motet became free in form. A motivic type of construction characterized melodic lines, and the lines themselves acquired a degree of harmonic direction, with parallel thirds and sixths abounding.

The term "motet" came to be applied to a wide variety of compositions. Although it was not part of the liturgy, the motet could be sung during church services. With a secular text, not uncommon in the fourteenth and fifteenth centuries, a motet was often sung in civic, national, or other secular festivities where its topical, patriotic, or adulatory text was appropriate. In general, any work except one on a text drawn from the Ordinary of the Mass, if composed in the style of a sacred motet, was given the name. Settings of longer texts, such as extended psalms, or the Canticle of the Virgin in the Office of Vespers

EXAMPLE 9   Gombert, motet, *Super flumina*

(Tr.: "[Sing us one] of the songs of Zion. How shall we sing. . . .")

From Davison-Apel, *Historical Anthology of Music*, Vol. I. Used by permission of Harvard University Press.

(Magnificat; see Appendix 2e), were often further identified by the first words of their respective texts. But with these exceptions, the term "motet" is flexible and general.

Obrecht

As he did in his Masses, Obrecht revealed both old and new style characteristics in his motets. A few of them contain multiple texts, a holdover from the fourteenth-century practice. He also made considerable use of other stylistic devices inherited from earlier composers, including free nonimitative counterpoint, thus indicating his relationship to Okeghem and other earlier Franco-Flemish composers. But in most other respects Obrecht was a forward-looking composer, making use of style elements that marked a break with the past. Chief among those elements is a more varied texture set in clear, well articulated forms.

EXAMPLE 10   Obrecht, motet, *Pater noster*

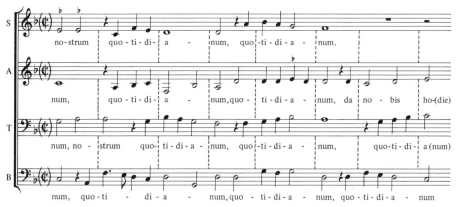

(Tr.: "Give us this day [our daily bread].")

From Davison-Apel, *Historical Anthology of Music,* Vol. I. Used by permission of Harvard University Press.

Perhaps the most obvious difference between Obrecht's style and Okeghem's is the former's use of short and well balanced phrases set off by clearly defined cadences that often employ full triads (see Example 10). This in itself gives a feeling of lightness to the music, a lightness that was seldom characteristic of Okeghem's. Further, in place of the nondirected, rambling harmony often found in Okeghem, Obrecht employed harmonic progressions that impart a degree of forward motion to his music. His considerable use of what later generations would call dominant-tonic cadences provided him with a way of checking that forward motion—and, incidentally, of creating the sectional form that is characteristic of his music.

Josquin

The 70-odd chansons and about 120 motets and related compositions of Josquin can be listened to with keen satisfaction today, for they are among the earliest examples of music that is expressive and emotionally rich to our ears. Josquin's fusion of Franco-Flemish and Italian styles, seen in the Masses, is particularly evident in the motets.

It is significant that Josquin, with his boundless imagination and interest in experimentation, found the motet a more congenial form than the Mass in which to write. Liturgical requirements and a fixed text probably contributed to Josquin's relatively limited interest in composing Masses—a feeling that was apparently shared by many later composers, Orlando di Lasso, for example. Later in the century the motet replaced the Mass as the form in which composers provided the greatest amount of musical innovation.

In Josquin's motets the use of imitative counterpoint became the outstanding stylistic feature. It became Josquin's general practice to compose a separate motive or melody for each section, paragraph, or sentence of the text and, in turn, often to apply devices of imitation to each melody. Thus the motet became in effect a series of connected sections—connected in that phrases usually overlapped at each section's end; such a section is called a "point of imitation." In many of his motets a section heard once is recapitulated or returns as a variant of the original section (see Example 11). Thus Josquin was able to impart a high degree of unity to what would otherwise be an essentially amorphous structure because of the continuous prose text on which the form was based. The point-of-imitation device became standard for motets even in his own time; in fact, a work (even a Mass movement) written in this manner is said to be "in motet style." As an offshoot of the sectional form favored by Josquin, many motets based on extremely long texts were sometimes composed in several parts or movements separated by decisive cadences. (Several of Josquin's psalm settings, to be discussed below, are written in two or more parts, for example.)

The element of "word-painting," in which a word or phrase of the text is given illustrative or symbolic treatment, became important in Josquin's motets also; his well-known motet *De profundis* (*Out of the Depths*) is especially rich in this regard. In his settings of the texts he sought for the exact musical means that would best disclose the personal significance the texts held for him. In this respect too he was a typical man of the Renaissance, for individual expression became a factor to be reckoned with. His work in developing word-painting devices remained influential for two centuries, to the time of Bach and Handel.

At an earlier time, when the total compass of a choral group was relatively limited and it was desirable to be able to distinguish one voice from another in the complex of tones, it was necessary to give each voice its own melodic contour and rhythmic scheme (see Example 5, page 15, for a typical passage). The expansion of that compass, begun a few decades before Josquin's time, was carried further in the late fifteenth and early sixteenth centuries. By increasing the use of techniques of imitation, composers were able to distribute the vocal lines across that larger compass; this in turn made it unnecessary to write each voice part in a different rhythmic style from that of its neighbors. As we saw in the account of the Masses, Josquin excelled in the use of imitation, and he also developed a high degree of rhythmic homogeneity in his motets.

In view of the flexibility enjoyed by the term "motet" in Josquin's time, it is appropriate to consider his settings of psalms under that term. According to Reese (*Music in the Renaissance*, p. 246), psalm settings in polyphonic style cannot be dated earlier than the beginning of the sixteenth century; perhaps the earliest example is a setting by Antoine Brumel, a contemporary of Josquin. Brumel's setting was published in 1514 by Petrucci in Venice in a volume that also contains the setting of a psalm by Josquin—the earliest that can be ascribed to him.

The Josquin work, Psalm cxviii (119), contains near its end a variant of the material heard near the beginning, a treatment similar to that seen in Example 11. (The Psalms are numbered differently in the Latin Catholic and King James Protestant Bibles; musical writings generally give both numberings: the Latin

EXAMPLE 11   Josquin, motet, *Ave Christe immolate*

(a) Part I, meas. 1–6

(b) Part II, meas. 57–63

From Friedrich Blume, *Das Chorwerk*, Vol. 18, edited by Friedrich Blume. Used by permission of Möseler Verlag, Wolfenbüttel and Zurich.

in Roman numerals followed by the King James in Arabic numerals.) Elsewhere Josquin's characteristic virtuosity in the use of imitative techniques is everywhere apparent. Psalm XCII (93), *Dominus regavit* (*The Lord is King*), is particularly open and transparent in its texture. Virtually every phrase of the text is given its own melodic line within its own section or point of imitation; pairs of voices then alternate in singing those melodies, and a full four-voice sonority is generally reserved for the climactic moments of the psalm. In Psalm CXXIX (130), *De profundis* (one of two settings he composed on that text), variety of textures is the outstanding feature. Extended passages in a low register for only two of the four voices, passages in block chords, others with long intertwined melismas, still others in which the tenor is consistently set above the alto, many repetitions of the phrase *et in saecula* ("world without end") culminating in a rousing *Amen*—with such elements the Psalm develops great emotional intensity and rises to dramatic climaxes. Other psalm settings by Josquin contain comparable variety.

In other motets the paraphrase technique, so imaginatively employed in the Masses, becomes characteristic; in yet others the cantus firmus is used—sometimes in long notes as found in the music of an earlier generation, at other times combined with a second and contrasting cantus firmus. And in addition to employing in masterful fashion all the devices of imitation, Josquin does not neglect canonic techniques; a canonic context is likely to appear when a cantus firmus is used—almost as if that remnant of a remote past were in special need of elaboration and embellishment.

This brief account of a few of the technical practices found in Josquin's motets cannot hope to suggest the variety of expressive states the motets reflect. We can hope only to make a few valid generalizations that illustrate the means he employed. The musical experiences to be gained from hearing this music are beyond the scope of verbal description; the motets must be rehearsed, sung, and studied—then sung again—to gain a true appreciation of their musical quality.

Isaac

Of the large number of composers active during the time of Josquin and a generation later, one may be singled out for his notable contributions. Heinrich Isaac (c. 1450–1517), whose career was divided between Italy and Austria, is remembered chiefly for a large collection of motets on texts drawn from the Proper of the Mass and from the Offices for the Feasts and Saints. This monumental work, commissioned by the Cathedral at Constance in 1508 and known as the *Choralis Constantinus,* represents the Flemish aspects of Isaac's style. The individual motets, most of them set for four voices, employ the appropriate plainsong chants as cantus firmi. Reflecting a mixture of conservative and forward-looking style tendencies, the cantus firmi are used in a variety of ways: sometimes in the upper voice instead of the tenor, not always set in the old-fashioned long notes, and often given the same rhythmic character as the surrounding voices. The textures are usually somewhat continuous, imitation playing

EXAMPLE 12   Clemens, motet, *Vox in Rama*

(Tr.: "A voice was heard in Rama.")

From Davison-Apel, *Historical Anthology of Music,* Vol. I. Used by permission of Harvard University Press.

an important role in them, and the lower voices give some evidence of having been written with instrumental performance in mind. Remaining incomplete at Isaac's death, the *Choralis Constantinus* was completed by his pupil, Ludwig Senfl (c. 1490–1542).

Clemens non Papa

In addition to his Masses, Clemens composed more than two hundred motets, as well as several books containing polyphonic settings of the Psalms in Dutch, designed for use in the Calvinist church. In general, his motets reveal that extreme contrasts in the rhythmic shape of the various voice parts had given way to essential uniformity of rhythms—a consequence of the considerable use of imitation in all voice parts, as in Josquin's music. And with imitative techniques in virtually every phrase, melodic motives (see Example 12), and similar rhythmic structures throughout the texture, the dominance of one voice over the others in Clemens' motets virtually disappeared. Their varied, sonorous texture, compounded of imitative counterpoint and chordal writing, became the common property of all Renaissance composers who set sacred texts to music.

3

Music for the Catholic Church 1525–1600

The sixteenth century saw a number of developments of great significance in the evolution of choral music. Following the accomplishments of Josquin des Prez, the Renaissance style reached its highest point in the works of three composers; the Italian Palestrina, the Flemish Lasso, and the English Byrd. At the same time a school of composers in Venice, beginning their work in the style of the Renaissance, moved away from that style and developed a distinctive Venetian manner of composing that anticipated in some respects the style of the seventeenth-century Baroque period. The continuing influence of the humanistic movement encouraged interest in secular texts, so that secular music came to rival sacred music in both its quality and quantity. Finally, the events set in motion by Martin Luther in Germany in 1517 and Henry VIII in England in 1534 split the Roman Catholic Church and gave rise to Protestant and Anglican churches that developed their own musical styles and repertoires.

Mass

Morales

In the late fifteenth and early sixteenth centuries Rome was known throughout the Christian world for the excellence and variety of its church music. The Papal Chapel had assembled perhaps the most outstanding choir in Christendom; its members were recruited largely from foreign countries and at various times included many eminent Franco-Flemish composers—Josquin chief among them—as well as numerous Spanish musicians (the musical connections between Italy and Spain being close in the sixteenth century).

The most important Spanish composer in Rome early in the century was Cristóbal de Morales (c. 1505–1553). He became a member of the Papal Chapel Choir in 1535, remained about ten years, and then returned to Spain. Among his works are 21 Masses and numerous motets, most of them published in Rome and presumably composed there. Based on the Franco-Flemish style, Morales's music was typical of the Spanish music of the period; it was conservative in its use of contrapuntal devices—with few melismatic passages, for example.

The majority of Morales's Masses are based on borrowed melodies—Gregorian chants, various contemporary motets, and Spanish and French popular songs. The cantus firmi are used in many ways, sometimes in the tenor exclusively and at other times in all the voices. Imitation and canonic writing are characteristic, and parody technique is approached at times in that two or three voices of the borrowed material are paraphrased together; yet when fragments of Gregorian chant are used, Morales usually adheres to their original shape and avoids excessive ornamentation. In such cases he quotes the chant exactly and adds appropriate and dignified counterpoints. Throughout these Masses, a restrained style remains basic; the intense aspects of Morales's style are found more often in the motets, which will be discussed below.

The Council of Trent

The discussion in the previous chapter indicated that the musical style which originated in the Duchy of Burgundy and the general area of the Netherlands had gradually come to dominate musical activities of Church and court alike in many parts of western Europe. Two elements of that style, as we have seen, are imitative counterpoint, in which text phrases are usually overlapped, and the parody technique, in which a variety of secular material is introduced into liturgical music. Conservative leaders of the Church became increasingly disturbed by such developments, for in the one case, the text was made largely unintelligible because of the text-phrase overlappings, and in the other, the sanctity of worship was diluted by the presence of popular tunes and secular madrigal fragments in the sacred forms.

The series of events that began with Martin Luther's activity in 1517 had led to the Protestant Reformation and to the recognition that certain practices of the Church needed revision. In 1545 a general council of the Church was called at Trent to deal with these problems. The Council lasted, with numerous long interruptions, until 1563, the relationship between music and sacred texts coming under discussion in its final year. Although the recommendations that resulted were very general and went no further than calling for greater intelligibility of the text and the avoidance of impure (that is, secular) influences in the music, they did hasten the development of a restrained, pure, and balanced style, introduced by Jacob Kerle (1531–1591) but carried to its highest point by Palestrina.

Palestrina

Born Giovanni Pierluigi about 1525 in Palestrina, a small town near Rome, the composer later added the name of his birthplace to his own. His entire professional career from 1551 developed in Rome—at the Julian Chapel in St. Peter's, at St. John Lateran, at Santa Maria Maggiore, and for his last 23 years again at the Julian Chapel until his death in 1594. His works include over 100 Masses, about 250 motets, and more than 200 other sacred compositions—Magnificats, Offertories, hymns, and sacred madrigals among them—plus 83 secular madrigals that are not representative of the type then developing (and which will be discussed in Chapter 5). The Mass, with its fixed text and its important place at the center of the Roman Catholic liturgy, occupies a high place in Palestrina's works; unlike Lasso, who seems to have favored motets, Palestrina was apparently more attracted to the Mass than to the motet, for many of his most expressive and representative works appear among the former.

Palestrina's style is based largely on elements drawn from Franco-Flemish music—a mixture of imitative counterpoint, canonic writing, and considerable amounts of chordal writing—to which he added some of the easy melodiousness characteristic of Italian music. These elements are so perfectly fused and handled with such restraint, refinement, and serenity that they give rise to an impersonal and objective kind of music dedicated solely to one purpose: to enhance the understanding of the texts to which they are set. Palestrina's style is consistent, and completely free of virtuosic effects—in fact so perfectly adapted to the liturgical texts that it sometimes seems to disappear (see Example 13).

Palestrina's essential conservatism is revealed by the large number (41) of four-voice Masses he wrote at a time when settings for five or more voices were much more common. On the other hand, he made full use of the variety of Mass types popular in his day, composing an abundance of parody Masses, and only a sprinkling of the older cantus firmus or canonic types. There are also a few that are *sine nomine* ("without name")—that is, presumably composed freely and not based on preexisting material.

Palestrina's melodic contours show a close kinship to those of Gregorian chant. Based on a mixture of leaps and stepwise progressions, his melodies reveal great care in their construction. It is a fundamental musical principle that a melodic leap attracts attention, and that a leap in a high voice or in the high range of any voice attracts more attention than in a low. Thus if two leaps in the same direction occur in a Palestrina melody, the higher interval is most often smaller than the lower one. Generally, however, Palestrina turned a melody containing a leap gently back upon itself in stepwise motion before allowing a second leap. His concern was always to minimize anything that would distract attention from the sanctity of the texts; his melodic procedures accomplished this purpose (see Example 14).

Dissonance treatment is another element that Palestrina kept under perfect control. In a basically consonant context, a dissonance is a strong attention-attracting device; the more extreme the dissonance, the more attention it attracts,

EXAMPLE 13   Palestrina, *Missa Tu es Petrus*

EXAMPLE 14   Palestrina, *Missa Papae Marcelli*

and the longer the tone providing the dissonance, the more obvious its effect.
The types of dissonance most common in Palestrina's music are the passing tone
(which forms a brief dissonance between two other tones that are themselves
consonant, as in Example 15a) and the suspension (which is a tone held over
from a previous chord in which it was consonant, as in Example 15b). In keeping
with his principles of dissonance treatment, Palestrina most often uses passing
tones in melodies that are moving rapidly—the more rapidly the better for his
purposes, and the passing tone is rarely placed on an accented beat, where its
presence would be even more obvious. Similarly the suspension, arising out of
a consonance, is absorbed into the next following consonance by downward
stepwise motion, and is virtually never accented—that is, never sounded afresh
at the moment of dissonance, but always tied to the consonant portion of the
sound.

EXAMPLE 15   Palestrina, (a) *Missa Brevis*; (b) *Missa Papae Marcelli*

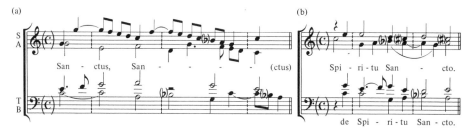

Palestrina treated all other musical elements with similar care. Without ever violating normal voice ranges or the natural progression of his melodies, he nevertheless produced a large variety of highly imaginative vocal combinations, each with its own coloration and distinctive sonority. In three-voice passages, for example, the alto is sometimes set above the two sopranos, and sometimes between them; or all three voices may be set close together at the top or bottom of the range. The addition of the fourth and fifth voices adds many other spacing possibilities: widely spread, crowded near the bottom, the top separated from the bottom, and so on. Such purely musical effects were for Palestrina a potent means of providing variety and expressiveness in his music, and they are among its most attractive features.

As for the texts, they are invariably set with regard for their proper accentuation, each text phrase thus acquiring its own rhythmic scheme. Yet Palestrina so spaced the text accents in the contrapuntal context that an overall duple (occasionally triple) meter results. The harmonic organization of the music shows a logical progression of chords—from supertonic to dominant to tonic, for example—across extended passages, and later passages are closely related to or even harmonic repetitions of earlier ones. Thus with rhythmic scheme and harmonic organization under firm control, his music has a high degree of unity.

It must be said that Palestrina was not alone in his century in his manner of employing the elements of composition. Other composers too had been careful to control the contours of their melodies, and had restricted their dissonance treatment. But Palestrina is set above his contemporaries by the consistency of his stylistic practices, by the rigor with which he controlled every attention-attracting device, and by the degree to which he avoided elements foreign to his purpose. His success lay in composing reverent, restrained, and technically flawless music perfectly suited to a single purpose: to enhance the sacred texts in accord with his own sense of appropriateness.

Other Roman composers

Palestrina's style was reflected in the music of several of his contemporaries, among whom Giovanni Maria Nanino and Felice Anerio may be mentioned. Nanino (c. 1543–1607), probably a pupil of Palestrina's, served as his successor at Santa Maria Maggiore and later moved to St. Peter's. Anerio (c. 1564–1614), at first a choirboy under Palestrina's direction, later succeeded him as composer to the Papal Chapel. Although he composed numerous Masses, his chief accomplishments are disclosed in his motets and madrigals. His style resembled Palestrina's so closely that several works formerly thought to be by the master of the Roman school are now correctly attributed to Anerio.

Of far greater importance, however, was Tomás Luis de Victoria (c. 1549–1611), who lived in Rome from 1565 to about 1584, after which he returned to his native Spain. Like Morales more than a generation earlier, Victoria composed in an emotionally rich and fervent style. Twenty Masses, a number of motets, and many other sacred compositions were published during his lifetime, but no secular music is included in his work. In a style that is essentially remote and dignified, Victoria introduced many dramatic and illustrative effects, but did so primarily in his motets.

The majority of Victoria's twenty Masses are of the parody type, and are based on his own motets as well as motets by Morales, Palestrina, and others. A comparison of the Masses with the motets on which they are based shows that he used the parody technique imaginatively, often altering the borrowed melodies to reflect the sense of the Mass text. In the Masses, Victoria sometimes uses more voices than were used in the borrowed material; melodies employed imitatively in the model he may set canonically in the Mass; he may change the time interval between pairs of voices in imitation, and so on.

Occasionally, Victoria will add a descriptive touch of the kind typical of the secular madrigals of the time (see Chapter 5); his *Missa O magnum mysterium* provides an example: in the Credo, at the passage beginning *Et resurrexit tertia die* ("On the third day He rose again from the dead"), the meter shifts from duple to triple and only three voices sing the words *tertia die*. But such touches are rare, as are all similar devices—technical or musical—that would offend Victoria's deep reverence for the Mass. Yet a few of his Masses are set for two choirs with *basso continuo* (see page 68) and are composed in the Venetian manner (see page 45) with shorter note values than usual and with chordal passages containing many repeated notes. One late work, his *Missa pro Victoria*, for double choir of nine voices plus *continuo*, is obviously modeled on the Venetian Masses of the time, which are in turn harbingers of the Baroque style of the following century.

Lasso

The long line of Franco-Flemish composers that began with Binchois and Dufay in the fifteenth century came to its highest point in the works of Orlando di Lasso (also referred to as Orlandus Lassus and sometimes Rolande de Lattre). Lasso was born in Mons in 1532, and as a boy was known for the beauty of his singing voice. After several years in Rome and elsewhere in Italy as a choir singer and composer (his first compositions were published in Venice in 1555), he moved to Antwerp. In 1556 he entered the service of the Bavarian court at Munich, where he remained until his death in 1594.

Orlando di Lasso with his singers and instrumentalists. Contemporary painting, artist unknown.

Lasso was one of the most prolific composers of his time; his surviving works include more than fifty Masses and many hundreds of sacred and secular compositions in a great variety of forms. At first showing himself to be a typical man of the Renaissance in his enthusiasms, experimental attitudes, and interest in expressing a variety of emotions in his music, Lasso later (after about 1560) became more restrained and serious in his composing, possibly because of the impact made by the Counter Reformation in Church affairs and sacred music generally.

In Lasso's Masses the parody technique is greatly in evidence, with the borrowed material treated in a number of different ways. Melodic motives are sometimes derived from the tunes and are freely imitated to form independent sections within a Mass movement. The material is often lengthened or shortened, and free counterpoints are composed to fit. In shorter Mass movements the borrowed material is sometimes not used; in longer ones it may appear several times. The end result is a series of Masses that are well proportioned, varied, and elegant in all details. Yet with all their quality, they are overshadowed by his motets, which will be discussed below.

Composers in Venice

Whether because of its unvarying text, its special liturgical function, or its centuries-old structure, the sixteenth-century Mass remained essentially a conservative form. Even in Venice, which in the middle 1500s saw the rise of a new motet style characterized by antiphonal writing and general brilliance, the Mass was stylistically rooted in the past. For example, the Masses of Adrian Willaert (c. 1490–1562), Cipriano de Rore (1516–1565), Andrea Gabrieli (c. 1520–1586), and Claudio Merulo (1533–1604) are not far removed from the style of Josquin. Largely of the parody type, they are full of solid counterpoint and a considerable use of canon; a high level of competence is everywhere apparent in them. But it is not to the Mass that we must look for the color and splendor associated with the Venetian style; it is to the motet (see page 73).

Composers in England

The second half of the fifteenth century had marked a politically unstable period in English history. A war of almost thirty years' duration, ending with the accession of Henry VII to the throne in 1485, had served to isolate England to some extent from continental influences. Few Franco-Flemish composers moved to that country until after the beginning of the sixteenth century, and many of the stylistic elements in their music were slow to appear in English music, since conditions for composing were not favorable. In the 1520s, the picture changed with the emergence of a group of native-born composers who made notable contributions to the English scene.

Toward the middle of the sixteenth century, in England as well as on the Continent, composers began to write Masses that required less time to sing than the large festival Masses and that could be performed in churches with more modest vocal resources than the large cathedrals enjoyed. In Masses of this type, the Kyrie and sections of the Credo were often omitted, melismas and text repetitions were kept to a minimum, and the whole was generally set in a simple, often chordal style. Such a Mass was called a *Missa brevis* or "short Mass," and many examples may be found in English music of the time, notably a number by Nicholas Ludford (died c. 1540).

Of greater importance is John Taverner (c. 1495–1545), organist at Oxford University from 1526. Among his surviving works are eight short Masses, one of which includes the use of a secular cantus firmus, "The Western Wynde"; the work represents one of the rare uses of a secular tune in an English Mass. The presence of extremely long melismas is characteristic here, as it is of his music in general; thus this Mass is not typical of the *brevis* type.

Taverner was probably the last prominent English composer to adhere entirely to the Roman Catholic liturgy. His contemporaries and successors divided their interest between the old faith and the requirements of the newly formed Anglican church which arose after 1534, when Henry VIII withdrew his allegiance and that of the English people from the authority of the Pope. For several decades thereafter, several English composers found themselves in a precarious position. In spite of their official employment within the Anglican church or at the Chapel Royal, they composed settings of liturgical texts in Latin even as they contributed to the creation of new musical forms on English texts.

Christopher Tye (c. 1499–c. 1572) served as organist of Ely Cathedral from about 1540 and made notable contributions to the new form of the anthem, which will be discussed below (see page 52). But he wrote for the Roman Catholic liturgy as well; four Masses and several motets are among his works on Latin texts. The influence of Franco-Flemish composers on Tye is seen in his generally contrapuntal style that includes many elaborate melismas. And Tye was among the first composers of the time in whose works differences between Roman Catholic and Anglican styles can be discerned.

Thomas Tallis (c. 1505–1585), organist at Waltham Abbey, then from about 1540 to his death a member of the Chapel Royal, composed with equal facility for both services. Two Masses may be mentioned for the melodic unity they exhibit. In one, a five-part parody Mass, *Missa Salve intemerato* ("Hail, Unblemished"), every movement begins with the identical motive in the two lower voices, after which all the voices go their various contrapuntal ways. The other, a four-part *Missa sine nomine,* employs essentially the same device, but with a slightly greater degree of freedom. In other respects the Masses are typical of their time.

Of far greater importance are three Masses by William Byrd (1543–1623), the most significant English composer of the sixteenth century. Throughout his long life Byrd remained a staunch Catholic, in spite of his service as organist of Lincoln Cathedral from 1563 and his membership of almost fifty years (from 1570) in the Chapel Royal, where he was closely associated with Tallis. The Masses are for three, four, and five voices, respectively; and all three are constructed in a fashion similar to the Masses of Tallis, in that each Mass has a prominent motive at the beginning of each of its movements. In other respects, however, the Masses reveal individual characteristics. The first is reserved and filled with a meditative air. The second is rhythmically diverse and vocally colorful with eloquent melismas and elaborate counterpoint, but it too is a meditative work. The third, longer and more powerful than the others, rises to dramatic heights; a fusion of chordal and contrapuntal passages occurs here (see Example 16), yet the several movements flow from beginning to end with few internal divisions. All three Masses contain a full share of wonderfully expressive melodies; even when sung out of context, the latter reveal the kind of beauty that is typical of virtually all of Byrd's choral compositions (see Example 17).

Motet

Morales

The variety of elements Morales used in his Masses appears also in his motets. Contrapuntal textures similar to those of Josquin but with fewer melismas, voices

EXAMPLE 16   Byrd, *Mass for Five Voices*, Credo

EXAMPLE 17   Byrd, *Mass for Five Voices*, Credo

used in pairs, and a constantly changing sonority are typical. One practice, however—the use of double texts—recalls Medieval style characteristics. Many of Morales's motets use a different text in one voice from the one on which the motet is based; in Morales's hands the added text serves a dramatic purpose without being a distraction, provides an appropriate commentary on the main text, and contributes to the intensity of expression for which Morales is noted.

One of his best-known motets, *Emendemus in melius (Let us make amends)*, illustrates the emotional fervor that is characteristic of these works (the motet is printed in *Historical Anthology of Music [HAM]*, No. 128). The text, from a response for the service of Ash Wednesday, is carried by four voices in traditional fashion; but to this a fifth voice, based on the text "Remember, man, that thou art dust" adds a mystical and penitential note. Dissonances, caused mainly by suspensions, are confined largely to words or phrases that are particularly signifi-cant, such as "sin," "death," and "mercy," and enhance the emotional effect of the whole.

Palestrina

More than four hundred works of various types, all of which may be grouped under the general term "motet," were composed by Palestrina. About 250 are true motets; a large number are Offertories, from the Proper of the Mass; others are Magnificats, from the Office of Vespers; still others are settings of such texts as psalms, hymns, and litanies. Although these works have many individual characteristics and differ according to type, as a whole they embody the principles that animated Palestrina throughout his lifetime and that we saw at work in his Masses. Restrained, unsensational, free of secular encroachments, eloquent in their sensitivity to their texts and the purposes of the liturgy—such characteristics are basic to the motets, as they are to the Masses.

Possibly because of the more varied texts, stylistic elements appear in Palestrina's motets that had not been prominent in the majority of the Masses. Some motets, for example, are largely in chordal style, notably the well-known *Stabat mater*. In a number of motets the sectional form (a consequence of giving each phrase of the text its own melodic material, which is then treated imitatively) is modified by repeating or varying each section after its first appearance; in the motet *Veni sponsa Christi* (*Come, Thou Spouse of Christ*), for example, Palestrina develops a form in which every even-numbered section is a transposition of the preceding odd-numbered part.

Palestrina's 35 settings of the Magnificat (grouped into four sets of eight with each member of a set being based on a different psalm tone° plus three additional settings) reflect an age-old tradition in the performance of plainsong. Alternate verses retain the Gregorian chant, while the other verses are set polyphonically. Settings range from three to eight voices, and in some cases devices of canon are employed. A set of Offertories spanning the entire Church year differ from earlier works (those of Lasso excepted) in that they are not merely polyphonic settings of the corresponding chants, but are freely composed and do not quote or paraphrase the Gregorian material. The Offertories are rich in examples of word-painting in appropriate passages, and illustrate the extent to which tonal° (as opposed to modal°) considerations had led to an increasing use of full triads. But the concept of modern major and minor tonalities is not yet apparent in Palestrina's music; that concept developed elsewhere than in Rome.

Victoria

The dramatic aspects of Victoria's style are generally handled subtly and discreetly. Many of his motets, for example, employ illustrative effects: a fondness for minor seconds in the motet *O vos omnes* (in *HAM*, No. 149) to express the lamentations of Jeremiah; leaps of diminished fourths to reflect grief; a stepwise upward progression through an octave to delineate the ascension of Christ; passages in chordal style when the text introduces the words "all" or "many"; and changes of meter from duple to triple when the idea of the Trinity is introduced.

The majority of Victoria's motets are settings for four, five, or six voices; but

others, particularly several settings of the Magnificat and settings of four antiphons in honor of the Virgin Mary, are for two or three choirs, each choir usually
for four voices. Some of these works are supplied with organ in *continuo* fashion
(see page 68)—without, however, adopting the short-phrased chordal style of
the Venetian school. But occasionally in moments where the text suggests emotional stress, Victoria did not hesitate to use many repeated notes within a phrase,
thus producing a dramatic touch in the Venetian manner. The texts in such works
are set antiphonally in the majority of cases, with alternate verses or text phrases
sung by the two choirs in turn.

Lasso

Lasso's vast contribution to the sacred and secular literatures of the sixteenth
century includes hundreds of motets (one set alone, the *Magnus opus musicum*,
contains no fewer than 516) along with several hundred secular pieces in various
forms. To a greater extent than virtually any of his contemporaries, Lasso became
a truly international composer. He was able to absorb all the various national
styles then being formed, composing Italian madrigals, French chansons, German
polyphonic lieder, and Flemish motets, as well as traditional settings in Latin—
with due regard for the essence of each style and with equal facility in all.

Lasso's sensitivity to the expressive possibilities of whatever text he was setting
is one of his outstanding characteristics. This is seen in a negative way in his
Masses, in which the invariability of the text seems not to have inspired him
equally at all times. In the motets, however, with a virtually unlimited range
of texts on many subjects available to him, he rose to his best efforts. His
imagination seemed inexhaustible in devising the exact kind of musical treatment
best suited to the literal sense of each text as well as its underlying meaning.

Among his first published works in this category is a set of motets for five
and six voices printed in Antwerp in 1556. These works reveal that Lasso had
absorbed the changes in musical style that took place about the middle of the
sixteenth century. Many composers now chose texts in which biblical figures were
personally involved with grief, suffering, and the like; larger philosophical
concerns were less often reflected in motets. In the interest of textual clarity,
a chordal style of writing with texts set in syllabic fashion (each syllable receiving
one note) often took the place of involved polyphony. And probably as a result
of the chordal writing, development of the vertical dimension of music grew
stronger: circle-of-fifths progressions,° tonal rather than modal cadences, bass
lines moving in fourths or fifths, fewer cross relations°—such elements were
forerunners of the decline of the modal system and the beginning of the tonal
system that was to be developed in the following century. (The fact that one
cannot apply such generalizations to the music of Palestrina is in itself a mark
of the Roman composer's conservative spirit.)

Yet Lasso revealed many individual style traits as well. His personal temperament, exuberant and questing in large part, is reflected in a vigorous rhythmic
style in which syncopations, many dotted rhythms, cross accents,° and sudden

changes of meter are characteristic whenever such devices enhance or augment the sense of the text. Although he was perfectly capable of writing in strict imitative style and even in canon, he most often preferred to write freely, confining the imitation to the first few tones of a phrase. And a passage that gives the appearance of counterpoint is in fact often based on the manipulation or elaboration of a single triad, disguised by rhythmic diversity and many passing tones.

These and other aspects of Lasso's style are eloquently present in his set of seven *Psalmi Davidis poenitentiales* (*Penitential Psalms of David*), composed about 1560, shortly after his move to the Bavarian court at Munich. The *Penitential Psalms* have long been held to represent one of the high points of sixteenth-century music as well as the greatest work of this Flemish master. The psalms included in the set are VI, XXXI, XXXVII, L, CI, CXXIX, and CXLII (6, 32, 38, 51, 102, 130, and 143). Each of them is concluded by the Lesser Doxology (*Gloria patri*). Lasso subdivides his texts in such a manner that the complete setting of the seven *Penitential Psalms* comprises no less than 132 motets.

Many passages in the *Penitential Psalms* are predominantly harmonic; the bass in such passages traces several steps in the circle-of-fifths (see Examples 18a and 18b), or else the harmony remains virtually static for several measures (Example 18c). In decided contrast to such harmonically oriented passages are others in which all the arts of polyphony are eloquently revealed. Imitative passages begin at various intervals and after different time spans; not confined to the fifth or octave, as was the general practice of the time, the imitation may be carried forward at any scale step. And most often the imitation is broken off after the beginning fragment has been imitated, to dissolve into free counterpoint (see Example 19a). Although much of the writing is chordal and texts are set in syllabic style, Lasso often composes long melismas for expressive or illustrative purposes, especially in passages for two or three voices; scarcely any extended passage is without a florid section in two or more voices simultaneously. These melismas give Lasso's music its flowing, mellifluous charm, and serve to a large degree to differentiate it from the music of his contemporaries.

EXAMPLE 18   Lasso, (a) First Penitential Psalm (VI), 5;
                              (b) Fourth Penitential Psalm (L), 10;
                              (c) Sixth Penitential Psalm (CXXIX), 5

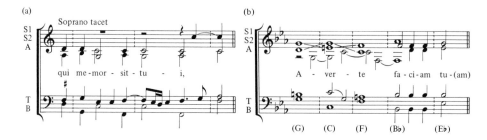

(c)

(Tr.: (a) "[For in death there is no] remembrance of thee."
(b) "Hide thy face [from my sins]."
(c) "My soul waits [for the Lord].")

Throughout the motets, text and music are closely related in a way that enhances the expressiveness of both components. Certain obvious devices, which abound in the music of the sixteenth century, are frequently found in Lasso's works, such as a passage in rapid notes to illustrate *velociter* ("quickly"), a descending melodic line to carry the idea of *profundis* ("deep"), or a leap upward on the word *coelum* ("Heaven"). But there are subtler examples of Lasso's felicitousness, such as the passage in Psalm No. V, Motet 8, where the words meaning "I am as a sparrow alone" are set in a long melisma; in Psalm No. IV, Motet 6, on the text "And thou forgavest the iniquity of my sin," where the setting is a song of jubilation; or in Psalm No. V, Motet 14, on the text, "Thou shalt arise and have mercy upon Sion," where the middle voice graphically illustrates the verb (see Example 19b).

EXAMPLE 19   Lasso, (a) Seventh Penitential Psalm (CXLII), 13;
                              (b) Fifth Penitential Psalm (CI), 14

(a)

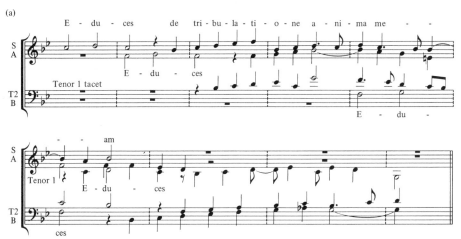

(Tr.: (a) "Bring my soul out of trouble."
(b) "Thou shalt arise and have mercy on Sion.")

The gradual encroachment of tonal devices became ever more prominent as the sixteenth century progressed. *Musica ficta°* had long since been established, of course, and had contributed to the weakening of the differences between one mode and another. Full triads, containing either a major or minor third, were being employed with increasing frequency. Bass lines often served a harmonic rather than a melodic function and progressed by fourths and fifths; above such root tones, then, the primary and secondary triads could be constructed, and progressions from dominant to tonic were customary in many works.

Lasso's music illustrates all the new harmonic practices of the time. It is significant that cross relations, which were a characteristic feature of older modal music, become increasingly rare in Lasso's work, while circle-of-fifths progressions are relatively common, as we saw in Example 18b. The sum of these and similar harmonic practices was to hasten the demise of modality and speed the full establishment of tonality with its system of major and minor scales. The latter system, it should be said, advanced more rapidly in secular works than in sacred. But there too Lasso was in the ranks of the progressive composers, as we shall see in Chapter 5.

Venetian Motet

Rome, the center of the Roman Catholic faith, was a city with a devotional, somewhat mystical air. Its music, especially that of Palestrina and his contemporaries, was inclined to sobriety and reserve. Venice, on the contrary, was opened out to the brilliant and ornate world of the East; Venetian traders had made their city-state the principal port for traffic with the Orient, and Venice reflected all the splendor, wealth, and active life of a cosmopolitan city. Thus the musical style of Venetian composers, influenced by a more colorful way of life, developed in quite another fashion than did the style of Roman composers— except in the Mass.

The chief ornament of Venice was (and is) St. Mark's Cathedral, with its gold-encrusted Byzantine domes, its profusion of mosaics and sculptures, and its architectural plan that made possible two choir lofts, each with an organ. Music was at the center of every Venetian ceremony, whether religious or civic. Even in the seventeenth century, when Venice had reached the lowest point of her commercial and political fortunes, the first public opera house was established there, and much of the time several opera companies were active simultaneously.

In the sixteenth century the post of chapelmaster at St. Mark's Cathedral was among the most honored positions in the musical world, and a long line of eminent composers occupied that position or the virtually parallel position of first or second organist. Adrian Willaert (c. 1490–1562) served as chapelmaster from 1527 and became the founder of a specific Venetian style. That style was characterized by the use of double choir; the presence of the two facing choir lofts in St. Mark's doubtless encouraged the idea of antiphonal singing, an old Byzantine tradition with which the far-traveling Venetians were acquainted. The indication *"cori spezzati"* ("broken" or "divided choirs") had appeared in two fifteenth-century manuscripts from Modena, containing mostly works by Franco-Flemish composers. Thus, while composers of Willaert's generation did not introduce the idea of double choir, they developed it and made it a feature of their music.

Antiphonal writing, with its implication of a double or divided choir, appears in many of Willaert's motets, psalms, and other works. A necessary feature of this technique, apparent in these works, is a series of short phrases set in block chords instead of a contrapuntal texture. Given the vast reaches of a cathedral like St. Mark's and the acoustical problems that a polyphonic composition would face there, it is clear that a chordal style would be more effective and would be entirely suitable to antiphonal performance with the two choirs placed in the facing choir lofts.

The motets of Willaert's principal successors—Cipriano de Rore, Claudio Merulo, and Andrea Gabrieli—develop the style far beyond Willaert in their variety of vocal color and special antiphonal effects—such as echoes—in the two opposing groups, and sometimes (later in the century) in their use of instruments.

Gabrieli

The Venetian style reached its highest point of development in the works of Giovanni Gabrieli (c. 1557–1612), a nephew of Andrea. Gabrieli succeeded his uncle as second organist at St. Mark's in 1585, after having been a colleague of Lasso's in Munich a few years earlier; his style was to become quite different from that of the older Flemish composer, however. Gabrieli is noted especially for his imaginative use of tone color—both vocal and instrumental; for his part in developing a chordal style based on short and incisive phrases that move freely within the texture, from low voice to high, from one choir to another; and for his accomplishments in bridging the gap into the next style period, the Baroque.

Published in several sets between 1587 and 1615, Gabrieli's works expanded the concept of double choir to embrace polychoral writing: among his motets and other sacred compositions are some for as many as four or five separate accompanied choirs. When he composed for a single choir he sometimes wrote for as many as eight voices, and then did not use the antiphonal style. In works for two choirs, however, he generally used no more than five or six voices in each; while in those for three or more choirs, four voices in each usually sufficed. Contrapuntal writing is often abandoned in those larger multivoiced works in favor of a chordal style; as we have seen, ensemble and acoustical difficulties arising from the separated choirs in the vast spaces of the Cathedral and the adjoining Piazza San Marco (for much of the Venetian music was used for civic ceremonies held out of doors) contributed to the development of a chordal style (see Example 20).

EXAMPLE 20   G. Gabrieli, *Hodie completi sunt*

(Tr.: "Today [the days of Pentecost] are ended.")

Gabrieli carried the Venetian love of elaborateness and pomp even further by providing instrumental accompaniments for many of his works, writing parts not only for the two organs in the choir lofts but for string and wind instruments as well. These parts were not confined to supporting or doubling the vocal parts, as had most generally been the earlier practice, but they often included independent melodies and short passages in which instruments were used alone (such a passage was called a *sinfonia*). Deploying this complex of voices and instruments in masterful fashion, Gabrieli brought colorful display and magnificence to his music, and a wealth of sonority that was admirably suited to the occasions for which it was written.

To a greater extent than any composer before him, Gabrieli exploited the principle of contrast. He delighted in the sound of high voices against low, in the interplay of contrapuntal and chordal passages, and in the drama of a strongly rhythmic moment opposite a quiet one. All these practices had become standard in Venetian music, of course. But the addition of an independent instrumental force greatly increased the possibilities of contrast, and Gabrieli took full advantage of it. Instrumental groups are often set opposite vocal groups or solo voices; or various sections of the instrumental ensemble engage in antiphonal performance, with the distinctive tone colors of the differing instruments themselves providing contrast. (In the seventeenth century, this methodical alternation of opposed and contrasting forces would be expanded, given the name *concertato*, and would eventually become basic to an important instrumental form, the *concerto*.)

The emphasis on contrast in Gabrieli's music is one of the several elements that transcends the style of the Renaissance. Thoroughly grounded in the music of the sixteenth century and taking his point of departure from the music of Josquin and other Franco-Flemish composers, Gabrieli brought Venetian music to a peak of emotional richness and excitement and carried its style forward into the Baroque period. With the music of Gabrieli, the long domination of musical development by composers from the north came virtually to an end. A period of domination by Italian composers began, to last almost a century and a half.

Motet in England and Germany

Thomas Tallis, whose Masses were mentioned above, contributed outstanding motets also. His sensitivity to the meaning of his texts was greater perhaps than any of his contemporaries' and, at the same time, his melodies were invariably of rare beauty. One of his 30-odd motets, the massive *Spem in alium* (*Hope in Another*), set for 40 voices grouped mostly into eight choirs of five voices each, shows Tallis's mastery of imitative counterpoint: its first section presents one phrase heard in 20 voices in succession, and in a later section 28 voices in various groupings present other phrases. Elsewhere, free counterpoint is employed, again with various vocal groupings, and the work ends with all 40 voices in counterpoint. Other Latin works by Tallis exhibit similar technical and expressive mastery. They include responsories, Marian motets (whose texts are based on insertions in the Gloria of the Gregorian Mass that venerates the Virgin Mary), Magnificats, and Lamentations. Canonic devices are present in some, chordal writing in others; even cantus firmus appears on occasion. Always an interplay of high and low voices adds rich color effects to the music.

One other composition of Tallis's deserves mention, as an experiment in the style of the prechoral days of the fourteenth century. His setting of the responsory *Audivi vocem* (*I Heard a Voice*), is built of sections set alternately in polyphonic and monophonic textures (reprinted in *HAM*, No. 127). The polyphonic sections, set for four voices in imitative style, are performed by a group of soloists, while the monophonic sections of plainchant are designed for a choir singing in unison (see page 10).

Byrd

The 30-odd motets and related compositions on Latin texts by William Byrd include some of his finest works. Published in several books between 1575 and 1607 and set for five to eight voices, they reveal a great variety of textures, expressive types, and technical means. Imitative writing dominates in most of them, but various examples of involved canonic techniques also appear. Byrd's sensitivity to textual implications is everywhere apparent, often extending as far as detailed word-painting. Considerable repetition of significant words, striking dissonances on words having emotional connotations, rising or falling melodic lines when the text suggests such motion (on "arise," "descend," "sleep," and the like), abrupt changes from long to short note values (at the word "suddenly")—such touches are typical.

Byrd's motets are often characterized by wide melodic leaps, considerable diversity of note lengths, and mixed textures. His *Ego sum panis vivus* (*I am the Bread of Life;* see *Masterpieces of Music before 1750* [*MM*], No. 25), for example, with its many melodic leaps of fifths and octaves, its range of note values from a whole note to a sixteenth, its shifting rhythmic scheme, and its frequent short melismas, is full of jubilation. Such expressiveness is everywhere characteristic of Byrd's motets and contributes largely to their high musical quality.

Hassler

Hans Leo Hassler (1564–1612), in spite of having been a German Protestant, was responsible for the music in a Catholic church in Augsburg; thus in the course of his duties he composed several Masses and a number of motets. In one of the latter, *Quia vidisti me* (*Because Thou hast seen me*), the passages in imitation are intertwined with short motivelike phrases, sung alternately by high and low voices (see *HAM,* No. 164). This and similar works, presumably among his early compositions, are somewhat influenced by the style of Lasso. Later, adopting the polychoral style of Gabrieli, Hassler composed motets that brought to Germany the grandeur and large-scale sonority of the music of Venice.

An example of Hassler's Venetian style is his motet *Laudate Dominum* (*Praise Ye the Lord,* reprinted in *A Treasury of Early Music* [*TEM*], No. 28). The work is set for two four-voice choirs of different color and range—sopranos and altos in the one; alto, two tenors, and bass in the other. Hassler achieves a number of textures in this setting; the first phrases are sung by Choir I in imitative style; the next are heard in alternation between Choirs I and II, but each choir has its own music, only the text being alternated; the final section is set for eight parts, again in chordal style and with much text repetition, and the whole rises to a sonorous climax. Hassler makes dramatic use of his vocal colors by alternating the high voices with the low in the first two sections, and the brilliant effect of the motet is entirely in keeping with the spirit of the Psalm.

4

Music for the Protestant and Anglican Churches 1525–1625

The Protestant Reformation, begun by the Augustinian monk Martin Luther in Wittenberg in 1517, greatly influenced the sound and shape of church music in northern Europe, but the full effects of the change were not felt for several decades. Even in Germany, where the Reformation first took root, the alteration of the Roman Catholic liturgy and the emergence of the Lutheran proceeded slowly. In some areas, notably those that maintained capable choirs at the larger churches, the service remained largely in Latin and, following the suggestions made by Luther in his publication of a *Deudsche Messe* ("German Mass") in 1526, polyphonic settings of certain Mass items were retained.

Luther's main purpose in preparing his version of the Mass was to involve the congregation in singing appropriate sections of the service. To this end he sought to make the text understandable for those who knew no Latin—certainly the great majority of the participants. The text of the Ordinary was therefore sung in German; the Gloria was omitted, however, and German versions of the Credo, Sanctus, and Agnus Dei (differing in many respects from the Latin text) were substituted. The Proper of the Mass was similarly modified by substituting German songs with appropriate texts for the Gradual and Offertory, and providing several options for the omitted Communion.

The German Mass was entirely optional, however, and the flexibility of the emerging Lutheran liturgy made possible any number of individual or regional alternates. Latin texts were permitted along with or in place of German texts; an appropriate German song could be substituted for any item of the Ordinary; prose texts could be spoken instead of sung—especially in rural areas where high musical skills were not to be expected—and so on. Thus, rather than attempting to prescribe a uniform liturgy in all parts of Protestant Europe, Luther and his followers encouraged a flexibility of liturgical observance that took local differences into account; this freedom was maintained into the early years of the eighteenth century.

Chorale and Chorale Motet

The Lutheran version of congregational song played an important role in the future course of choral music. In 1524 at Wittenberg, Johann Walther (1496–1570), Luther's friend and musical advisor, published his *Geystlich gesangk buchleyn* (*Little Book of Sacred Songs*) containing 38 songs with German texts (23 of the texts by Luther himself) and five Latin motets. This historically important work was issued in several editions up to 1551, with additional songs in each edition. The settings of the German melodies, for three, four, and five voices, are all in cantus firmus style, with the principal melody in the tenor in all but two cases (see *TEM*, No. 24). About half the songs present free counterpoints above and below the melody, while the other half are written predominantly in a chordal style that includes a well-marked cadence at the end of each line of the text. This publication was followed by other similar collections containing works by a number of Lutheran composers, and within fifty years some 200 sacred songs were available.

The sources of the texts and melodies were varied. As we have seen, Luther wrote many of them himself, including *Ein' feste Burg* (*A Mighty Fortress*); others were translations of Latin religious songs, and still others were adaptations or parodies of secular song texts with the words changed to express an appropriate religious sentiment. Thus the words of a song by Isaac, "Innsbruck, I must now leave thee," became "O world, I must now leave thee" and became one of the best-known texts in the Lutheran repertoire. Melodies were derived in similar fashion: some were taken over directly from popular songs and supplied with new texts; others were adapted from various sources, and many new melodies were composed in the general style of the old.

A sacred song of this type became known as a *chorale*. Usually 12 to 16 measures in length and having a text consisting of several four-line stanzas, the chorale was at first sung as a single-line melody by the congregation. Soon, however, various other methods of performance were adopted, and more elaborate chorale settings resulted. One common setting was in four fully harmonized parts, with the melody in the top voice; in this form the successive verses were sung alternately by the choir in parts (schools and adult singing societies were organized for the purpose of training the participants in this activity) and by the congregation in unison. By about 1600, organ or other instrumental accompaniment was usually provided. For separate use by the choir, the chorale melody was often employed as a cantus firmus in a motetlike composition in which freely composed sections, melodic elaboration, and imitative counterpoint were min-

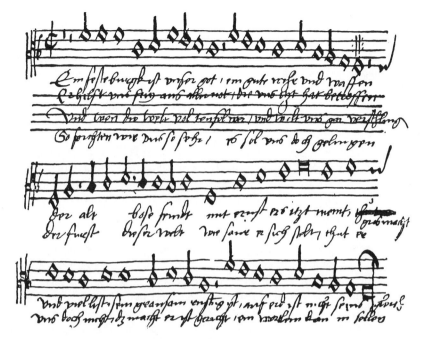

Autograph copy of Martin Luther's *Ein' feste Burg.*

gled. Such *chorale motets* became important items in the newly emerging
Lutheran church music of the seventeenth century, contributed to the rich
literature of the eighteenth, and rose to their zenith in the music of Bach.

Notable among the composers of the early chorale motet was Johann Eccard
(1553–1611), who studied with Lasso in Munich, then became professionally
active in Berlin. His chorale motets, some for four and some for five voices,
brought the Franco-Flemish style to the music of the Lutheran church. Another
was Hans Leo Hassler (1564–1612), who worked in Nuremberg and Dresden,
after having studied with Gabrieli at Venice. In addition to writing conventional
motets, Hassler also composed a number of secular songs of various types; one
of the latter, *Mein gmüth ist mir verwirret* (*My spirit is troubled*), was supplied
with a sacred text shortly after Hassler's death. The melody of that song subsequently became one of the treasures of the chorale repertoire; known by the
text "O sacred Head now wounded," it was used five times by Johann Sebastian
Bach in his *Passion According to St. Matthew* with different harmonizations and
different texts.

A number of Hassler's contemporaries and immediate successors introduced
new style characteristics that belong properly to an account of the Baroque
period. Among them were such notable figures as Michael Praetorius (1571–1621),
Johann Herman Schein (1586–1630), and above all, Heinrich Schütz (1585–1672).
The music of these composers will be discussed in Chapter 6.

Calvinist Psalm Settings

Quite separate from these Lutheran developments are those that took place under the influence of Jean Calvin, at first in Geneva and other parts of Switzerland, later in France and elsewhere in northern Europe. Adherents of Calvin's reforms opposed themselves to the Roman Catholic liturgy and theology more strongly than the Lutherans, and decreed against the singing of any nonbiblical texts. Thus, the texts of the psalms came to occupy a central place in the Calvinist form of worship. The Calvinists prepared rhymed metrical French translations of the Book of Psalms, which were set to melodies adapted from secular tunes or else composed for the occasion. The psalms were then sung unaccompanied by the congregation in unison. The contributions of Claude Goudimel (c. 1505–1572) were especially important in this connection (see *HAM*, No. 126a).

A more elaborate type of psalm setting was permitted in devotional services in the home, however. For this purpose the melody was supplied with three or more accompanying parts, arranged either chordally or in a contrapuntal style similar to the motets of Lutheran Germany; a setting of Psalm xxxiv (35) by Claude Le Jeune is found in *HAM*, No. 126b, and two versions of Psalm xxii (23) by Goudimel are in *TEM*, Nos. 25 and 26. The chordal settings, with the melody in the top voice, gradually found their way into the Calvinist church services as well; some of the settings—notably the tune known as "Old Hundredth," composed by Louis Bourgeois about 1551 and sung either to Psalm 100 or to the Doxology—still survive in Protestant hymnals. In other settings the melody was placed in the tenor and surrounded by melodic lines in the three other voices; here again Bourgeois provides an example (see *HAM*, No. 132).

Because the Calvinists looked with disfavor on an elaborate musical apparatus in the church, psalm settings like Bourgeois's were not subject to the kinds of elaboration enjoyed by the chorales in the Lutheran church; for the most part, they remained in the more modest confines of the hymnals.

Anthem

Among the contributions of English composers active in the period after 1534—the time when the Anglican church was establishing a liturgy distinct from that of the Roman Catholic Church—was the development of a new form, the *anthem*, a term probably derived from the "antiphon" of the Roman liturgy. That form soon assumed a particularly important place in the services of Protestant denominations. Various texts translated into English from the Roman Catholic Offices and other portions of the liturgy were set in a style made up of chordal writing and counterpoint, with the former more common. The anthem was generally set in syllabic style in the chordal sections, but with long melismas in the contrapuntal parts. Two types were soon distinguished: the *full anthem* for choir throughout, and the *verse anthem*, which included passages for solo voice or voices. Instrumental accompaniment was usually provided, and settings for five or six voices (as opposed to the customary four voices of the continental style) soon became the most usual.

As with the motet, a term rather generally applied to a large number of compositions whose texts reflected a variety of sources, so with the anthem. Adaptations of works that had appeared originally with Latin texts, Englished paraphrases of psalm texts, a variety of religious poems with only a faint relationship to the liturgy—all were (and are) referred to as anthems. A clear definition of what constitutes an anthem text was apparently never drawn up, and the term remains somewhat elastic.

The composers to be discussed in this section, from Tye to Gibbons, share a characteristic that appears often in English music—a conservative attitude toward new developments. For example, the use of cross relations had declined on the Continent in the second half of the sixteenth century, as we saw in the music of Lasso, and composers had largely moved toward harmonic rather than linear° considerations. In English music, however, the cross relation remained a striking feature in secular and sacred music alike; thus linear (that is, modal) thinking seemed to concern English composers for at least two generations longer than it did composers on the Continent.

Tye

The Masses of Christopher Tye, generally in contrapuntal style, were mentioned above. Very different from them are his Anglican anthems; now a chordal style dominates and syllabic treatment is the most typical. This type of setting followed the recommendation of Thomas Cranmer, Archbishop of Canterbury, whose work was decisive in establishing the form of the Anglican liturgy in 1544. The official body of chant was set one note to one syllable, and it was generally assumed by the Archbishop that polyphonic settings of these chants (in the form of anthems) would also adopt the one-for-one style.

But Tye and later composers did not restrict themselves entirely to this style. In one of Tye's well-known anthems, *I Will Exalt Thee*, passages in imitative or free counterpoint are often set between chordal passages, and in the first part of that work the counterpoint is flowing and somewhat melismatic. The second part, on the other hand, is largely chordal, with all voices approaching their cadences simultaneously and with the structure marked by well-defined sections separated by rests. In another major work by Tye, a setting of the Acts of the Apostles, containing versified settings of about half of the biblical text, the separate numbers are almost entirely in chordal style, conforming completely to Cranmer's injunction.

Tallis

The 17 anthems of Thomas Tallis, although the one-for-one chordal style is present, are especially notable for their contrapuntal passages, which reveal that the imitative style, sparsely present in English music before about 1550, had now become thoroughly assimilated. Tallis' anthem *Heare the Voyce* (reprinted in

TEM, No. 27) is similar in every respect to the continental motet except for its English text. Several points of imitation occur, each given to one line of the text and each with its own melodic phrase subject to imitation in all four voices; unity is provided by the fact that the beginning of each line includes a prominent leap of a fourth or fifth, a characteristic that is maintained in each of the imitating voices.

Tallis occasionally employed the English version of antiphonal technique, as in the anthem *If Ye Love Me*. Here, two four-voice groups, placed at opposite sides in the choir stalls, sing both alternately and together. But contrary to Italian antiphonal practice, the union of the two groups seldom results in true eight-voice writing, for the four parts most often are merely doubled. Essentially, therefore, the "antiphonal" components of this and similar compositions consist of two semichoirs or a full choir, and the sonorousness caused by an increase in the number of separate voice parts is lacking.

Byrd

The surviving works of William Byrd include numerous anthems and four Services for the Anglican church, as well as works on Latin texts and secular compositions. In all these works Byrd revealed himself to be a consummate master of the art of composition, with an astonishing variety of styles and techniques at his command. Lyric melodies set in the midst of involved contrapuntal textures, brilliance and dramatic power in chordal passages, refinement in every aspect of text setting—all are typical of his many compositions.

This variety comes to eloquent expression in Byrd's anthems. In one such work, a setting of Psalm cxvii (118), *Teach Me, O Lord*, verses are set alternately for solo voice and for choir; the solo settings are generally accompanied by organ, while the unaccompanied choir verses are most often harmonized chordally with triads in root position.° His setting of *Behold, O God* is written for two solo voices and choir and contains an interplay of solo, duet, and full choral passages. Still another, *Arise, O Lord*, consists of two parts, one for five-voice choir and one for six-voice; here solo writing does not appear, and expressive variety is achieved by changes in contrapuntal texture and in rhythm.

EXAMPLE 21   Byrd, *Christ Rising Again*

(accompaniment omitted)

From Davison-Apel, *Historical Anthology of Music*, Vol. I. Used by permission of Harvard University Press.

An example of Byrd's sensitivity to his texts is seen in his verse anthem *Christ Rising Again* (reprinted in *HAM*, No. 151), for two solo voices and six-voice choir, accompanied by four viols. The work is characterized by a generally rising inflection; virtually all the phrases begin with an ascending contour, and each upward leap in the first three entrances is larger than the one preceding, thus heightening the effect (see Example 21). Solo and choral passages overlap, so that a continuous musical flow results, and the mixtures of solo voices, choral passages, and independent instrumental accompaniments are eloquently blended.

Byrd's anthems are further distinguished by his use of varied instrumental colors. This additional element enabled him to express fully his essentially subjective approach to the texts. In this respect he may be contrasted with his great continental contemporaries: Lasso, whose exuberance seemed unbounded at times until it changed into a profound, almost mystical approach to the words he set; and Palestrina, whose liturgical appropriateness and disciplined objectivity remained key characteristics.

Tomkins

Thomas Tomkins (c. 1572–1656), after studying with Byrd, served as organist of Worcester Cathedral from about 1596 to 1646, but also became a member of the Chapel Royal in 1621. The majority of his most significant composition was done before 1620; thus he may be placed with the important group of sixteenth-century English composers. Ninety-three anthems have survived, with full anthems representing slightly more than half the total. The full anthems continue the polyphonic texture of earlier periods, and in that texture Tomkins shows himself at his best.

His five-voice setting of *When David Heard* (reprinted in *HAM*, No. 169) poignantly reflects the grief of David at the death of his son Absalom. Full of minor seconds, a traditional way of expressing lamentation, it rises to dramatic heights through Tomkins' tendency to repeat text words or phrases over and over again (see Example 22). Resourcefulness in the use of imitative techniques, great facility in employing rhythmic counterpoint in the form of cross accents, and a touch of the grandiose, as in a twelve-voice setting of *O Praise the Lord,* are characteristic of Tomkins' anthem style.

Gibbons

The English composers discussed above are representative of a large number of their contemporaries who also composed sacred music, but whose major contributions were in the field of secular music. The most prominent of these composers, including Thomas Morley, Thomas Weelkes, John Wilbye, and Orlando Gibbons, will be discussed in Chapter 5. Gibbons (1583–1625), however, belongs in this chapter as well. Writing his sacred music entirely for the Anglican service, he composed about 15 outstanding full anthems, as well as about 25 verse anthems. Gibbons' music is equally expressive in both contrapuntal and chordal textures; imitation is an important element of his contrapuntal writing, usually serving to build a dramatic climax after a section set in chordal style. Melismatic writing is relatively rare in the anthems, probably as a consequence of Gibbons' technique of repeating a text phrase several times in an extended

EXAMPLE 22   Tomkins, *When David Heard*

From Davison-Apel, *Historical Anthology of Music*, Vol. I. Used by permission of Harvard University Press.

passage, in a manner similar to Tomkins'. We can see this technique in one of his smaller anthems, *O Lord Increase My Faith* (reprinted in *HAM*, No. 171), as well as in such larger works as the six-voice *Hosanna to the Son of David*.

The verse anthems are best represented by his setting of *This Is the Record of John* (reprinted in *HAM*, No. 172), for tenor soloist and five-voice choir; the solo sections are accompanied by four instruments (probably viols) in contrapuntal texture, while the choral passages are unaccompanied and are written in mixed style. In this anthem each choral passage repeats a portion of the preceding solo text but the music is new each time.

Gibbons' anthems testify to his position as a composer living in a transitional time between major style periods. On the one hand, he became the last great representative of sixteenth-century polyphony in England; his full anthems give ample evidence of his skill and expressiveness in that style. On the other hand, he adopted—even if tentatively—certain of the elements that were to mark the style of seventeenth-century Baroque music: solo passages with an independent instrumental accompaniment, a freely moving melodic line that at times almost takes on the character of recitative, a form made up of short and separated sections. All these elements, found in his verse anthems, were to characterize the vocal music of the seventeenth century.

5

Secular Music
1450–1600

Choral music was defined in Chapter 1 as music written in parts designed to be performed with several voices on each part. The great majority of the works discussed in this book conform to that definition and require, on each part, a number of voices to produce the desired quantity of sound. Related to choral music is *vocal chamber music*, which has different essential requirements: this music can be performed—and in fact through much of its existence has been performed—with only a single voice on each part. In terms of our definition, therefore, such music scarcely belongs in this book. Yet we can justify its presence here when we consider how performance conditions have changed in the centuries since the music was composed.

Much vocal chamber music—including primarily the chanson, madrigal, and related forms—was designed for entertainment in a palace chamber or in the home, where it was performed in an atmosphere of intimacy. Relatively small rooms have different acoustical properties than present-day concert halls, so that one singer on a part was both feasible and desirable in vocal chamber music. But in recent times a substantial amount of that music has entered the repertoire of concert groups and is heard in larger halls under acoustical conditions often very different from those of earlier centuries. As a purely practical measure, consequently, the parts have come to be performed with two or three singers on each; no violence is done to the music thereby, and such performances are embraced in our definition of choral music. Thus, vocal chamber music has its place in this book.

One other point having to do with present-day performance should be mentioned. Vocal chamber music, because of its generally transparent texture, lightly accented rhythms, and relatively subtle expressiveness, presupposes flexibility in dynamic shading, a fine blending of voice qualities, and absolute precision in performance. By definition, such finesse is seldom attained by a massive choral group; thus there is an intrinsic difference in idiom between choral performance and vocal chamber music performance. With the high level of musical competence that exists today, however, the requirements for the proper performance of vocal chamber music by a *small* choral group can generally be met.

Chanson

The chanson as it appeared in the works of the fifteenth-century Franco-Flemish composer Gilles Binchois was briefly described in Chapter 1. There it was seen as a work for three voices largely in contrapuntal or fauxbourdon style, with the treble voice dominant and the two lower voices written in an angular fashion that strongly suggests instrumental performance. At the end of that century, in the works of Josquin and many of his contemporaries, the chanson underwent a series of changes and became extremely popular among all classes. Virtually every composer of the time contributed to the literature; almost one hundred chansons of various types, written by late–fifteenth-century composers, became the subject of the first printed collection of polyphonic music, the *Harmonice musices odhecaton A*, published by Ottaviano de' Petrucci at Venice in 1501. The collection includes works in a variety of styles and reveals that in the chanson many composers first used the stylistic devices that were to characterize the music of the sixteenth century. One of the types, to become important later in the century, was the *contrapuntal chanson*. In its development, Josquin's chansons served as models.

The contrapuntal chanson was generally composed for three to six voices, with five-voice settings being the most usual. Imitative counterpoint became an important element of its structure, and variety was achieved by brief passages in chordal style. The texts are often humorous or ironic, and deal with subjects of universal appeal: fidelity and faithlessness, fulfilled and unrequited love. A noteworthy feature is the blend of popular tunes and scholarly counterpoint, in which a popular tune, borrowed for use as a cantus firmus, undergoes all kinds of complicated canonic treatment, yet the chanson as a whole never loses the relaxed and unsophisticated charm of the popular melody.

In the chansons of Josquin, both the literal and underlying meanings of the texts are scrupulously respected, and proper accentuation is always observed; no matter how light the text's subject matter, it is provided with eloquent and expressive music (see Example 23). Duple meter is most usual in Josquin's chansons, as it was in much of the popular music of the time, as opposed to the triple meter that prevailed in earlier, especially sacred, music. Miniature works of art, the chansons by Josquin are on the same high musical level as his motets.

The contrapuntal chanson was popular with most Franco-Flemish composers

EXAMPLE 23   Josquin, *En non saichant*

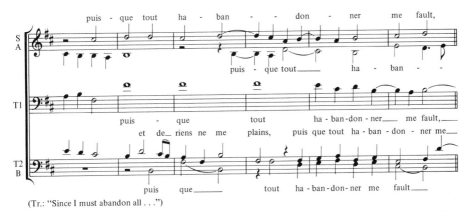

(Tr.: "Since I must abandon all . . .")

From Friedrich Blume, *Das Chorwerk*, Vol. 3, edited by Friedrich Blume. Used by permission of Möseler Verlag, Wolfenbüttel and Zurich.

and enjoyed wide geographical distribution, culminating in the work of Lasso in Munich. This sensitivity to all shades of textual meaning was combined with the utmost musical expressiveness in the music, and a perfect blend of the two resulted (see Example 24).

EXAMPLE 24   Lasso, *O faible esprit*

(Tr.: "O ardent heart, be not consumed!")

From Friedrich Blume, *Das Chorwerk*, Vol. 13, edited by Heinrich Besseler. Used by permission of Möseler Verlag, Wolfenbüttel and Zurich.

In France, meanwhile, a second type of chanson had become a great success. Called the *Parisian chanson*, this type was characterized by four-part, mostly chordal, writing, as opposed to the five-part contrapuntal style of the Josquin type. The Parisian chanson was designed for popular rather than aristocratic consumption, so its texts were light lyric poems in three or four verses, on sentimental or humorous themes. A single publisher, Pierre Attaingnant, issued 2,000 of these chansons in the twenty years after 1528, a fact that attests to their enormous popularity. Claude Sermisy (c. 1490–1562) was among the earliest composers of the Parisian chanson, and his many chansons did much to define the form and set standards for others to follow.

A light and lilting rhythm is one of the main characteristics of the music. A dactylic motive (long-short-short) often begins a chanson of the Sermisy type, to be followed by new syncopated motives that carry the tune briskly forward to its cadences. The chanson often breaks away from the prevailing duple meter with short sections in triple, and repeated notes, repeated chords, and a deft and fast-moving articulation all contribute to the prevailing lightness of the music. Phrases are well separated with pauses occurring simultaneously in all the parts, giving clarity to the structure of the piece; to this clarity is often added a pleasing symmetry, provided by similar beginning and ending phrases. Elegance, good humor, and sharp wit are in general characteristic of the Parisian chansons.

A third type, the *program chanson*, is best represented in the works of Clément Janequin (c. 1485–c. 1560), who also composed Parisian chansons. The "programs" in his chansons are such simple things as bird calls, street cries, and other easily imitated sounds, and Janequin gave the chansons such fanciful titles as *Cries of Paris*, *Song of the Birds*, *The War*, and *The Fall of Boulogne*. Short phrases filled with repeated notes move about from voice to voice in a quasi-imitative manner, and chordal style virtually disappears. Rhythmic vitality is provided by many repetitions of nonsense syllables ("fa-la-la" and the like), and Janequin's cheerfulness and humorous approach to his material are everywhere apparent. (One program chanson by Janequin is reprinted in *HAM*, No. 107.)

Madrigal

Destined to become perhaps the most influential secular vocal form of the sixteenth century, the madrigal also became one of the tools with which Italian composers threw off the domination of Franco-Flemish elements and developed an indigenous Italian style. The madrigal was preceded, in the middle of the fifteenth century, by another form, the frottola, sung primarily at the courts and in aristocratic circles. In the frottola short poems of an amorous nature, but treated humorously or satirically, were set in three or four parts in chordal style. The upper part, carrying the lighthearted melody, was designed to be sung, whereas the two or three lower parts were to be played. A typical text consists of a few six-line stanzas each followed by a four-line refrain.

About the 1530s the frottola became frivolous and salacious; a reaction set in and the form lost favor. A new type of text appeared, consisting of a single stanza of dignified character. Such a stanza was usually of ten lines, rhymed according to any of a number of patterns, with each line containing either seven or eleven syllables. Cardinal Pietro Bembo, the leader of the reaction, himself provided text models for the new type, which a host of minor Italian poets imitated. The poems were then set for four or five voices in chordal style; phrases were generally separated by rests, but occasional bits of imitation at phrase ends caused the phrases to overlap so that the form was integrated.

To this form the term *madrigale* was applied, the derivation of the term being unclear. According to one version, it is related to *matricale* (having to do with "mother tongue") because the texts were in Italian rather than Latin; according to another, it is derived from *mandria* ("herd") or *mandriano* ("herdsman") because pastoral love and its problems became conventional subjects in the texts.

The earliest composers of madrigals included Philippe de Verdelot (died 1550), a Flemish singer active at Venice and Florence; the Italian Costanzo Festa (c. 1490–1545), a member of the Papal Chapel; the Flemish Jacob Arcadelt (c. 1505–c. 1560), active in Rome; and Adrian Willaert, the founder of the Venetian school. Several hundred madrigals resulted from the activities of this first generation of madrigal composers; four-voice settings that contain short passages in triple meter are in the majority, and the style, while containing a few passages in imitative writing, is basically chordal (see Example 25).

EXAMPLE 25   Arcadelt, *Voi ve n'andat' al cielo*

(Tr.: "[While I] would rise in flight, remain saddened in sorrow.")

From Davison-Apel, *Historical Anthology of Music*, Vol. I. Used by permission of Harvard University Press.

In Willaert's later madrigals, after about the 1540s, a second stage of development began. The existing texts for madrigals became somewhat stereotyped, and Willaert chose the sonnets and *canzoni* of Petrarch (1304–1374) for his settings. Petrarch, one of the earliest of the humanists and the author of refined and exquisite love poems, became a text source for an entire generation of madrigal composers. Willaert's later madrigals were set mostly for five voices, a setting adopted by the majority of the composers who followed him. Counterpoint again became an essential ingredient of madrigal style, and imitative writing interspersed with chordal passages was typical. In this development Willaert was followed closely by Cipriano de Rore (1516–1565), also Franco–Flemish and also active in Venice.

The madrigals of Willaert and De Rore, together with those of many of their contemporaries, now also began to adopt some of the descriptive practices common to motets of the time. Word-painting became characteristic in the later madrigal; Willaert and De Rore led the way. A text phrase implying quick motion or psychic agitation was illustrated by rapid rhythmic motion, for example; a mood of solemnity or sadness was suggested by voices moving slowly in their lower ranges, while violent emotions, such as rage or anguish, were expressed by chromatic° alterations (see *HAM*, No. 131). All these practices, present to some degree in the madrigals of the period about 1540 to 1580, became common at a later stage of development.

Still representative of the second stage are many hundreds of madrigals by Orlando di Lasso in Munich, Philip de Monte (1521–1603) in Vienna (perhaps the most prolific of all madrigal composers; more than 1,100 of his works in this form have survived), Giaches de Wert (1535–1596), mainly in Mantua, the two Gabrielis in Venice, and many other composers equally widespread geographically. Each composer's madrigals have a flavor all their own, with differing uses of contrapuntal and chordal style, a variety of rhythmic devices, more or less use of chromatic embellishment, and so on—a tribute to the versatility of the form. But all the madrigals share a strong concern for appropriate setting of the texts; the use of the descriptive device of word-painting is to be found in the music of all these composers, along with alterations in the number of voices used (two high and two low in antiphonal passages, for example, or temporary omission of one of the five voices in other passages) wherever the nature of the text required.

One subtype of this period's madrigal is important for the influence it had on later English composers. Giovanni Gastoldi (c. 1556–1622), the successor of Wert at Mantua, became known primarily as a composer of *balletti*, which are lighter versions of madrigals, essentially. The lightness consists of dancelike rhythms; a deft, predominantly chordal, style; and a form consisting of two short sections, both repeated. A refrain filled with nonsense syllables ("fa-la-la") similar to those of the program chansons of Janequin became a feature of Gastoldi's *balletti* and contributed greatly to the gaiety that characterized the form (see *HAM*, No. 158).

A third stage in the development of the madrigal is primarily the accomplishment of two Italian composers, Luca Marenzio (1553–1599) and Carlo Gesualdo, Prince of Venosa (c. 1560–1613). Marenzio published seventeen books of madrigals in the years after 1580; although several of his works are for four or six voices, five-voice settings dominated. He employed every stylistic device of the time, including counterpoint, chordal writing, a kind of chordal recitative also used by Giovanni Gabrieli, free counterpoint in some voices and chordal writing in others, and an advanced harmonic scheme in which diminished triads, transient modulations°, and pungent dissonances were characteristic. All these devices served one objective: to clarify and enhance the meaning of every word and phrase of the text; in this objective he was eminently successful.

Marenzio's madrigals deal with a wide range of emotions, drawing on verses by Petrarch, Ariosto, Tasso, and other major poets. In addition to the customary poems about love and lovelorn states, Marenzio selected texts full of grief, anguish, or death. His ability to find the musical counterpart of this wide range of emotional states—and of physical objects as well—enabled him to compose eloquently and expressively. Word-painting, too, was developed to a high degree by Marenzio, and he was quick to use changes of meter and changes in notation (for example, half notes in a context of quarter notes to suggest open eyes) to wring the last bit of pictorial possibility from his texts. All Marenzio's devices were used with keen discrimination, the result being a body of madrigals of rare beauty and power (see Example 26).

EXAMPLE 26 Marenzio, *Madonna mia gentil* ("My Gentle Lady")

(Tr.: "Being on earth, I seem to enjoy Paradise.")

Gesualdo carries to an extreme degree Marenzio's discreet chromaticism, and there is little place in his madrigals for the gentler emotions. Gesualdo, not trained as a professional musician, was unconcerned with restraint and balance; he experimented ceaselessly to find the musical means that would mirror the emotional extremes he favored, and in doing so he carried the use of chromatically related chords further than any of his contemporaries. Typical devices include triads built on roots a half-step apart (on G and G sharp, for example), wild angularity in melodic lines—with leaps of diminished octaves, say—and melodies based on chromatic fragments. Gesualdo's madrigals, with their hyperexpressiveness and daring harmonic effects, employ little word-painting; they hold their position in the literature primarily because of their chromaticism, their single-minded concentration on a few emotional states, and their air of extravagant fantasy (see Example 27).

EXAMPLE 27 Gesualdo, *Moro lasso*

(Tr.: "I die, alas, from my pains, and who can give me life?")

Reprinted from *A Treasury of Early Music*, compiled and edited by Carl Parrish. By permission of W. W. Norton & Company, Inc. Copyright © 1958 by W. W. Norton & Company, Inc.; and by permission of Faber and Faber, Ltd., publishers.

Hyle that the Sunne with his beames

, hot, fcorched the fruits in vale & moun-

taine: Philon the fheperd late forgot,

fitting befides a Chriftall fountaine,

fitting befides a Chriftall fountaine, in fhadow of a greene Oke   tree,

vppon his pipe this fong playd   he;   vntrue loue, vntrue loue, vn-

true loue, adew loue, adew loue, your minde is light,   :||:

A page from an early edition of a madrigal by William Byrd.

The English madrigal

Early in the reign of Elizabeth I, about 1560, Italian music began to be well received in England. The madrigal became particularly popular and within two decades was a staple of English musical fare. Books of Italian madrigals were translated, *Musica transalpina*, 1588, and *Italian Madrigals Englished*, 1590, among them; these were followed a few years later by anthologies containing madrigals by Marenzio and Gesualdo. The result was a host of English madrigals modeled on the Italian and, a bit later, madrigals with a specifically English style. The large number of madrigals written by English composers in the age of Elizabeth I constitutes a high point in the history of English music.

A main characteristic of English madrigals is that their texts (mainly pastoral in content) were drawn from the works of minor and popular poets, as opposed to the Italian madrigals that consistently drew upon the literary masterpieces of the day. From the beginning, therefore, the English madrigals enjoyed wide popular appeal, were immediately approachable, and were sung by everybody— not only by the aristocrats. Accordingly, the English madrigal emphasized simplicity of texture (with no involved counterpoint), directness of rhythm (with predominantly dancelike patterns), and melodies that were simply and clearly harmonized.

Thomas Morley (1557–1602), among the first composers in the field, called many of his works "canzonets." The settings are mainly for three voices, with an essential element of the texture a series of lighthearted short phrases that move freely from voice to voice in chordal style. Other works by Morley closely resemble the *balletti* of Gastoldi with even sprightlier rhythms and with refrains based on nonsense syllables. Morley called them "balletts," and many of the works that are still performed are of this type; such balletts as *Now Is the Month of Maying*, *My Bonny Lass She Smileth*, and *Sing We and Chaunt It* are typical.

Morley often introduced sections of contrapuntal writing, lengthened the form, and briefly changed meters from duple to triple (see *HAM*, No. 159).

Thomas Weelkes (c. 1575–1623) composed balletts on the Morley model, but also wrote true madrigals in which the influence of Marenzio is to be seen. Several sets of his works (1597, for three to six voices; 1598, for five; and 1600, for five and six) contain madrigals that often exceed Morley's in extensiveness, expressiveness, and dramatic quality. The changes of meter found occasionally in Morley become characteristic in Weelkes (see Example 28); and contrasting meters heard simultaneously in different voice parts add a new degree of rhythmic complexity to Weelkes's works and to the English madrigal in general.

EXAMPLE 28   Weelkes, *Hark All Ye Lovely Saints*

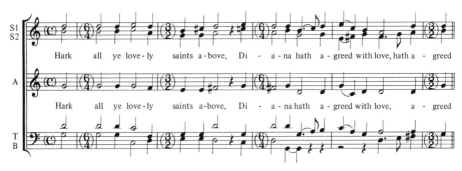

From Davison-Apel, *Historical Anthology of Music*, Vol. I. Used by permission of Harvard University Press.

Many other composers added their individual touches to the form, notably John Wilbye (1574–1638) and Orlando Gibbons (1583–1625). On the whole, though, the madrigal retained essentially the same style, kind of content, and aesthetic appeal in the works of the later composers that it had in the earlier. Some twenty years after its arrival in England, it declined in popularity and soon became virtually obsolete.

6

Music of the Early Baroque
1600–1675

At the end of the sixteenth century, a series of influences radically altered the forms, textures, and techniques of all music. As at other comparable times in the history of music, these influences were more obvious and immediate in some fields than in others. Consequently, there followed a period of stylistic uncertainty that lasted for several decades, with the old, conservative, and traditional existing side by side with the new, radical, and innovative. Merely for the sake of convenience, we are using the date 1600 to mark the point at which these stylistic differences were clearest.

The old practice was represented best by the contrapuntal style developed by generations of Franco-Flemish composers and modified according to individual needs by musicians such as Palestrina. That style had become virtually international in church music of the sixteenth century, as we have seen, and lived on in many sacred compositions of the seventeenth century as well. Other compositions in the same field, however, turned to the new style, as we shall see below.

The new style had varied sources. One source was the long-standing opposition on the part of many Italian composers to the very notion of counterpoint. The "learned" aspects and the inner discipline imposed by counterpoint symbolized a style—Franco-Flemish in its origin—that ran counter to Mediterranean musical instincts, which preferred natural melodiousness and direct expression over the contrived and involved expression typical of the northern style. Further, in a contrapuntal setting, several words or phrases of the text were almost necessarily performed simultaneously, with the result that textual clarity and understanding were endangered; this too was seen as a defect by the Italians. Yet so powerful was the hand of tradition that counterpoint remained a dominant style in the composition of church music far into the seventeenth century.

Another source may be traced to the growth of the humanistic movement in Italy. The leaders of that movement included men whose interest lay in secular rather than sacred writings, and who sought openly to rediscover the past by turning to the works of Homer, Plato, Cicero, and other authors of classical Greece and Rome. As the sixteenth century ran its course, the humanists became interested in the music of ancient times as well; believing that music and poetry had been closely related in those times, they sought to restore that supposed connection. Since only a few fragments of the music were available and theoretical books offered little clear help, they resorted to speculation. Beginning about 1580, a group of noblemen, poets, and musicians met at the home of Count Giovanni Bardi in Florence to work toward that end. In a series of writings and compositions, this group, known as the Florentine Camerata, set forth aesthetic principles and musical examples of a new kind of music that was to be of enormous importance in the seventeenth century and was to give rise to a new style.

Yet another source leads back to the experiments of Venetian composers in the last years of the sixteenth century. Works for double choir had been followed by multichoral works, especially by Giovanni Gabrieli, and compositions of massive size had often resulted. The majority of those huge works had included parts for instruments as well as voices, and often antiphonal style had been applied to the two components. Out of this developed a type of composition with a structure comprised of short phrases heard alternately in the various sections of the ensemble. This style, in which vocal and instrumental groups in a sense competed with each other, soon came to be known as the *concertato* style (from the Latin *concertare*, to contend or strive). These four aspects of Venetian music—antiphony, massive size, instrumental elements, and the concertato principle—became influential in the new music of the seventeenth century.

An essential difference between the old and new styles (called *prima prattica* and *seconda prattica* by Monteverdi, *stile antico* and *stile moderno* by others) lay in the respective relationships between text and music. In the older style, the *prima prattica*, the music was felt to dominate the text, with musical considerations of phraseology, texture, and form taking precedence over considerations of text, such as clarity of understanding, repetition or nonrepetition of words, and the like. In the new style, the *seconda prattica*, modern composers sought to make the text dominate the music; clear enunciation so that every word could be understood, and a doing away with the confusion that occurs in polyphony when two or more text phrases are sung simultaneously—these were among the ideals to be worked toward. And this in itself required a recasting of the technical means of composition.

The most immediate result of the recasting was the establishment of a texture consisting of a melody and a bass line; in performance it was understood that a series of chords would be constructed on the notes of the bass line to provide harmonic support for the melody. With an instrument capable of playing sustained tones (such as a cello, bass, bassoon, or trombone) doubling the bass line, the improvised chords were performed on a lute, theorbo, or keyboard instrument. A system of notation was developed to indicate the desired harmonies, using a series of figures and symbols whenever something other than a triad in root position was required. This combination of bass line with symbols ("figured bass"), fundamental instrument, and supporting instrument was called *basso continuo* or *continuo*, and a principal occupation of keyboard players until the middle of the eighteenth century was the "realization" of such figured bass lines in the continuo parts. Considerable freedom in these realizations was both permitted and expected; adding passing tones, supplying bits of melodic imitation, embellishing chords, and other evidences of the improvisatory spirit were a normal part of the continuo player's function.

The seventeenth century was a period of contrasts and polarities. Aside from the basic contrast in prevalent composing styles, characterized by the terms *prima* and *seconda prattiche*, there were, in the latter, the polarity of melody and bass, and the competition between two elements in the concertato style. These are two of the pairs of opposing factors. Two different rhythmic styles constitute yet another pair. One style, derived from the dance rhythms of the Renaissance period, resulted in the regularization of basic rhythmic patterns and the notation of these patterns by barlines; thus the "measure" as we know it came into being. Each measure consisted of a pattern of strong and weak beats, with the whole comprising a work in metrical rhythm.

The other rhythmic style, very different from the first, resulted from the application of the aesthetic principles formulated by the members of the Florentine Camerata. In a series of *Discourses on Ancient Music and Good Singing,* written about 1580 probably by Vincenzo Galilei, the father of the astronomer and one of the first composers in the new style, the author had urged the composer not to imitate "the musicians of today who think nothing of spoiling it [the verse] . . . or cutting it to bits to make nonsense of the words. . . . In composing, then, you will make it your chief aim to arrange the verse well and to declaim the words as intelligibly as you can." As for the rhythmic setting of the verse, "it will be neither too slow nor too fast, but will imitate the speech of a man magnificent and serious" (Strunk, *Source Readings in Music History,* pp. 294–96). Elsewhere Galilei suggests that composers learn from actors how to express emotion by adjusting the speed and pitch level of the speaking voice. Out of these suggestions, then, grew a type of setting in which the melodic line imitated the normal inflections as well as the rhythms of the speaking voice. This style, being characterized by prose rhythms rather than by dance patterns of regularly recurring strong and weak beats, favored the development of unmetrical rhythm, and a declamatory or reciting musical line (*stilo recitativo*) resulted (see Example 29).

A number of works in a variety of forms were composed in the first decades of the seventeenth century that embodied the new principles of recitative style, melody-bass polarity, and basso continuo; the opera is the most important of the new forms, and the earliest operas were composed by members of the Florentine Camerata. But composers found the recitative style in its ideal form

EXAMPLE 29   Peri, *Euridice*

E voi,   deh per pie - tà del mio mar-ti - ro   che nel mi-se-ro cor di-mo - ra e - ter - no

(Tr.: "And you, alas, pitying my martyrdom that in misery stays in my heart eternally.")

unduly limiting; they were not all willing to subordinate their purely musical instincts to a textual imperative. Within a few decades of its inception, pure recitative was modified. Monteverdi had led the way in the recitative passages of his operas. He often inserted short sections of lyric melody in the midst of his recitatives, and he sometimes introduced melodic motives in the declamatory melodic line, which were imitated in the fundamental bass line. The purely melodic sections were at times given two- or three-part forms, or were extended through the use of ornamental variations. Gradually the new melodic type, called *bel canto,* was separated from the recitative sections and developed its own stylistic integrity.

A typical bel ·canto melody owes nothing to the text to which it is set. It develops its own melodic contours, follows a rhythmic scheme that is not bound by textual rhythms, is usually set in metrical rhythm, most often avoids harsh intervals such as augmented fourths and major sevenths, and is harmonized simply (see Example 30). First in opera and other secular forms and eventually in church

EXAMPLE 30   Hassler, *Chorale Concerto*

Er - schie -nen_ ist__ der_ herr - li-che Tag, dran sich__ nie - mand gnug freu - en   mag

(Tr.: "Such a glorious day has dawned that no one can describe his joy.")

music, the *bel canto* style rose to prominence in all parts of Europe. It existed parallel to the recitative style, and it became customary to set a text in two contiguous sections: one narrative or expository in recitative style and the other lyric or dramatic in bel canto style. This "recitative and aria" pair would remain an ingredient of large vocal and choral forms for almost two centuries.

Still another element of the new style needs mention here. In the course of the first few decades of the seventeenth century, primarily in forms other than opera, imitative and nonimitative counterpoint gradually found their way back into musical texture. No longer the counterpoint based on the modes that had prevailed through the earlier centuries, however, it was rather a harmonically derived counterpoint based on the system of tonality that marks the great majority of music from the seventeenth century to the beginning of the twentieth. Chords resulted from the interaction of the melodic lines, of course, as they had in modal counterpoint, but now all the chords were ordered in the context of a prevailing tonal center or keynote, with specific harmonic functions in their progressions—especially those leading to cadences. Transient modulations to other keys became possible, but always within the framework of the basic key, and the use of chromaticism also became subject to the requirements of that key. Finally, having a tonal center as a consonant base to which to return, dissonance itself came under greater control than earlier in the century; since dissonances now resolved to consonances, they could afford to be farther reaching and more pungent. The end result was a system in which every musical nuance could be expressed harmonically.

Many of the developments we have been discussing required several decades to make their full impact. The tonal system, for example, some elements of which had emerged as far back as the fifteenth century, took form only slowly, and it was not until 1722 that a theoretical basis explaining and justifying what was happening in music was formulated by Jean Philippe Rameau; even at that time certain modal inflections were still to be found in works by conservative composers. Yet the general impact of these stylistic innovations marked a clear break with the style of the Renaissance. Historians in the eighteenth century, writing about somewhat parallel developments in the other arts, described them with the term *baroque*. Later music historians applied the same term to works composed in the style described above, and eventually the entire period from about 1600 to 1750 became known as the Baroque period.

Mass

Monteverdi

In the early seventeenth century the Mass was treated more conservatively than other choral forms. A number of composers associated with Rome, Nanino and Anerio chief among them, wrote Masses in the style perfected by Palestrina. Away from Rome composers could not—or did not wish to—avoid the attractiveness of the new style. The most prominent of such composers, and one of the great masters of all time, was Claudio Monteverdi (1567–1643). Born at Cremona, Monteverdi became a pupil of Marc'Antonio Ingegneri, and in his earliest works showed his mastery of vocal counterpoint. Moving to the court of Mantua in 1590, Monteverdi composed several books of madrigals in which the harmonic innovations of Marenzio were carried forward. At Mantua too he composed the first seven of his operas—of which *Orfeo* is the earliest great masterwork in that field. Still at Mantua, he published his first considerable collection of sacred music.

In 1613 he was elected chapelmaster at St. Mark's in Venice—one of the most prestigious positions in the musical world of the time—where he remained until his death, thirty years later. Many sacred compositions were composed at Venice, along with the continuo madrigals and operas on which his fame so largely rests. His part in developing the new Baroque style and his position as the first major composer in that style are the foundation stones of his great reputation.

Among the sacred works, his three Masses are noteworthy. The first, composed in 1610, is a parody Mass for six voices with continuo, based on themes from Gombert's motet *In illo tempore*. Monteverdi's major accomplishment in this Mass was to weld the elements of Franco-Flemish polyphony to the spirit of the Baroque. Using ten melodies taken from his model, he produced a masterpiece of imitative counterpoint in which the tonal harmonies of the seventeenth century come to full expression. The interval and distance of imitation vary frequently, passages in three- or four-part imitative texture are accompanied by two or three other voices in free counterpoint, and many long melismas in several voices at once add a flowing and elaborate expressiveness to the Mass text.

The second, a four-voice Mass with an unfigured continuo, was published in 1641 as part of the collection *Selva morale e spirituale* (*Moral and Spiritual Forest*) though obviously written earlier. This collection also includes five spiritual madrigals, several Mass movements, and about thirty miscellaneous sacred compositions. The works are varied; some are for two choirs with instrumental accompaniment, others for a single voice with accompaniment, and still others (the Mass among them) are for four-voice choir accompanied only by continuo. The Mass is in the *stile antico* and is based almost entirely on the use of imitative counterpoint; only a few passages in the Credo approach chordal style. The counterpoint is in the eloquent style of Lasso, and as the continuo does no more than support the lowest voice and can therefore be omitted in performance, it does not weaken the sixteenth-century flavor.

The third Mass by Monteverdi, published posthumously as part of another collection in 1651 but also belonging to the post-1613 period, resembles the second in again being for four voices with continuo and in containing many elements of the *stile antico*. But the melodies of the various movements of this third Mass are closely related; either they outline a descending fourth or they are based on a gently undulating chromatic line (see Example 31a), and thus a high level of thematic unity is assured. The ever-changing texture contains at times canonic imitation, free counterpoints, chordal writing, some use of cantus firmus, and even examples of fauxbourdon (see Example 31b). The whole, with its eloquent melismas (often in four parts at once), frequent changes of meter at dramatic high points, and a high level of rhythmic complexity, is a monument to the quality of Monteverdi's skill and imagination.

Other composers

Many other composers adopted the polychoral elements of Venetian style to a greater extent than did Monteverdi, including Paolo Agostino (1593–1629) and

EXAMPLE 31   Monteverdi, *Missa*, 1651

Orazio Benevoli (1605–1672), both of whom were active in Rome. Benevoli spent several years in the 1640s at the Imperial court in Vienna. For the consecration of the Cathedral in Salzburg in 1628 he composed a Mass for two eight-voice choirs, six separate groups of string and wind instruments, and continuo parts— the whole work consisting of fifty-three separate lines. Other and later works by Benevoli, most of them written for St. Peter's in Rome, call for four or more choirs with continuo. Such works took advantage of the architectural features of the churches for which they were written; the various choirs were placed in different parts of the church, so that the element of spatial separation added a new dimension to the antiphonal style in the Baroque period.

The Masses of a number of Austrian composers reveal a gradually increasing use of the concertato style mixed with traditional choral writing, along with the use of new formal elements—some derived from the opera. Later in the century, for example, passages for one or more solo voices are sometimes included in choral movements. The longer Mass movements, notably the Gloria and Credo, are sometimes divided into separate sections, which are then set for solo voice, solo ensemble, or choir. Sometimes an instrumental movement called a *sinfonia* is placed before the Kyrie, and often the Amen which ends both the Gloria and Credo is set as a long and elaborate section in fugal style. The composers active in this development, especially Johann Stadlmeyer (1560–1648) and Christoph Strauss (c. 1580–1631), were generally associated with the Imperial court at Vienna, where elaborate choral and instrumental forces were available. Later Viennese composers included such men as Antonio Bertali (1605–1669), Johann Heinrich Schmelzer (c. 1623–1680), Johann Kaspar Kerll (1627–1693), and Heinrich Biber (1644–1704), many of whom were active in the operatic field as well.

In many of the Masses of this group of composers, instrumental accompaniments became the rule. Using the principles of the concertato style, the Masses were often set with short interludes for instruments between choral passages; brass ensembles and timpani lent a festive air, and other colorful effects (such as the use of bells in the accompaniment to a Kyrie) were common. And in keeping with the new instrumental resources and the separation of Mass movements into shorter sections, the whole often became known as a "concertato Mass" or "cantata Mass."

In the seventeenth century the Mass in France, England, and Germany moved from a dominating musical position to one of lesser importance. During the 67-year reign of Louis XIV (1643–1715, and King from 1648), French composers were strongly under the influence of their ruler and his court. And while opera flourished and developed a distinctive French style, especially under the virtual dictatorship of Jean-Baptiste Lully (1632–1687), composers of sacred music were forced to reckon with the personal tastes of the King, who did not favor elaborate high Masses (that is, Masses that were sung throughout), and who substituted a spoken low Mass at the court. But since the low Mass service lacked the elaborateness and display to which the King had become accustomed in opera and ballet, sections of music with non-Mass texts were often inserted. Thus arose the *Messe basse solenelle* (solemn low Mass), which provided a framework for the performance of the motets of Lully and his contemporaries.

In England, during the troubled reign of Charles I (1625-1649) and the period of the Commonwealth (1649–1660) under the Lord Protector Oliver Cromwell, all aspects of Roman Catholicism—including its music—gradually fell victim to the zeal of the Anglicans and the Presbyterians. And in Germany the series of religious and political wars known collectively as the Thirty Years' War (1618–1648) further reduced the areas in which Catholic music could flourish. Thus in all three countries the composition of Masses was greatly lessened and thereafter remained a negligible factor in large parts of Europe.

Motet

From the high point of its development in the works of Lasso, the Renaissance motet underwent a series of changes parallel to those in the Mass. A set of compositions by Ludovico da Viadana (1564–1645), *Cento concerti ecclesiastici* (*One Hundred Ecclesiastical Concerts*), published in 1602, was in a sense a forerunner of the Baroque motet. In selecting appropriate items from this work for performance, a choirmaster no longer found it necessary to replace missing voice parts by instruments, as had been the custom in the Renaissance, for the *Cento concerti* were composed for one to four voices with continuo. Later composers went beyond Viadana in using other factors of the new style, notably monophonic writing and the concertato principle.

A notable work of the period is the *Vespro della Beata Vergine* (*Vespers of the Blessed Virgin*), composed by Monteverdi in 1610. The work includes twelve motet settings of the Psalms appropriate to that Office, and two different settings of the same Magnificat; the Mass *In illo tempore*, discussed above, was published at the same time as part of the collection. The motets are set for one to eight voices, with two of them requiring double choir; one of the latter is for eight voices (SATB, SATB),° the other for ten (SATTB, SATTB). Each of the twelve motets is supplied with an instrumental accompaniment, the instrumental groups ranging from continuo alone to an ensemble requiring thirteen instruments. The motets are generally based on traditional plainsong themes and contain a large quantity of contrapuntal devices, but passages of coloratura writing, advanced triadic harmonies, recitativelike melodic lines, and stirring orchestral effects bring the motets well into the seventeenth century.

The practice of introducing many varieties of vocal color into motets was continued through much of the seventeenth century. This is seen in three motets by Alessandro Grandi (died 1630), a pupil of Giovanni Gabrieli and a colleague of Monteverdi at St. Mark's in Venice (the motets are reprinted in *Das Chorwerk*, No. 40). In one of these, *Plorabo die ac nocti* (*I Shall Cry Day and Night*), set for four voices and continuo, the first passage is for bass and alto in imitation; this is followed by a short section for alto, tenor, and bass, and later by a section for tenors alone. The four voices come together only in two passages (separated by a section for sopranos alone) near the end of the motet. In another motet, *Ave regina coelorum* (*Hail, Queen of Heaven*), set for two sopranos, mezzo soprano, alto, and continuo, a constant interplay of motives, coloratura passages, and short imitations for two or three voices is characteristic. Only in two short sections near the middle and end of the motet are all four voices heard together.

North of the Alps a variety of styles in motet composition prevailed for several decades. A number of psalm settings by Jan Pieterszoon Sweelinck (1591-1652) may serve as an example. Sweelinck, long identified with Amsterdam as an organist, is known primarily as a composer of imaginative instrumental music. His psalm settings are for five-voice choir, generally in a conservative contrapuntal style that recalls the sixteenth century; only occasionally does he introduce chordal passages. Johann Christoph Demantius (1567–1643), on the other hand, brought many of the devices of madrigal composers into his motets. Illustrative treatment of text passages abounds in his motets and psalm settings. In one such passage, on the text "As Moses lifted up the serpent in the wilderness," long and sinuous melismas in all six voices simultaneously give evidence of Demantius's concern with the sense of the text.

In another style, the many motets of Hans Leo Hassler (1564–1612) reveal a fondness for the massed vocal effects typical of Venice. Active in Augsburg and Nuremberg as an organist, Hassler studied with Andrea Gabrieli, and even in his earliest motet collection (published in 1588) he composed for eight and twelve voices. In a collection of 1607 he used chorale melodies in 52 elaborate chorale motets. In another chorale collection, published in 1608, settings in simple four-part hymn style are typical. And again, Johann Hermann Schein (1586–1630) composed choral works in which the Venetian style is combined with the use of basso continuo, but with German texts instead of Latin.

Schütz

Heinrich Schütz (1585–1672), one of the most significant figures in German music, occupies a unique position in the development of musical style. He was born in Hesse, studied with Giovanni Gabrieli in Venice from 1609 to 1612, and

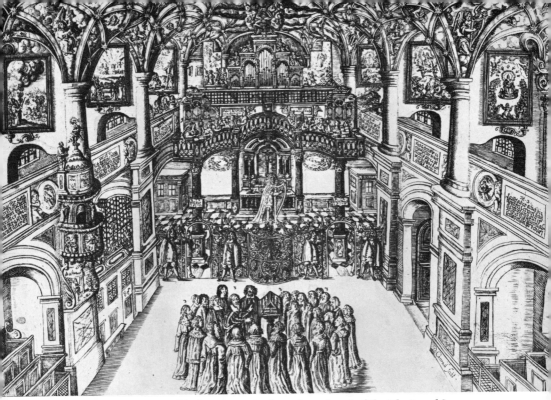

Heinrich Schütz surrounded by his singers in the palace chapel of the Elector of Saxony in Dresden. Contemporary engraving.

in 1617 was made chapelmaster to the Elector of Saxony in Dresden. He remained in the service of the court for 55 years until his death at the age of 87, and some of his most important works were composed when he was in his eighties. He lived through the ravages caused by the Thirty Years' War, taking a few leaves of absence in Copenhagen and making trips to Italy to renew his contacts with Monteverdi.

Schütz's works fall into several categories, motet collections and oratorios being chief among them, and except for a few madrigals and other secular pieces, they are all dedicated to the purposes of the Lutheran Church. The first major collection, *Psalmen Davids* (*Psalms of David*, 1619), consists of 26 psalm settings in German, some for as many as four choirs totaling 21 voice parts, and all including continuo supplemented by other instruments. In the larger psalms the setting often varies from verse to verse; for example, in Psalm VIII (8) verses or half verses are set in the following sequence: both choirs, second choir, first choir, both, second, first, and so on. In other cases solo voices are added, as in Psalm CXX (121): soprano soloist, choir, alto soloist, choir, tenor, choir, bass, and choir. Schütz was greatly interested in contrasting one vocal color against another and in writing antiphonally for massed choral forces—both being practices of the Venetian style, of which his teacher Gabrieli was so great an exponent. That interest comes to eloquent expression in *Psalms of David*, Schütz's largest work.

In 1625 Schütz published a set of 35 *Cantiones sacrae* (*Sacred Songs*, that is, motets), with five more in an appendix. Texts are drawn partly from the Psalms, partly from other sources (notably St. Augustine), and all are set in Latin.

Significantly, the settings are all for four-voice choir with continuo; but the latter was added at the publisher's instigation and against the composer's inclination. Repeatedly in his prefaces Schütz inveighed against the use of continuo—largely because many organists of his time realized the figured bass in a slovenly manner not in accord with the composer's intentions. The motets in this collection reveal first of all Schütz's mastery of counterpoint; close imitations, free counterpoints, melismatic passages, declamatory writing, motivic manipulation, and rhythmic counterpoint are wonderfully blended here. This colorful variety of textures is dedicated to the inmost meanings of the several texts, and a fervent, spiritual tone pervades the entire set. Yet the work does not represent merely an example of sixteenth-century style; the advanced harmonic touches, many mediant° modulations, augmented or diminished fourths in the melodic line, and the continuo itself all reveal Schütz's awareness of the harmonic developments of his time.

From 1628 to about 1644 Schütz traveled widely: his second Italian trip, three extended stays in Copenhagen, and a period of service to the court of Hanover fall in that interval. One result of the Italian visit was the first set of *Symphoniae sacrae* (*Sacred Symphonies*), published in Venice in 1629; that work contains twenty settings of Latin texts for one to three voices and instruments. It is mentioned here primarily because it illustrates Schütz's adoption of the concertato principle and the further influence of Monteverdi's style on him. Somewhat similar to the *Symphoniae sacrae* are two sets of *Kleine geistliche Konzerte* (*Small Sacred Concerts*, 1636 and 1639) with texts in German and with settings ranging from one to five solo voices with continuo. Typical here is a masterful use of melodic declamation within smoothly flowing rhythmic structures, a feature Schütz developed even more highly in his later works. A second set of 27 *Symphoniae sacrae* (1647), this time with German texts, rounds out four collections of vocal chamber music in which Schütz attained the final synthesis of Venetian and German styles; continuo textures, declamatory writing, and advanced harmonies are all modified to meet the needs of a style that is essentially contrapuntal.

In the *Geistliche Chormusik* (*Sacred Choral Music*) of 1648, with 29 choral settings mainly of New Testament texts in German, Schütz returned to the choral genre that interests us most. The settings range from five- to seven-voice; with regard to the use of continuo, the composer describes them on the title page as works "in which the *bassus generalis,* according to advice and desire, not, however, from necessity . . . is also to be found." Schütz, feeling that mastery of contrapuntal techniques was the essence of musical art, had often expressed his concern that a new generation of German composers would arise without approaching that mastery; the Preface to the *Geistliche Chormusik* is eloquent on this point, and the work was a worthy model for younger composers to follow.

Here is a purposeful renunciation of the sharp melodic contrasts, pictorial writing, and massive sonorities characteristic of the *Psalms of David,* composed nearly thirty years earlier. In place of such spectacular elements come passages of flowing counterpoint with interwoven voices, a restrained use and control of dissonance, and balanced phrase structures. The whole reflects quiet reverence and a sense of personal involvement with the sacred texts; it can be called a musical metaphor of Christian faith.

Finally, with the publication of the third set of *Symphoniae sacrae* in 1650, Schütz revealed his renewed interest in the concertato style. Containing 21 motets with German texts mainly from the Bible, the collection includes settings for a variety of solo voices (from three to six), with a single or double choir in 16 of the motets and with continuo and supplementary instruments in all. Short *sinfonie* often appear between choral or solo passages; and the moods of the various texts, ranging from deepest sorrow to jubilation, reflect restraint, simplicity, or dramatic intensity as the occasion demands. One of the composer's greatest single works, the motet *Saul, was verfolgst du mich?* (*Saul, Why Do You Persecute Me?*), is contained in this collection.

French composers

The use of basso continuo appeared relatively late in French sacred music. Among the first composers to specify continuo was Henri Dumont (1610–1684) in a set of *Cantica sacra* (*Sacred Songs*, that is, motets), composed about 1652 for two- to four-voice choir with instrumental accompaniment. Dumont became chapelmaster at the Royal Chapel in 1665; his motets were among those inserted in the low Mass for the enjoyment of the King. Here all the elements of concertato style are present: instruments are combined with voices in a variety of ways, short motives instead of long phrases are used, and instrumental interludes become typical.

Once having found its place in French music, the concertato style was used by later composers almost exclusively—for example, by Jean-Baptiste Lully, the dominant figure in the development of French opera. Born in Florence, Lully came to Paris as a boy of twelve, soon found favor with the young King Louis, and rose rapidly to an important position as violinist, composer of ballets and operas, and eventually master of music to the royal family. Through his skill as a courtier he quickly rose to a preeminent position in France and ruthlessly drove his competitors from the field. His sacred music (several motets, a *Te Deum*, and smaller works) exhibit many of the same qualities that made his operas objects of imitation for half a century.

Lully had a superb sense of the theater and was able to apply that sense to his motets as well. The motets range from limpid sweetness to powerful drama— always in keeping with the sense of the texts—and the melodies are characterized by a blend of Italian intensity and French grace. The use of counterpoint is limited; in its place comes a masterful control of the rhythmic element, with reiteration of rhythmic patterns becoming a major dramatic feature. Lully favored the use of a single five-voice choir when several soloists were also required—for example, in the motet *Pie Jesu*, for five soloists, choir, and orchestra; and two five-voice choirs when few or no soloists were needed—as in *Plaudate, laetare*. A short-phrased style with many internal cadences gives his motets the effect of being in several sections or movements, and the resemblance to choral cantatas (see below) is marked.

Other Forms

We mentioned in Chapter 2 that the term "motet" was a stylistic rather than a formal identification and was applied even to works carrying lengthy texts and those that had specific places in the liturgy. During the course of several centuries a few such texts were set repeatedly by many composers. Among them, three deserve special mention for the number of times they were set as well as for the variety of their settings: the Te Deum, the Stabat Mater, and the Magnificat. Although the treatment those texts received in the seventeenth century often resulted in forms that bear only a slight relationship to the original form of the motet, they are still related to that form in at least two important respects: they are settings of sacred—if not scriptural—texts, and they have a firm place in the liturgy. Thus it is appropriate to consider them as offshoots of the motet.

Te Deum

This text, attributed to Bishop Nicetas and written near the end of the fourth century, has been used ever since as a hymn of praise or thanksgiving in church services as well as on days of secular jubilation. (The Latin text and traditional plainsong melody are found in *Liber usualis,* p. 1832; a translation is given in Appendix 2c.) In the Roman Catholic Church it is used in the Office of Matins; it may be used in English translation as part of the Morning Prayer of the Anglican service, and in the Lutheran Church it was used as early as 1529 in a German translation made by Luther himself.

Sung in plainsong for many centuries, in due course the Te Deum attracted the attention of a host of choral composers; one of the earliest settings is for eight-voice choir by Jacobus Vaet (died 1567), a Flemish composer who served as chapelmaster at the Imperial court in Vienna. Orlando di Lasso composed a six-voice setting in 1568, and thereafter, in the later sixteenth and early seventeenth centuries, the Te Deum is prominent in the works of William Byrd and Orlando Gibbons in England, Hans Leo Hassler and Johann Hermann Schein in Germany, and Jean-Baptiste Lully in France.

Stabat Mater

One class of Gregorian chants, on the text *Alleluia,* is distinguished by an extremely florid line, and in many of them the final syllable of the word is itself extended in a melisma to embrace two dozen or more tones set in an undulating contour (see Example 32). Possibly out of a desire to make the final melisma easier

EXAMPLE 32   *Liber usualis,* p. 405

to commit to memory, rhymed texts were often set to them; and thus arose the *sequence* (called *prosa* in France, from PRO se<i>quentia</i>). Hundreds of sequences were composed from the tenth to the thirteenth century, and the sanctity of the liturgy was endangered thereby. The Council of Trent moved to abolish all but four of the sequences, one of which, *Dies irae (Day of Wrath)*, retained an important place in the Requiem Mass; a fifth, on the text beginning *Stabat Mater* (see Appendix 2d), was given a place in the liturgy early in the eighteenth century.

In the general loosening of liturgical structures that took place in the early seventeenth century (marked also by the introduction of the concertato Mass, often with operatic overtones) the Stabat Mater was sometimes sung either before or after the Credo; indeed, in the latter location, as the item dedicated to the Offertory, a wide variety of solo or choral works with bravura effects was often inserted. Eventually, then, the Stabat Mater assumed its place on certain specified festivals.

The text is concerned with the Seven Sorrows of the Virgin Mary standing beneath the Cross. The full text (found in *Liber usualis*, p. 1634v) consists of ten pairs of verses rhymed AAB, CCB in each pair. The first four pairs (eight verses) are descriptive, while the remainder, beginning with the phrase *Eia mater*, constitute in essence a prayer; thus a two-part form is suggested. This moving poem has affected composers for several centuries, and many choral settings exist in a profusion of styles.

Even before its liturgical position was fixed, the Stabat Mater attracted the attention of major Renaissance composers, the poignancy of its text providing a suitable vehicle for expressive music. One setting by Josquin, composed late in the fifteenth century, was highly regarded and was often reprinted in the sixteenth. Josquin's setting, for five voices, is divided into two sections, as the structure of the text suggests. Imitative textures dominate, with each verse having its own motive in keeping with the motet technique of Josquin's day, and with each verse thus constituting a point of imitation. His sensitivity to changes of vocal color to fit the changing moods of the text, illustrated so frequently in his motets, is very much present here as well. The tenor is based on a cantus firmus derived from Gregorian chant, and there is some evidence that the part was performed instrumentally; hence this setting is often listed as being for four voices with instrumental cantus firmus.

A setting of the Stabat Mater by Palestrina for two four-voice choirs represents one of his rare uses of eight-voice writing. The work is almost entirely in chordal style and is characterized by the same emotional reserve typical of his other works. (Another setting for three choirs, often attributed to Palestrina, was probably composed by Anerio.)

Magnificat

Opposed to freely written (that is, nonbiblical) poems, such as the Te Deum and Stabat Mater, are certain scriptural texts drawn either from the Old or New Testament; the text of the *Magnificat*, taken from Luke 1: 46–55, is chief among them (see Appendix 2e). Used in the Office of Vespers in the Roman Catholic service and at Evensong in the Anglican, it is a canticle of the Virgin Mary. Polyphonic settings were composed as early as the fourteenth century; since the text is composed of a series of short contrasting sections, it was most often set with the odd-numbered verses chanted and the even-numbered verses sung—at first by an ensemble of soloists and later by a choir. The cult of the Virgin Mary enjoyed high esteem among the laymen of the time, and the text honoring her was set repeatedly. In the sixteenth century, for example, Palestrina composed about 35 settings and Lasso almost 100.

Many of the older settings, including some of Palestrina's, employed the traditional plainsong melody as a cantus firmus, around which other voices were set in imitative counterpoint. Those by Lasso are often freely composed and reveal an eloquent use of short descriptive melodies. The harmonic richness and approach to tonal harmony Lasso revealed in his motets is even more strikingly evident in his settings of the Magnificat. Lasso often set the text for women's voices alone, undoubtedly because the text was attributed to Mary by the writer of the Gospel.

A Magnificat was included in Monteverdi's collection of 1610, the *Vespro della Beata Vergine*, mentioned above. The work is there present in two versions: one for seven-voice choir, five soloists, and orchestra; the other, a simplified one adapted for smaller churches, for six-voice choir and organ. Even the latter is full of dramatic power and elaborate in its variety of vocal combinations. Yet this variety has a common denominator, for the work is unified by a cantus firmus that appears in virtually every section. The whole is a masterpiece of expressive writing in which the concertato style with its operatic overtones is here seen to be suitable for the setting of sacred texts.

Magnificat settings continued through the seventeenth century, especially in the German-speaking countries. Many composers, Hassler and Schein among them, set the text in a concertato style similar to Monteverdi's. Modifications in the setting continued to be made by major composers as the century ran its course, as we shall see in Chapter 7, and in virtually each case the resulting work reflects the style of its country and its decade.

Oratorio

Shortly after the middle of the sixteenth century and under the leadership of St. Filippo Neri (1515–1595), a series of informal devotional services was instituted in Rome. It became customary, after a session devoted to sermons and prayers, to sing hymns (*laudi*) and other works in Italian; eventually, by the beginning of the seventeenth century, works in monodic style were introduced and the musical portion of the service was elaborated into a somewhat dramatic form. A narrator (*testo*, literally "text") provided scriptural readings and bits of narrative to explain and connect the other texts, and his part was often written in recitative style; on a few occasions sections for choir were also included. These devotional meetings were held in the oratories (prayer halls) of churches; the resultant musical form thus came to be called *oratorio*. The oratorio was originally intended for the common man, hence the use of the vernacular, Italian; but by the middle of the seventeenth century it had attracted the attention of aristocrats and churchmen as well, and for them Latin came to be used instead.

The first considerable work in which the future dramatic form of the oratorio was foreshadowed was performed in Rome in 1600. *La rappresentazione di anima e di corpo* (*The Representation of the Soul and the Body*), a kind of sacred opera, was composed by Emilio de' Cavalieri (c. 1550–1602); it included characters representing the Spirit, Time, the Body, and similar allegorical figures, who were given parts largely in recitative style (a scene from this work is reprinted in *TEM*, No. 37). Other composers went further in adopting operatic devices such as the aria and *arioso* (a form in which bits of lyric melody were inserted into a piece largely in recitative style), and the roles of the testo and the choir were gradually enlarged. The testo narrated the action, three or more soloists took roles of characters, the choir commented on and reflected on the unfolding of the story, and an orchestra provided a sometimes elaborate accompaniment.

Giacomo Carissimi (1605–1674), with 15 Latin oratorios, became the first major composer of the form. In a typical work by Carissimi, significant episodes in the life of a biblical figure are set in dramatic form. His *Judgment of Solomon* (a scene is reprinted in *MM*, No. 32), *David and Jonathan, Job, Abraham and Isaac,* and his masterpiece, *Jephtha,* are representative. The choir was given a major role in the dramatic action; with phrases harmonized simply but reflecting great dramatic drive, it became the element that transformed the oratorio into a choral drama. The recitatives at times approached lyricism and developed a degree of melodic integrity. The parts for soloists often resembled the bel canto passages employed in the opera of the time; and imaginative ensemble settings and even passages for double choir gave a considerable variety of vocal color to the whole. Finally, instrumental preludes, *sinfonie,* and *ritornelli* (regularly recurring instrumental interludes), played by an orchestra consisting only of violins and continuo, added instrumental color as well. Often an oratorio came to resemble an opera—except that the former was seldom staged and the latter made little use of choir.

A number of Italian composers wrote oratorios in the form Carissimi developed, among them Stefano Landi (c. 1590–c. 1655), Michel Angelo Rossi (c. 1600–c. 1660), Domenico Mazzocchi (1592–1665), and Giovanni Legrenzi (1625–1690). Notable composers and representative oratorios of the second half of the Baroque period will be discussed in Chapter 7.

Passion

The Passion as a musical form is often closely related to the oratorio of the seventeenth century, although its history extends much further back. A dramatic portrayal of the events in the life of Christ from the Last Supper through the betrayal to the Crucifixion, summarized in the phrase "the Passion of our Lord," was a favorite subject in the repertoire of Medieval sacred drama. Musical versions of the Passion are even older, with plainsong settings dating back to the fifth century. In those settings the participants taking the roles of the Evangelist (that is, the Narrator), the Saviour, and various other individuals sang melodies that were closely akin to the melodic formulas that were used in psalmody. To about the fifteenth century the plainsong Passion remained virtually unchanged in musical style.

At that time, polyphonic settings of portions of the text were gradually introduced. A Passion was reputedly composed by Binchois in 1437, but the music has not survived; two English manuscripts (the composers are unknown) date from about the same period. In these and a few similar early works the Latin text is retained; a mixture of plainsong (for the parts of the Narrator and the words of Christ) and ensemble passages in chordal style and with simple harmonies (for the other characters) is most usual. After the Protestant Reformation, when many texts were translated into the vernaculars, the tradition of combining plainsong with chordal passages was retained. In the first German example, by Johann Walther, composed about 1525 on a text from the Gospel of St. Matthew, the part of the Evangelist is sung by a tenor, that of Christ by a bass, other characters by an alto, and those of the *turba* ("crowd") by a four-voice choir.

In a St. John Passion composed by Antonio Scandello (1517–1580) at Dresden about 1560, a new feature was introduced. The texts for all characters except the Evangelist (that is, Jesus, Pilate, the High Priest, etc.) as well as those in the *turba* were set in short choral passages for two to five voices; the chordal texture became less rigid and often included cantus firmi and passages in imitative writing. This work became a prototype for many Passions written by major and minor composers in Germany and Austria through much of the seventeenth century.

One example is seen in a St. Mark Passion by Ambrosius Beber, a German composer about whom little is known except that he was active in Naumburg at the turn of the seventeenth century and that he composed this Passion (his only surviving work) about 1610. (The Passion is reprinted in *Das Chorwerk*, No. 66.) In Beber's setting the Narrator sings in plainchant in a style that recalls the recitation of psalmody. Texts given to Jesus are set for a four-voice ensemble of soloists, those for the other chief characters are set variously for two to four solo voices, and those for the crowd for five-voice choir. A noteworthy distinction exists between the chordal style of the choral passages and the freer contrapuntal style that characterizes many of the passages given to the soloists. And parallel to Protestant German Passions such as those by Scandello and Beber are Roman Catholic settings composed elsewhere, most of which return to the Latin text; those by Lasso and Byrd are of the latter type.

Eventually the part of the Narrator was often also set in chordal or contrapuntal style; thus the Passion became in effect a series of motets. An example is found in the six-voice St. John Passion by Christoph Demantius (1567–1643), active in Saxony. This setting (reprinted in *Das Chorwerk*, No. 27), for two sopranos, alto, two tenors, and bass, presents the relevant parts of the Gospel in somewhat shortened form; here all sections of the text—those of the Narrator as well as the others—are set polyphonically and sometimes imitatively, with passages for three or four voices used antiphonally within the six-voice settings. The style on occasion reveals considerable rhythmic complexity, as seen in Example 33.

EXAMPLE 33   Demantius, *St. John Passion*

(Tr.: "Not this one, but Barabbas.")

From Friedrich Blume, *Das Chorwerk*, Vol. 27, edited by Friedrich Blume. Used by permission of Möseler Verlag, Wolfenbüttel and Zurich.

Harmonically, the work suggests that Demantius was acquainted with the music of Gesualdo and Monteverdi. Chromatic alterations, chord progressions moving directly from A major to C minor, augmented triads, melodic inflections in which augmented seconds are present, and similar touches show how much progress Demantius had made on the path away from modality and toward the tonal system; but cross relations are also present.

Related to the Passions are the works that set into music the events from the Entombment to the Resurrection. Known as "Resurrection History" or "Easter Oratorio," a work of this kind had a text usually compiled from the four Gospels and ended with the words from I Corinthians 15: 57 beginning, "Thanks be to God who giveth us the victory." A work in this form by Antonio Scandello, composed about 1568 as a continuation of his St. John Passion, served as a model for later composers and was reprinted many times through the seventeenth century.

Perhaps the most outstanding early example is the *Auferstehungs-Historie* (*Resurrection History*) by Heinrich Schütz. Composed in 1623 on a German text, it includes parts for a tenor (the Evangelist), eight other soloists, a six-voice choir that is expanded to eight-voice in the final chorus, and continuo. In the Preface to the work Schütz gave specific directions about the way the continuo is to be realized, and expressed the hope that, if possible, four *viole da gamba* be used in place of the organ continuo; further, he wanted only the Narrator and viols to be seen, with the remaining soloists and choir placed near the organ and concealed from view. Thus Schütz sought to retain the idea of spatial separation that had been characteristic of the Venetian school half a century earlier.

Schütz's text is based on that used by Scandello, and is derived from the four Gospels. The part of the Narrator is cast in free recitative style; again Schütz specified that he sing "without actual meter as seems comfortable to him, and does not hold any syllable longer than one essays to do in slow and understandable speech." The recitative style resembles that of the Florentine monodies with, however, notable modifications at points where the drama or pathos of the text requires (see Example 34). Other passages (those of the High Priests, Cleophas

EXAMPLE 34   Schütz, *Resurrection History*

(Tr.: "And behold, there was a great earthquake; for the angel of the Lord descended from heaven, and came and rolled back the stone from the door"—Matthew 28:2.)

and his servant, the three Marys, etc.) are set as duets or trios either in parallel thirds and sixths or in imitative style. But the words of Jesus are also set as duets—for alto and tenor—in keeping with an old tradition of setting all such partial texts in motet style. The full choir is confined to an introductory chorus, a section near the end in which the Resurrection is announced, and the closing chorus in which the choir is divided into two four-voice groups singing the traditional final words antiphonally in chordal style. And to the second of these groups the voice of the Narrator is added, reiterating in free rhythm the single word *victoria.*

In this work especially, but to a large extent in earlier and later works as well—most notably those on German texts—it is important to mention Schütz's great gift for adapting his melodies to the accentual characteristics of the language. Inflected syllables, accented vowels, and even unstressed ones, are wonderfully mirrored in the vocal lines, whether in recitative or lyric style. Tones may be higher or lower than their neighbors, long or short, carry metrical accents or avoid them—always in accord with the requirements of the words to which they are set. Rarely has a composer been so successful in balancing his musical requirements against the needs of his texts.

Organized in somewhat similar fashion is Schütz's setting of *Die sieben Worte unsers . . . Jesu Christi* (*The Seven Words of Jesus Christ on the Cross*), written in 1645. The musical means are of the simplest: five-voice choral settings of the Introit and Conclusion with instrumental *sinfonie* set after the one and before the other; a series of narrations preceding each of the Seven Words, and the Words themselves; and three comments by the two thieves crucified with Jesus. Yet the whole breathes an air of devoutness and sorrow unmatched in the Baroque period. The sense of the text is wonderfully enhanced by the halting motives given to the voice of Jesus, as well as by the expressive variety of the settings of the Narrator—given variously to one or another of the solo voices and occasionally to the four together, somewhat in the old fashion of a motet for four solo voices. The work is unified by the figured bass, which serves as a link between the diverse styles (instrumental, monodic, and contrapuntal) that carry the texts. Schütz's poignant reserve is here eloquently revealed, and the work is a fitting monument to his religious fervor.

We return now to the Passion proper, as set by Schütz. Some twenty years after the composition of *The Seven Words*—Schütz was then in his eighties—he composed three settings of the Passion on the texts of Matthew, Luke, and John, respectively. (The setting of the St. Mark text, formerly attributed to Schütz in early editions, is now known to be spurious.) Unlike his other oratorios, which employ continuo or instruments or both, and unlike the motetlike Passion by Demantius, Schütz's Passions are unaccompanied throughout. In a series of recitatives of varying lengths, interspersed with short choral interjections, the eventful story unfolds. The Narrator, Jesus, several disciples, Pilate, and other participants in the sacred drama are given recitatives; various groups such as the High Priests, the Elders, and the soldiers are presented in four-voice choruses usually no more than a few measures in length. The whole moves forward relentlessly to the final scene, after which a reflective chorus brings the work to a conclusion. Although all three Passions are similar in structure and style, there are notable differences in individual treatment—reflections of the differences in the texts themselves.

As in the *Resurrection History* and *The Seven Words,* Schütz's Passion recitatives are neither adaptations of the old psalmody nor imitations of Florentine monody. Rather they represent a new type of melody composed of many tone repetitions, expressive melismas, and free rhythms, differences in range and general contour serving to delineate each character sharply from the others. And the choruses in brief compass provide the dramatic or intense or reflective moments that the texts require (see Example 35). In returning to a severe,

EXAMPLE 35   Schütz, *St. Matthew Passion*

(Tr.: "Lord, is it I?")

unaccompanied style, Schütz seemingly reverted to an earlier century. Yet his settings of the Passion reflect a perfect amalgamation of sixteenth- and seventeenth-century practices in their dramatic fervor, tonal inflections, and restoration of contrapuntal writing. The works are unique in the century; although Schütz had no followers, the influence of his Passions on later composers of sacred music was profound.

Continuo Madrigal

Secular music in the first half of the seventeenth century developed somewhat differently from sacred music, notably because of the increasing emphasis given to new instrumental forms, textures, and performing media. As for choral music, we must recognize the fact that it was overshadowed by solo song, chamber cantata, and opera in the works of secular composers. There is one exception to this fact: the madrigal continued to flourish. This form, as developed by Marenzio and Gesualdo in the sixteenth century, found an admirable champion in Monteverdi. The madrigal had become a form capable of expressing a wide range of emotions in a style that made considerable use of chromaticism and—in the case of Marenzio—word-painting.

Building on that foundation, Monteverdi composed eight books of madrigals across the long time interval between 1587 and 1638. In them may be seen the gradual fusion of the hyperexpressive style of Marenzio and Gesualdo with the concertato style and other aspects of Baroque music to constitute a body of works that have few parallels in the literature.

The first four books (1587, 1590, 1592, 1603) take their point of departure from the madrigals of Marenzio. The style is in general a judicious mixture of counterpoint and homophony; wide-ranging harmonies and chromatic touches are typical (without approaching Gesualdo's freedom), and the sense of the texts is everywhere observed. Yet even in these early madrigals Monteverdi's awareness of developments in the new monodic style is evident; he often departed from the concept of equality of voices by setting two or three voices against the bass, which established the harmonic framework, and these voices were often set in a kind of harmonized recitative or declamatory style. The result was a flexible and expressive texture in which the subtleties of the text were brought to eloquent expression.

The last four books of madrigals (1605, 1614, 1621, 1638) show the gradual introduction of continuo writing (beginning with the last six madrigals of Book V) and occasionally other concertizing instruments. In those works the polarity of melody and bass is fully established; inner voices are made free to engage in melodic interplay, to introduce independent motives, and to enter or leave the four- or five-voice texture as the composer's expressive needs dictated. Instrumental parts are on occasion made independent of the voices; introductory *sinfonie* and *ritornelli* appear, and a virtual dialogue between voices and instruments, carried by short rhythmic motives, becomes typical. This dialogue is of course basic to the principles of concertato style. Throughout these later madrigals, the settings range from solo voice with continuo to large choral works with instrumental accompaniment. Based on a fusion of the old madrigal style with the new monodic style and a tight integration of solo and ensemble forces, Monteverdi's madrigals represent a new formal organization. At the same time, it is with Monteverdi that the concertato madrigal reached its highest point of development.

7

Music of the Late Baroque
1675–1750

The importance of secular music that was characteristic of the first half of the Baroque period continued into the second half, with secular forms flourishing and exerting an ever stronger influence on sacred music. Instruments were used with voices in a more elaborate fashion than earlier in the century, and the operatic style found a regular place in sacred forms. While the separation between the Roman Catholic and Protestant liturgies grew wider, certain formal developments took place in the one that were sometimes paralleled in the other. Thus the stylistic distinctions between Catholic and Protestant music, between sacred and secular music, and even between liturgical and nonliturgical music become increasingly difficult to draw.

Motet

In France the motet style inaugurated by Lully was carried forward principally by Marc-Antoine Charpentier (1634–1704). A native Parisian, Charpentier studied with Carissimi in Rome and, after serving as organist at several churches in Paris, became director of music at Saint-Chapelle in 1698. He composed almost a hundred motets, hymns, and psalm settings, as well as important oratorios.

Charpentier's motets differ greatly in length, ranging from the relatively short *Laudate Dominum* of about three minutes to the massive setting of Psalm L (51), *Miserere me, Domine,* lasting some 45. The extent of his instrumental requirements varies as greatly: from organ alone in *Oculi omnium* to an orchestra of twenty string and wind instruments and continuo in several others. And the vocal forces range from motets for a single four-voice choir to works that require five soloists and two four-voice choirs. These facts suggest a relationship between the nature of the text and the size of the musical forces.

The texture of the motets is generally chordal, with contrapuntal writing most often reserved for climactic moments or section endings. Charpentier's melodies are somewhat angular, based on tones of the triad, and are distinguished by his concern for balance and grace, a concern that is not hampered by his fondness for phrases of irregular length, as we shall see below. And the orchestration is characterized by considerable doubling (flute, oboe, and violin on the same melodic line, for example)—a practice that leads to great volumes of sound and a rather thick tone color.

Michel Richard de Lalande (1657–1726), a colleague of Charpentier and one of the most eminent seventeenth-century French composers, spent much of his career at the Royal Chapel of Louis XIV, for about twenty years as its director; in addition, he served a secular function as director of the King's chamber music. As a composer he was active in several fields, composing many ballets, several instrumental suites and short pieces, and 42 motets for soloists, choir, and orchestra.

Lalande's setting of Psalm CIX (110), *Dixit Dominus* (*The Lord Says*), illustrates his imaginative approach to his texts. After an instrumental introduction, a section for soprano soloist is followed by one for tenor; this leads into an ensemble section for six soloists frequently interrupted by short solo interludes, with the full choir then reworking and amplifying the material. Succeeding verses are sung alternately by a soloist and the choir; the forward flow of the music is often checked by dramatic reiteration of phrases, and significant words are sometimes isolated by pauses. Imitation is often employed but with no loss of textual clarity, and elsewhere solid chordal writing rises to sonorous climaxes.

During the course of the Baroque period, several factors seem to have brought about the gradual transformation of the motet from a single movement to a work of several movements. From the sixteenth century came the device of giving each section of the text its own melodic motive and imitating that motive within its section, thus giving rise to a series of sections called points of imitation. Sectional settings also resulted when each verse or half-verse of psalm texts was set separately, sometimes with different groupings of voices in each; or when the addition of continuo and other instruments in the seventeenth century made it possible for composers to insert an occasional sinfonia or ritornello for instruments alone between vocal movements. And we have also seen the general tendency, derived from the Venetian school, of alternating vocal groups—two choirs singing antiphonally, for example, or choir alternating with a group of soloists—which led to clearly marked sections. So did the natural division of certain texts into two or three parts, as we saw in the case of the Stabat Mater. Finally, when long texts such as the Te Deum were set in motet style, the result was often a series of movements; this practice may, in time, have influenced the setting of all extended motet texts into a similar form compounded of several separate short pieces. The end result was that a motet could take several forms:

a single unified movement, a movement cast in sectional form, or a series of long or short movements connected only by a unified text.

Buxtehude

Multimovement motets are found in the music of Dietrich Buxtehude (1637–1707), born in Denmark of German parents. As organist and composer he served from 1668 to his death at Lübeck, in northern Germany. There in 1673 he instituted a series of *Abendmusiken* ("evening concerts"), performances of organ, instrumental, and sacred choral music, on the several Sundays before Christmas. The *Abendmusiken* became famous throughout Germany and attracted the interest of many notable German musicians—Bach and Handel among them—who traveled to Lübeck to hear them. Among Buxtehude's surviving works are over a hundred settings of biblical and other sacred texts, the great majority of them in German.

A typical example is his *Jesu, meine Freude* (*Jesu, Priceless Treasure*), a setting of six stanzas of the chorale text for three soloists, a three-voice choir, and continuo amplified by two violins. After an extended instrumental sonata in three contrasting sections, the various stanzas are set as follows: choir, soprano soloist, bass soloist, choir, soprano soloist, choir; each stanza is separated from the next by a ritornello. Solo passages are appropriately florid, those for choir are largely in chordal style, and both are based on imaginative variations of the chorale melody itself. We shall examine Bach's treatment of the same text below.

In a setting of four stanzas of *In dulci jubilo* for three-voice choir, continuo, and two obbligato violins, Buxtehude presents the traditional Christmas melody in chordal style with extended melismas at the end of each phrase of the text, keeping its traditional mixture of Latin and vernacular. Here the melody is treated freely on each appearance, in the manner of a choral fantasy. Another treatment is seen in Buxtehude's jubilant *Das neugeborne Kindlein* (*The Newborn Babe*) for four-voice choir with continuo and three violins. Here, although there are both chordal and imitative textures and in spite of frequent changes of tempo and meter, the work is in one movement. The choral phrases, separated by instrumental interludes, are characterized by short energetic motives followed by pauses, in the style later made familiar by Handel.

Bach

The Baroque period had seen the growth of a great variety of styles, forms, and expressive elements—including the mystical tone that had been characteristic of German music for almost two centuries and that had underlain much of the music of Heinrich Schütz. Johann Sebastian Bach (1685–1750) was able to synthesize these diverse factors and compose works of the highest order and logic and of the highest expressive power. Bach's music, the greatest manifestation of the Baroque creative spirit, also marked its end. After Bach, a new style and a new approach to composition were required.

Johann Sebastian Bach as a young man. Painting by an unknown master, c. 1775.

Bach was born in Eisenach, one of the centers of Lutheranism, to a family that had been musically prominent in Thuringia for two centuries. Largely self-taught, he became an excellent violinist and superb organist, attaining his first major position as organist to the Duke of Weimar in 1708. In 1717 he became chapelmaster to the Prince of Anhalt at Cöthen, and in 1723 cantor at St. Thomas's Church in Leipzig, where he remained until his death. His principal duties differed widely in the three periods of employment, for he served successively as organist, master of a secular musical establishment, and choirmaster and musical administrator of a city's music. Directing his creative interests to the requirements of each position, he composed works for organ and other solo instruments, for orchestra and chamber music combinations, and for choir; throughout his life his religious spirit and zeal for composing to the greater glory of God remained steadfast. The works to be discussed in the present chapter include motets, the *Magnificat*, cantatas, Masses, oratorios, and two settings of the Passion.

Bach's six surviving motets are of different types. One, *Lobet dem Herrn* (*Praise the Lord*), a setting of Psalm cxvi (117), is for four-voice choir and continuo. Four others, *Der Geist Hilft, Singet dem Herrn, Fürchte dich nicht*, and *Komm, Jesu, Komm* (*The Spirit Helpeth, Sing to the Lord, Be Not Afraid*, and *Come, Jesu*, respectively), are set for two four-voice choirs without continuo, although the use of instruments to support the voice parts may have been permitted by the performance practice of the time. And the last, *Jesu, meine Freude* (*Jesu, Priceless Treasure*), is an elaborate work in eleven movements set for five-voice choir without continuo. With the possible exception of the first motet, all were designed as funeral music; in the Leipzig of Bach's day it was sometimes customary to replace the Vespers service with elaborate funeral services for prominent citizens. The motets were performed on those occasions.

Jesu, meine Freude beautifully illustrates Bach's unique ability to maintain a symmetrical setting with an ascending line of emotional intensity. The text of the work is based on six verses of the chorale combined with selected verses from Paul's Epistle to the Romans, Chapter 8. It is organized as follows:

No.	Form	Setting	Text	Length	Meter	Treatment
1.	Chorale	SATB	Verse 1	19 meas	4/4	Chordal
2.	Chorus	SSATB	Romans 8:1	84	3/2	Chordal and imitative
3.	Chorale	SSATB	Verse 2	19	4/4	Variation of Verse 1
4.	Trio	SSA	Romans 8:2	24	3/4	Contrapuntal
5.	Chorus	SSATB	Verse 3	63	3/4	Mixed texture
6.	Chorus	SSATB	Romans 8:9	48	4/4	Fugal
7.	Chorale	SATB	Verse 4	19	4/4	Variation of Verse 1
8.	Trio	ATB	Romans 8:10	23	12/8	Contrapuntal
9.	Chorus	SATB	Verse 5	106	2/4	Freely imitative; chorale melody as cantus firmus
10.	Chorus	SSATB	Romans 8:11	41	3/2	Begins like No. 2
11.	Chorale	SATB	Verse 6	19	4/4	Identical with No. 1

This wonderfully intricate form embraces an ever more concentrated expressiveness. For example, the variations (Nos. 3 and 7) become increasingly poignant (see Example 36), and No. 10 is only about half as long as No. 2, although based on the same material; conversely, No. 9, with the fifth verse of the chorale text, is several times longer than its equivalent, No. 3. Within the symmetrical form, these and other details gradually transform the tone from fear (No. 2) through

EXAMPLE 36   Bach, *Jesu, meine Freude*

jubilation (No. 6) and renunciation (No. 8) to comfort for the living (No. 10). In its control of structure, expressions of reverence and faith, and sheer musical beauty, *Jesu, meine Freude* is one of Bach's masterpieces.

Te Deum

Charpentier

In the late Baroque period many settings of the Te Deum were treated in a fashion similar to the longer motet texts; that is, they were composed for soloists as well as choir, were supplied with an orchestral accompaniment, and were divided into several sections or movements. One of several settings by Marc-Antoine Charpentier, a massive work requiring some 25 minutes in performance, reveals how consistently the composer made full use of these elements of Baroque style. This *Te Deum*, whose date of composition is unknown, is set for eight soloists (reduced to three in modern editions), four-voice choir, continuo, and an orchestra including flutes, oboes, English horn, bassoon, trumpets, timpani, and strings. Because the trumpets play such a large part in enhancing the brilliance of the orchestral sound, the work—like so many other works of the time—is in D major, a key especially suited to the trumpet used in the Baroque period. Charpentier's setting is divided into 13 sections or connected movements for the 29 verses of the text. The lengths of these sections vary greatly, however, and some are themselves divided into subsections distinguished by changes of setting, texture, or meter.

In all the passages given to the choir, the texture is largely chordal; only occasionally does a short melisma or a bit of imitative writing break their forward rhythmic drive. The passages for ensembles of soloists, on the other hand, are predominantly contrapuntal and often imitative, especially when the three string instruments add obbligato voices to the texture. A notable feature of Charpentier's melodic lines in general is a number of phrases of irregular length (see Example 37); such phrases, often of three, five, or six measures rather than the usual two or four, result from his fondness for repeating words of the text several times or prolonging a single syllable disproportionately. This device, in contrast to the regular flow of melodies of conventional length, goes far to give the *Te Deum* the rhythmic interest that is also characteristic of Charpentier's shorter motets.

Purcell

Henry Purcell (1659–1695), the most prominent English composer of the seventeenth century, was born in London; first a young chorister of the Chapel Royal, at twenty he succeeded John Blow as organist of Westminster Abbey, and a few years later became organist of the Chapel Royal. In his short life he composed one true opera, five or six quasi-operas, incidental music to over forty plays, quantities of secular vocal music, dozens of instrumental works, more than

EXAMPLE 37   Charpentier, *Te Deum*

(a) (meas. 42–46)

Te De - um, te De - um, te De - um, te De - um lau - da - mus

(b) (meas. 180–84)

Ple - ni sunt coe - li et ter - - - ra

(c) (meas. 389–93)

Te er - go quae - su - mus, fa - mu - lis tu - is sub - ve - ni

sixty anthems, and a large number of other sacred works. His setting of the Te
Deum in English, composed about 1694, is of special interest here.

The Chapel Royal of Charles II, possibly reacting against the repression of
music and art that had marked the period of the Commonwealth, adopted a
somewhat secular attitude toward church music, seemingly considering it primarily an attractive entertainment for the courtiers. Purcell, reflecting that
attitude, accepted the superficiality of the time but transformed it in the light
of his great skill as a melodist and as a composer of innate taste. While much
of his church music is perfunctory, many of his anthems and his setting of the
Te Deum rise far above the bulk of other music of the time.

Purcell's *Te Deum* is set for five soloists, a four-voice choir that is often
separated into two semichoirs, and continuo. The work is divided into 22 connected sections marked by constant changes in performing medium; the sections
range from three to seventeen measures in length. The full choir, which begins
and ends the work and sings five short passages within, is divided into halves
that are presented antiphonally in several passages, and these in turn are separated by solo groups set either for two sopranos and alto, or alto, tenor, and
bass. Textures vary in similar fashion: passages in four-voice counterpoint follow
others in chordal style, in imitation, or in mixed textures. And one notable passage
near the close is written as a double canon (see Example 38), giving evidence
of Purcell's accomplishments as a contrapuntist. Yet the most moving effects are
created by the choral sonorities resulting from Purcell's frequent use of a kind
of choral recitative, with all the voices virtually chanting a text phrase in thick
chordal style. We shall see other examples of this treatment in his *Magnificat*
and anthems below. Purcell's *Te Deum* was honored by almost a century of annual
performances in one or another of the major London churches, gradually to give
way to Handel's settings of the same text.

Handel

George Frideric Handel (the Anglicized form of the name, which he himself
adopted, 1685–1759) was born in Halle in central Germany. When still in his
teens he moved to Hamburg, where he was a violinist in an opera orchestra

EXAMPLE 38   Purcell, *Te Deum*

and began the composition of his almost forty operas. In 1710, after three years spent in Italy, he became chapelmaster to the Elector of Hanover (who later became George III of England), and from 1711 he was a resident of London. For a period of three years (1717–20), Handel served as musical director for the Duke of Chandos; with the exception of that appointment, he depended for his livelihood on profits from his operas and lived as a free-lance composer, although he enjoyed a life pension from Queen Anne and was often in favor with the court. His operas were composed between 1705 and 1741, his twenty-odd oratorios from 1708 to 1757, and a huge number of other sacred and secular vocal works and large quantities of instrumental music fall early and late in his career. German born, largely Italian influenced, and a naturalized Englishman, Handel was enormously successful in assimilating various styles, adapting them to his own requirements, and creating an individual style. His oratorios will be discussed below; of interest here are his English settings of the Te Deum, which have remained in the repertoire, while those of his continental contemporaries have long since been forgotten.

The *Utrecht Te Deum,* so called in celebration of the signing of the Treaty of Utrecht in 1713, is modeled largely on Purcell's conception and arrangement. The work is again in D major, like so many others, and Handel's orchestral writing abounds in brilliant melodic ideas. Orchestral prelude, postlude, and interludes are designed to enhance the festive nature of the text, and a division of the roles of instruments and voices results in passages in which the former express jubilation at the same time as the latter carry forward the stately song of praise. A similar division occurs in the double vocal fugue "All the Earth," where one fugue theme mirrors the reverence of the text phrase while the other is jubilant in tone. Other choruses range from exuberant magnificence to simple devoutness, notably the six-voice "Day by Day," with its succession of short motives used antiphonally, alternately, or sequentially. And in the closing chorus, "O Lord, in Thee Have I Trusted," a combination of a quasi-plainsong melody with a variety of other melodic fragments is raised to dramatic heights by the breathtaking orchestral accompaniment.

Additional settings of the Te Deum by Handel include another in D, one in B flat (the *Chandos Te Deum*), and one in A major, which is simply a transposed, transformed, and somewhat shortened version of the B flat setting. Much later, about 1743, Handel composed the *Dettingen Te Deum*, in honor of the victory of the British and the Hessians over a French army in one of the battles constituting the War of the Austrian Succession (1740–48). One of Handel's most brilliant works, this setting is comparatively modest in its vocal and instrumental requirements: a five-voice choir, alto and bass soloists, and an orchestra consisting of oboes, bassoon, trumpets, strings, and continuo with organ. Yet the work is magnificent in its expression of majesty and reverence. Along with sonorous chordal writing, as in the first chorus, "We Praise Thee," are sections set for soprano soloist and semichoir of men's voices in an eloquent lyric style. Often short rhythmic motives or melodic fragments separated by pauses—a device of which Handel was particularly fond—animate an entire chorus. We can see this practice, for example, in "Thou Didst Open the Kingdom of Heaven to All Believers"; here the phrase "to all" is carried by a short figure that pervades virtually the entire texture (see Example 39). Elsewhere are solos or duets that express the reverent text phrases in melodies of purest bel canto style. And underlying all are the dramatic power and rhythmic drive that transform a Handel choral work into a great musical experience for every singer and listener.

EXAMPLE 39   Handel, *Dettingen Te Deum*

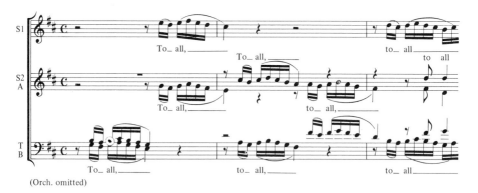

(Orch. omitted)

Magnificat

Purcell's English *Magnificat* differs in many respects from his *Te Deum* and from Magnificat settings by other composers. The work is for four-voice choir, continuo, and six soloists, no more than four of whom sing at any one time. Occasionally the soloists are used antiphonally in short passages. Sections are not definitely marked, being distinguished primarily by changes of vocal color; thus the effect is that of a single long, continuous movement. The final section, on the text of the Doxology ("Praise God from whom all blessings flow"), gives another example of Purcell's contrapuntal mastery; it is set in three-voice canon at two different time intervals (alto at a fourth above the tenor after four beats, soprano at the octave after six beats) with an independent and freely moving counterpoint in the bass. The chief attractiveness of this work lies in its choral sonority, its passages in imitative style, and its variety of vocal color.

Bach

Of quite different nature is Bach's Latin *Magnificat*, composed in E flat for the Christmas season of 1723, and then modified, transposed to D major, and somewhat shortened about 1730. In the latter version it stands as one of Bach's most joyful, majestic, and expressive works. It is set for five-voice choir, four soloists, and an orchestra consisting of two flutes, two oboes interchangeable with *oboi d'amore* (pitched a third lower than the normal oboe), bassoon, three trumpets, timpani, strings, and continuo with organ. The setting consists of twelve separate movements, several of considerable length, with five movements for choir, five for various soloists, and one each for duet and trio.

The first movement opens with an orchestral prelude, followed by a chorus and an orchestral postlude. Based on two or three short motives that appear in several keys, for many instruments, in all pitch ranges, and often in imitation, the whole resembles a brilliant concerto movement; full of buoyancy and jubilation, it is overwhelming in its effect. The second part of the last movement, on the text *Sicut erat in principio* ("As it was in the beginning"), appropriately recapitulates motives from the first chorus with the same jubilance. Internal choral movements are varied in treatment: No. 4, *Omnes generationes*, is entirely imitative and approaches fugal writing; No. 7, *Fecit potentiam*, is based on a fugal exposition that contains many overlappings and interweaving accompanying contrapuntal voices, continues with developments of short motives, and ends dramatically with a few measures in slow tempo to emphasize the sense of the text; No. 11, *Sicut locutus est*, is in mixed imitative and chordal style, and except for the continuo is unaccompanied.

The solo movements are similarly varied. A series of motives connected by sequence repetition° or elaborated into chains of melismas is basic to all of them, but the instrumental accompaniment and general mood of each are different. The first solo aria, No. 2, *Et exultavit spiritus*, for Soprano II, is accompanied by strings and is appropriately joyful in tone; No. 3, *Quia respexit*, is set for Soprano I with obbligato provided by *oboi d'amore*. No. 5, *Quia fecit*, for Bass soloist, is provided only with a continuo accompaniment, and so on. In every case Bach's choice of setting unfailingly enhances the meaning of each text phrase. Whether the words express joy or sorrow or reverence, the musical details are always marvelously appropriate, and a masterwork results.

Anthem

The English anthem, represented so eloquently in the works of Tallis, Byrd, and Gibbons, continued to be an important form in the late Baroque period. The outstanding composers of the form were Purcell and Handel.

Purcell

As discussed earlier, two forms of the anthem had developed in the sixteenth century in England: the full anthem for choir, and the verse anthem for soloists and choir. Purcell obviously preferred the verse anthem, as all but 13 of his 63 anthems are in this form. This fact may be attributed in part to the growing popularity of the musical theater (plays with incidental music) at the English court and the influence of theatrical devices on church music. The liturgical solemnity characteristic of much German church music and the emotional intensity of its Italian counterpart were of little interest to the English court. Mindful of this fact, Purcell developed a style in which melodic grace in the solo passages was contrasted with great sonority in the choral. His texts are most often selected from the Book of Psalms.

The full anthems are written mainly for five to eight voices. Textures are generally either contrapuntal or chordal, and mixed textures (that is, those comprising three or more voices in counterpoint accompanied by other voices in chordal style) are relatively rare. In the chordal passages Purcell often employed a kind of choral recitative in which all voices follow the rhythm of the text phrase simultaneously (see Example 40). In spite of a few modal touches, the harmony is predominantly tonal; expressive dissonances, transient modulations, and the like are all based on the tonal system.

EXAMPLE 40   Purcell, *Lord, How Long*

The verse anthems are distinguished by the imaginative use of instrumental accompaniments. Typically the anthems begin with an orchestral introduction, motives from which are employed in the following choral section. Instruments are used to double the vocal parts, but often are also used in obbligato fashion to provide a countermelody for the vocal line; occasionally, especially with a joyful text, a type of concerto movement is introduced, in which the voices imitate the instrumental lines.

The solo parts in the verse anthems (most often given to men's voices) are distinguished by wide leaps and expressive dissonances, with considerable use of dotted rhythms to mirror accurately the rhythms of the text. In fact, the close correspondence of textual and musical accents is a striking feature of all Purcell's vocal writing in chordal, imitative, and canonic passages alike, whether written for solo voices or choir.

The ceremonial ode, a form related to the anthem, plays a somewhat minor part in Purcell's works. The odes, of which he wrote about sixteen, were occasional pieces, composed for royal birthdays, weddings, secular celebrations, and similar occasions. Often set quite elaborately for several soloists, five-voice choir, and orchestra on secular and sometimes trivial texts, they represent a perfunctory side of Purcell's work. Routine treatment abounds in them. They often illustrate one feature, however, that is not typical of the anthems—movements constructed over a "ground" or *basso ostinato*. In a movement of this type, a bass melody of fixed length is used repeatedly, sometimes in the upper voices and sometimes transposed to another key; over this ground other phrases enjoy an independent existence. One of his odes, *Hail, Bright Cecilia*, contains two movements of this kind as well as an excellent chorus in fugal style. Another ode, *Love's Goddess*, contains one of Purcell's most effective secular fugal choruses; the work was known to Handel and was of obvious influence on him.

Handel

A high point in the composition of anthems early in the eighteenth century was reached by Handel in his set of eleven anthems (some existing in two versions) composed during the course of his employment as chapelmaster to the Duke of Chandos. The texts are all taken from the Psalms, with each anthem using one or more soloists, a choir ranging from three to five voices, and a string orchestra with continuo (and occasionally flutes, oboes, and trumpets). The Chandos Anthems are among the first works Handel composed on English texts; consequently examples of unfelicitous accentuation are sometimes found. In all other respects, however, they reveal a master composer.

The third anthem of the set, *Have Mercy upon Me, O God*, is typical. Based on Psalm L (51), it is for soprano and tenor soloists, three-voice choir, orchestra, and continuo. The work begins with a French overture, consisting of an imposing slow section and a fast section in fugal style. Then follow a lengthy chorus in imitative texture and slow tempo, a slow duet for soprano and tenor solos, a recitative and aria for tenor, a fast chorus in imitative style, a slow solo for soprano, and a fast closing chorus again in imitative style. The first two and the last two movements are in C minor, the middle three respectively in E flat, F minor, and F major. Elements of unity are supplied by two types of melodic phrases: short phrases separated by pauses in the slow movements and rhythmically alive phrases containing many repeated notes in the fast (see Example 41). The basic tone of the anthem gradually changes from penitence to joy, in keeping with the sense of the text.

EXAMPLE 41   Handel, *Chandos Anthem No. 3*

(a) Adagio

Have mer-cy up-on me, O God, have mer-cy, have mer-cy, have mer-cy up-on me, O God.

(b) Moderato

and glad-ness, of joy and glad-ness, of joy and glad-ness, and glad-ness, and glad-ness, and glad-ness.

Other Chandos Anthems contain some movements that are contrapuntal and some that are predominantly chordal. Both types, characterized by considerable repetition of text phrases, lead directly to the massive choruses that are among the great glories of Handel's oratorios; in fact, certain of the anthems anticipate the choral effects, melodic turns, and general style of the later and larger works. The set of Chandos Anthems is unduly neglected and well deserves to regain its place in the repertoire.

Cantata

In Italy about 1620 the term *cantata* referred to a sung piece, as opposed to a *sonata*, a piece "sounded" on instruments. The four books of *Cantade e arie* (about 1620–29) by Alessandro Grandi mark one of the first appearances of the term; in this work the several stanzas of the text were essentially variations over a basso ostinato, set for solo voice with continuo, and the whole was often prefaced by a section in recitative style. Soon the cantata assumed its form of two or more pairs of recitatives and arias on dramatic texts concerned with love in one of its many manifestations. In that nonchoral form, the cantata was sometimes written for an ensemble of two or three soloists. In Germany, England, and France, where the cantata soon found its way, many eminent composers adopted it, in its solo or ensemble form; among them, Legrenzi, Stradella, Alessandro Scarlatti, Charpentier, and Clérambault may be mentioned.

In the late Baroque period a choral form roughly parallel to the cantata gradually emerged, and was called the *chorale cantata*. Typically it was set for soloists, choir, and orchestra, and often included a Lutheran chorale. The major developments leading to the chorale cantata took place in Germany after about 1640, when Franz Tunder (1614–1667, Buxtehude's predecessor at Lübeck) included a setting of a chorale in some of his cantatas. In subsequent developments by later composers, the principle of composing variations over a basso ostinato was discarded, sections or movements for choir found places along with the recitatives and arias, and the chorale cantata emerged. This new form of choral music generally included an instrumental introduction, several movements set variously as arias, duets, or choruses, and a stanza of a chorale as the closing movement. In that form, with texts generally adapted from the Bible, the Lutheran liturgy, hymns, or chorales, it became of major interest to a host of German composers in the late seventeenth and early eighteenth centuries, including Buxtehude, Johann Philipp Krieger (1649–1725), Johann Kuhnau (1660–1722), and Friedrich Zachow (1663–1712).

About 1700 a new type of text was introduced by Erdmann Neumeister, a Lutheran pastor at Hamburg. Neumeister wrote a series of poems that embraced the church year and were specifically designed to be used as cantata texts. He made paraphrases of appropriate biblical verses, combined them with meditative lines that illuminated the central thought of the chorale to which they referred, and cast them in free forms that were suited to composition as recitatives and arias. Following Neumeister's lead, a number of other poets wrote texts suitable for cantatas—Franck, Picander, and Rambach among them.

Bach

The greatest composer of chorale cantatas was Johann Sebastian Bach. Out of more than 300 cantatas Bach is known to have composed, over 200 have been preserved, 188 of which are sacred cantatas, of special interest to us here. About thirty of these were written during the course of his employment as organist to the Duke of Weimar (1708–17); the remainder date from the first two decades of his stay at Leipzig (1723–50). Bach's cantatas are an encyclopedia of all the formal and stylistic devices of his time, which it was his genius to absorb, improve, and transform. Based in general on the spirit of Neumeister's reforms, 8 cantatas use that poet's texts; 8 texts are derived from Martin Luther, 6 were probably arranged by Bach himself, 73 are by other poets, and the remainder are by unknown authors.

The great majority of the cantatas contain chorales and are set for soloists, four-voice choir, and orchestral accompaniment. It is immediately apparent that Bach used no standardized form, for few of the cantatas are exactly alike in their details—the number of recitatives and arias, instrumental movements, choruses, and so on.

The cantatas show first of all Bach's great ability to create new formal structures by assimilating and combining a host of unrelated styles. For example, fugal passages appear in an essentially concertato chorus; arias are cast in forms that resemble those of the instrumental concerto; a new type of vocal melody based on instrumental idioms is devised to express the spirit of the texts; the verses are set in a variety of ways—including arias, duets, and simple or elaborate choruses; sets of variations on the chorale melody appear frequently; an opening chorus is often set in the form of a great chorale fantasia. A large majority of the cantatas begin with such an extended choral movement on the first verse of the chorale and end with a simple four-part setting of the last verse.

In most of the recitative-and-aria pairs found in operas, cantatas, and similar works of the Baroque period, the aria is generally sung by the same voice that performs the preceding recitative, elaborating on and carrying forward the sense of the recitative. In Bach's cantatas, quite another situation is found: well over half the recitative-and-aria pairs are divided between two voices or between a solo voice and a duet or trio. In many cantatas two or three recitatives for various voices follow each other without intervening arias; in others, there is a succession of arias without recitatives. In every case we are made aware that Bach's purpose was always to enhance the expressive potential of his texts by casting their phrases in the most appropriate forms.

Taken as a whole, the chief characteristic of the cantatas is their variety. An array of imposing, brilliant, or profound choruses; a succession of expressive recitatives and melodious or virtuosic arias often provided with obbligato instruments; orchestral accompaniments in a variety of styles and expressive qualities; closing chorales that reflect the sorrowful, reverent, rejoicing, or triumphant tone of their texts—with such components brought together by an overwhelming technical facility, a peerless musical imagination, and a never faltering spiritual conviction, the Bach cantatas are a priceless treasure of the literature.

Mass

Italian and Austrian composers

While choral music continued to be written in Italy and Austria in the late Baroque period, much of it has remained unpublished and much is merely routine. Our general survey of the literature must take account of that fact. Thus of the many composers in these countries who wrote Masses in the late seventeenth and early eighteenth centuries, we shall discuss only two.

In Italy, Antonio Lotti (c. 1667–1740) was most highly regarded in his own time. Lotti was associated primarily with Venice, where he served at St. Mark's in a variety of positions from about 1689, becoming chapelmaster in 1733. His career as a church musician was not incompatible with composing operas; some twenty of his operas, composed between 1693 and 1719, were widely performed and led to his being invited to the Dresden court for a two-year stay in 1717-19. In his many Masses and other works on sacred texts Lotti bridged the gap between the old contrapuntal style of the sixteenth century and the dramatic, agitated, and opera-influenced style of the seventeenth. Many of his Masses, composed for voices alone (that is, without continuo), contain touches of chromaticism, especially in the Crucifixus and Agnus Dei. Lotti often cast his phrases in regular four-measure lengths, employed devices of sequence repetition, and made use of tonal harmonies—in a texture that is reminiscent of his great Renaissance predecessors. Two settings of the Crucifixus, one for six voices and one for eight, are still performed today, but as concert numbers rather than items in the liturgy.

In Austria, on the other hand, settings of the Mass occupied composers whose chief attainments were in the secular field—especially in Vienna, among composers associated with the Imperial court. Chief among the latter was Johann Joseph Fux (1660–1741). Fux rose above many of his Viennese contemporaries by virtue of his skill as a contrapuntist and by his harmonic imagination. At various times he served as chapelmaster at the Cathedral of St. Stephen, composer at the Imperial court, and later chapelmaster to the court. In these positions he composed hundreds of works in several fields—operas, keyboard music, some fifty Masses, eleven oratorios, and smaller sacred works among them. As the author of *Gradus ad Parnassum* (*Steps to Parnassus*, 1725), a compendium of rules of species counterpoint that purported to exemplify the style of Palestrina, Fux remained of great influence for almost two centuries. His outstanding *Missa canonica* reveals not only his great technical skill but also his melodiousness and his sensitivity to text nuances. In the various canonic sections of this Mass, the interval of imitation often changes in mid-course (from a fifth above to a second above, for example), in double canons two different intervals of imitation are present simultaneously (see Example 42), and so on.

EXAMPLE 42   Fux, *Missa canonica*, Credo

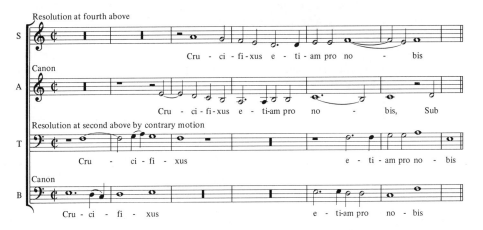

Bach

Johann Sebastian Bach must be placed in quite another category. As cantor of St. Thomas's Church in Leipzig and director of the city's church music—a Lutheran city, be it noted—Bach composed five Masses. Through the seventeenth and early eighteenth centuries the prescribed liturgy at Leipzig was in both Latin and German, alternating from one Sunday to the next; certain hymns and Mass items were specified at various services and festivals, and the order of service varied considerably from time to time throughout the Church year. (A detailed account is given in Spitta, *Johann Sebastian Bach,* English edition [1883–85], Vol. II, pp. 263–80.) The Kyrie and the Gloria were often used in these services, a fact that explains why four of Bach's Masses—in G major, G minor, A major, and F major—consist of only these two items.

The four Masses, attributed to the period about 1730–37, consist mostly of modifications of movements from Bach's cantatas. Bach often used music in one connection that he had originally composed in another, but such a practice represents far more than a mere arrangement or text substitution. Sometimes a four-voice choral passage is inserted into an instrumental sinfonia, or an aria is transformed into a four-voice chorus, or choral sections are lengthened or shortened to adjust to the new textual and expressive conditions. Yet in every case, whether the music is freshly composed or derived from a cantata, the result is always appropriate to its new text.

The F major Mass, perhaps the richest of the four in its expressive variety, is written for four-voice choir, with one aria each for soprano, alto, and bass soloists, and is accompanied by an orchestra consisting of two oboes, two horns, strings, and continuo. The Kyrie is for the three upper voices, over a bass cantus firmus derived from a liturgical chant, while the oboes and horns intone a Lutheran chorale, line by line. The Gloria begins and ends with two jubilant choruses in fugal style, between which are placed the three solo arias. The contrasts between the rhythmic vitality of the choral numbers, the expressive and florid aria for soprano, and the vigorous bass and alto arias, parallel the variety in the respective text phrases of the Gloria itself.

A characteristic of Bach's vocal writing that is found repeatedly in the cantatas and larger choral works is strikingly evident in this Mass—the transfer of instrumental idioms to the vocal line, with melodic figures outlining triads, and with angular lines and wide leaps (see Example 43).

EXAMPLE 43   Bach, *Mass in F Major*

Of completely different stature is Bach's huge Mass in B Minor, one of the greatest treasures of western music. The Mass fits the liturgical framework of the Roman Catholic service, but cannot be used in a service because of its size and length. And since it includes the entire Ordinary of the Mass, it was not entirely suited to the Lutheran church of his day. It remains an ideal work, growing out of Bach's religious faith—of, but not for, the Church.

The Mass was composed at intervals between 1724 and 1747; the Sanctus was apparently among the earliest numbers written, the Credo perhaps the last, and several of the movements contain some material originally written for the cantatas. Bach submitted the Kyrie and Gloria to the royal court at Dresden in 1733. While there is no evidence that these movements were performed at the court during Bach's lifetime, it seems certain that large portions of the Mass were sung in Leipzig shortly after the work's completion.

The B minor Mass is written for five soloists, five-voice choir (expanded to six in the Sanctus and to eight in the *Osanna*, but reduced to four in several other movements), and an orchestra consisting of two flutes, three oboes (interchangeable with *oboi d'amore*), two bassoons, three trumpets, *corno da caccia* (hunting horn), timpani, strings, and organ with continuo. The whole is divided into 25 movements, three of them in two contrasting parts.

This enormous work, requiring about two hours in performance, is an example of the so-called cantata Mass. The manuscript is divided into four sections, each with a well-defined form, and reveals a wealth of symmetrical and other relationships (see Karl Geiringer, *Johann Sebastian Bach,* p. 209). The table on page 106 gives an overview of its plan of organization, but cannot indicate all the subtle inner connections the Mass contains. One example may be mentioned: the first of each of the two pairs of choruses (Nos. 12 and 19a) that frame the large symmetry of the Credo reflect the presence of Gregorian chant: a melody derived from chant in the one (see Example 44b and compare 44c) and strongly suggesting the style of chant in the other.

Expressive variety ranging from deepest grief through majesty and power to utmost jubilation characterizes the Mass. The various movements include elaborate orchestrally accompanied fugues for choir, delicate settings for solo voices and a few instruments, and poignant short choral movements. In addition are many examples of Bach's use of symbolism. The suggestion of Gregorian chant in the midst of what may be called German Protestant counterpoint, as seen in the Credo, Nos. 12 and 19a, on the words *Credo in unum Deum* and *Confiteor unum baptisma,* express Bach's feeling of the oneness of the Creator. The symbolism is carried further in the duet No. 14, *Et in unum Dominum Jesum Christum Filium Dei unigenitum,* for here the soprano and alto begin in imitation at the unison and continue in canonic texture, thereby expressing the relationship between Father and Son. The *Et incarnatus est,* No. 15, is based on a hovering motive (see Example 44d) confined to the violins until the last few measures; there, at the phrase *Et homo factus est,* the motive appears in the cellos and basses, to give a graphic picture of the descent of the Spirit.

The most concentrated and expressive moments of the Mass are contained in the three choruses (Nos. 15, 16, and 17) at the exact center of the Credo, dealing with the Incarnation, Crucifixion, and Resurrection of Jesus. The solemnity of the *Et incarnatus est,* with its hovering motive symbolizing the Spirit, is followed by the *Crucifixus* in which a series of short phrases over a basso ostinato is set with poignant harmonies in a transparent contrapuntal texture; the effect is indescribably moving, and the anguish of the scene is reflected with the simplest of means. With the sharpest possible contrast the *Et resurrexit* begins forcefully and with the greatest joy (see Example 44e), reflecting the contrast of moods that animates the change from Good Friday to Easter; this is one of the most heartwarming and jubilant choruses in all of Bach. The Mass as a whole expresses

Bach, Mass in B Minor

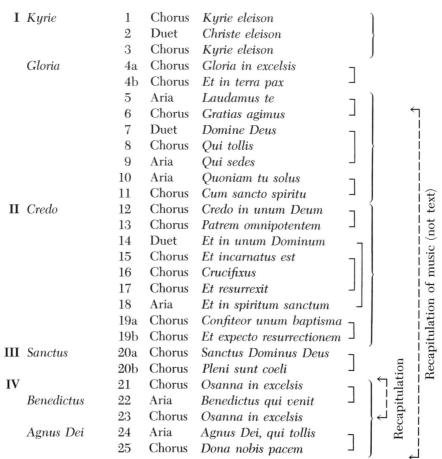

I *Kyrie*	1	Chorus	*Kyrie eleison*
	2	Duet	*Christe eleison*
	3	Chorus	*Kyrie eleison*
Gloria	4a	Chorus	*Gloria in excelsis*
	4b	Chorus	*Et in terra pax*
	5	Aria	*Laudamus te*
	6	Chorus	*Gratias agimus*
	7	Duet	*Domine Deus*
	8	Chorus	*Qui tollis*
	9	Aria	*Qui sedes*
	10	Aria	*Quoniam tu solus*
	11	Chorus	*Cum sancto spiritu*
II *Credo*	12	Chorus	*Credo in unum Deum*
	13	Chorus	*Patrem omnipotentem*
	14	Duet	*Et in unum Dominum*
	15	Chorus	*Et incarnatus est*
	16	Chorus	*Crucifixus*
	17	Chorus	*Et resurrexit*
	18	Aria	*Et in spiritum sanctum*
	19a	Chorus	*Confiteor unum baptisma*
	19b	Chorus	*Et expecto resurrectionem*
III *Sanctus*	20a	Chorus	*Sanctus Dominus Deus*
	20b	Chorus	*Pleni sunt coeli*
IV	21	Chorus	*Osanna in excelsis*
Benedictus	22	Aria	*Benedictus qui venit*
	23	Chorus	*Osanna in excelsis*
Agnus Dei	24	Aria	*Agnus Dei, qui tollis*
	25	Chorus	*Dona nobis pacem*

Recapitulation of music (not text)

Recapitulation

(Brackets denote paired or parallel forms; braces denote symmetrical patterns.)

EXAMPLE 44   Bach, *Mass in B Minor*

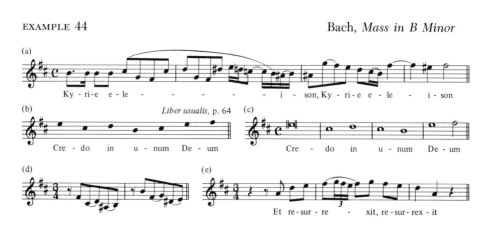

(a)

Ky - ri-e e - le - - - - i - son, Ky - ri-e e - le - i - son

(b)   *Liber usualis*, p. 64   (c)

Cre - do in u - num De - um   Cre - do in u - num De - um

(d)   (e)

Et re-sur - re - xit, re-sur - rex - it

the reverence that characterizes the great majority of Bach's choral music. In doing so, it transcends denominational and liturgical considerations; it remains one of the great monuments of the human spirit and one of the eternal master-pieces of western civilization.

Passion

Events in the history of the Passion from about 1665 to 1725 lead to a grow-ing resemblance to the oratorio form. The Gospel text remained as the center of the work, but it was often expanded by the insertion of sentimental, poetic passages that commented on the events of the betrayal, trial, and Crucifixion in a moralizing tone. Conforming to the spirit of the oratorio in general, composers often emphasized the incidents that enhanced the sheer drama of the Passion—such as Judas's betrayal, Peter's denial of Jesus, and the savage temper of the crowd. The orchestral accompaniment often verged on the programmatic, and recitatives acquired expressive contours, laden with emotion. Where the words spoken by Jesus appeared in the recitative, the accompaniment was generally given to a group of string instruments instead of only to the organ with continuo. Settings of the Passion (the St. Matthew text seems to have been favored over the other Gospels) are numerous; those by Thomas Selle (about 1642), Thomas Strutius (1664), Johann Sebastiani (1672), and Johann Kuhnau (1721) are among the more successful German works in that style.

With the rise of the popularity of the opera in Germany—especially in Hamburg—came a desire to select dramatic stories from the Bible and set them in quasi-operatic style. The Passion itself fell victim to this tendency: often the scriptural text was paraphrased in rhyme; peripheral events like the lament of Mary Magdalen or the tears of Peter were given dominant positions; and an allegorical figure, the Daughter of Zion, was introduced to carry the sentimental commentary forward. A setting of this kind by Reinhard Keiser (1704), under the title of *Der blutige und sterbende Jesus* (*The Bleeding and Dying Jesus*), enjoyed wide popularity.

Handel

A setting of the St. John Passion attributed to Handel (also about 1704), on a text arranged by Christian Postel, marked the beginning of a reaction against the operatic type. In Handel's version the biblical text is restored and given to the traditional figure of the Evangelist (that is, the narrator or *testo* of the oratorio form), lyric moments are provided in a succession of arias, and choruses reflect the pathetic or dramatic events in exemplary fashion. About 1716 Handel approached the Passion again, but now on a text arranged by Barthold Brockes, a town councillor of Hamburg. This version of the text, set by many composers in the early eighteenth century, consisted of a poetic paraphrase of the events of the Passion compiled from all four Gospels (mainly that of St. Matthew), but done with perhaps more reverence and taste than in the operatic versions. The text also included chorale verses, introduced by Sebastiani some 45 years earlier, which add a devout and meditative tone to the narrative. Handel's Passion of 1716 was known to Bach, who did not hesitate to adopt some of Handel's musical details in his own settings.

Telemann

Georg Philipp Telemann (1681–1767), one of the most prolific composers of the Baroque period, was associated principally with Hamburg, where he served as director of music for the five most important churches of the city from 1721 until his death. One of his duties was to compose a Passion annually; 46 settings resulted, of which about 20 have survived in manuscript. Following a Hamburg tradition dating from the late seventeenth century, he set each of the four Gospel accounts on a regular four-year cycle. Beginning with a St. Matthew setting in 1722 and ending with a St. Mark in 1767, Telemann applied his enormous energy and technical facility to the task. Only three or four of these settings have been printed, however. (See Basil Smallman, *The Background of Passion Music,* 2d ed., 1970, for details.)

In his many operas, his available orchestral and chamber music, and his few published cantatas, Telemann revealed himself a fluent, expressive, but somewhat superficial composer. The available Passion settings, on the other hand, show a composer sensitive to the dramatic qualities of the Gospel texts and imaginative in his approach to them. His settings keep the traditional elements of the Passion form—notably recitatives, arias, choruses, and chorales—but they occasionally omit such essential items in the Passion narrative as the Last Supper and the entombment. The narrative itself tends to take second place to an overweight of meditative arias and reflective choruses. Handel in his 1716 Passion on Brockes's text had composed solo arias that contained choral interjections in the form of short questions ("Why?" "When?" and so on). Telemann too used that device, as did Bach.

Bach

At an early stage of Bach research it was supposed that Bach had composed five settings of the Passion. Later studies revealed that a St. Luke setting, partly in Bach's handwriting, was not by him; and that only a few items from his St. Mark setting (1731) have survived (recovered in large part from Bach's other works, in which the items had first appeared). Two settings are complete: a St. John (first performed in 1723 or 1724) and a St. Matthew (1729); nothing is known about a fifth setting.

The *St. John Passion,* representing Bach's first essay in the form, is based on John 18–19, but also contains two passages from St. Matthew: in No. 18, after Peter's denial (John 18:27), Bach inserted a phrase (Matthew 26:75) describing Peter's weeping; and in No. 62, to introduce the scene of the earthquake after the entombment, Bach inserted verses from Matthew 27:51–52. The text items not contained in the two Gospels were derived from Brockes's text, and the composer himself may have written the texts of several arias. The work is set for four soloists, four-voice choir, and an orchestra consisting of two flutes, two oboes, strings, and organ with continuo; in several numbers additional instruments supply obbligato parts with eloquent effect. The whole is divided into two parts containing 68 numbers.

The St. John Gospel presents a highly dramatic account of the Passion events, emphasizes the demanding nature of the crowd, and is in general more concentrated in its dramatic portrayal than the other Gospels. Thus one of the essential elements of the Passion-oratorio—the number of meditative, devotional texts set as arias and chorales—is necessarily limited. These facts are reflected in Bach's setting, which draws sharp contrasts between the unruly crowd and the divine calm of Christ. Recitatives are poignant, intense, and dramatic in turn; many angular lines, leaps of augmented or diminished fifths and augmented seconds, phrases that outline intervals of sevenths or ninths—such elements give the recitatives a vigorous, animated contour that is appropriate to the dramatic intensity of the text.

The choruses are occasionally highly florid and contain passages in which elaborate melismas occur in all four voices simultaneously; such passages alternate with others in imitative style, sometimes based on abrupt or angular motives, at other times on smoothly flowing chromatic lines, as in Nos. 23 and 25. Opposed to the choruses are a number of meditative arias set in ornamental style with elaborate figurations provided by obbligato instruments, especially Nos. 32 and 63. And again in contrast to the arias are two passages, Nos. 31 and 62, set in arioso style; here a freely moving recitative set over a pulsating orchestral accompaniment provides a link between the narrative passages in recitative and the contemplative moods in lyric style. To these diverse types are added the chorales in four-part harmony, sung by the congregation in traditional performances, to add meditative commentaries and to reflect on the faith that underlies the entire Passion account.

Bach revised his *St. John Passion* on several occasions. He removed three arias, replaced a sinfonia by a recitative, arioso, and aria (Nos. 61–63 in the present version), shifted the closing chorus to Cantata 23 (replacing it by a chorale, No. 68), and shifted the original opening chorus to the end of Part 1 of the *St. Matthew Passion*. With the substitution of the present opening chorus, *Herr, unser Herrscher* ("Lord, Our Redeemer"), the mood of the original Passion was dramatically altered to one of triumph, of victory over degradation and death. In its present form the *St. John Passion* is a work of the first magnitude, full of Bach's religious spirit, his technical mastery, and his expressive power.

The *St. Matthew Passion*, based on Matthew 26–27 and first performed on Good Friday, 1729, is a larger work on several counts. It is set for two four-voice choirs (with an additional choir of boys' voices in the first chorus), four soloists, a number of additional singers for short solo passages given to various characters in the sacred drama, an orchestra often divided into two parts each with its own continuo and organ, and requiring *oboi d'amore, oboi da caccia,* and *viola da gamba* as obbligato instruments in various arias. The text is set in 78 numbers, 13 of which are themselves divided into two or more parts; thus a total of 104 separate numbers results, as opposed to the 68 of the *St. John Passion.*

The opening chorus begins with a majestic instrumental passage for divided orchestra; several motives form a tight contrapuntal texture over pulsating reiterated tones in the bass. The first choir's entrance on soaring melodies set in counterpoint is at times interrupted by sharp rhetorical questions from the second choir, over which floats a choir of boys' voices singing a chorale. It is a movement characterized by great dignity and absence of external effect, with a controlled fervor, simplicity, and vastness that wonderfully establish the tone of the entire Passion. Thereafter in a variety of choral movements—one of them, on the shout "Barrabas" (No. 54b), only one measure in length—fitting commentaries and profound meditations serve to illuminate the narrative carried in the Evangelist's recitatives.

The Matthew text contains a number of episodes not present in John—among them the conspiracy against Christ, the Last Supper, the repentance of Judas, and the earthquake after the death of Christ. In the recitatives that describe these and the other events of the Passion, Bach composed flowing and wide-ranging melodic lines that eloquently express the intense feelings evoked by the Gospel account (see Example 45). Set between the choruses, arias, and chorales, the recitatives move the listener profoundly as the dramatic story unfolds.

The range of expressive types found in the choruses is matched by that found in the arias. From the fervent yet simple soprano aria No. 19, *Ich will Dir mein Herze schenken* ("I Will Give You My Heart") through one of the most eloquent of all, No. 47 for alto, *Erbarme dich, mein Gott* ("Have Mercy, Lord"), to the elaborate bass aria with *viola da gamba,* No. 66, *Komm, süsses Kreuz* ("Come, Sweet Cross"), the arias provide many of the deeply reflective moments that make Bach's St. Matthew unique among Passion settings. Restraint and dignity characterize the arias, with the elaborate melismas found in the St. John setting not present here, and the use of the *viola da gamba* and *oboi da caccia,* as well as other obbligato instruments, adds greatly to their expressiveness.

Finally, the 13 chorales, placed at moments of greatest emotional tension such as the prophecy of resurrection, the arrest, the trial, and so on, emphasize the devotion and reverence that underlie the entire Passion. Bach's ability to balance the dramatic with the meditative elements even while giving full weight to the sense of the Gospel text is everywhere apparent. Lesser composers in the decades after Bach's time sought to emphasize the sentimental aspects of the added texts, and the musical settings of the Passion declined accordingly in importance and musical value.

Oratorio

The achievements of Giacomo Carissimi in developing the oratorio in Italy had major consequences in other countries. In France the principal composer of the form was Carissimi's student, Marc-Antoine Charpentier, who composed over

EXAMPLE 45   Bach, *St. Matthew Passion*

(Tr.: (a) "And he [Peter] went out, and wept bitterly."
    (b) "And he [Judas] cast down the pieces of silver in the
    temple, and departed, and went and hanged himself.")

thirty oratorios—many of them more elaborate than his teacher's. A set of 14 "sacred histories" deal with episodes in the lives of biblical characters; the scriptural texts, most of them in Latin, are paraphrased, set in dialogue form, and set for narrator, soloists, choir, and orchestra. Titles such as *Historia Esther, Filius prodigus, Judicium Salomonis,* and *La Reniement de St. Pierre* (a scene from the latter is reprinted in *TEM,* No. 42) reveal the direction of Charpentier's interests. As in his motets and *Te Deum,* Charpentier gave full rein to his dramatic sense in the choruses, and his melodies in solo numbers show his concern for refined expression. The recitatives at times revert to an early stage of development, for the part of the Narrator is sometimes set for solo voice, sometimes for a duet or trio, and at other times for choir.

After Carissimi's fundamental work in establishing a model for the form, composers in Italy brought the oratorio ever closer to the opera. The chorus, which loomed so large and played so important a role in German works, was given a smaller part in Italian oratorios. The greatest weight was given to the arias and ensembles for soloists, paralleling the practice in operas of the time. Italian rather than Latin again became the favorite language for the texts—some of them based on paraphrases of appropriate scriptural verses, others freely adapted from the biblical events.

Among the most important early eighteenth-century composers of oratorios in Italy was Alessandro Scarlatti (1660–1725). In more than twenty oratorios, composed between 1680 and 1722 mostly for Rome and Naples, Scarlatti introduced many of the same technical devices that made him one of the outstanding operatic composers of the time. His use of the *da capo* aria (an ABA form in which the third part recapitulates the first) added an element of formal structure to the often amorphous settings for solo voices. And his use of coloratura passages and emotionally suggestive harmonies (such as diminished triads and chromatic modulations) increased the poignancy and dramatic effect of appropriate passages.

Brief mention must be made of Antonio Vivaldi (c. 1675–1741). Famed in his lifetime and again at present as a composer of instrumental concertos, Vivaldi also wrote many operas, large quantities of church music, and at least two oratorios.

One of these, *Juditha triumphans* (*Judith Triumphant*), composed in 1716 for Venice, has remained in print. Set for five soloists and choir, its orchestra includes solo instruments performing as a concertino, and a group of oboes, brass instruments, timpani, strings, and continuo to form the tutti section. The other, *Beatus vir* (*Blessed Is the Man*), requires six soloists, double choir, and two orchestras each consisting of oboes, strings, and continuo. Here one may see the Venetian polychoral style brought into the eighteenth century; indeed, Vivaldi, as a native of Venice and long active there, was strongly influenced by the style that had originated under the Gabrielis and their school at St. Mark's. The dramatic fervor and rich play of orchestral color combine to place his oratorios among his outstanding works.

In the countries where Italian influence remained strong, notably in Austria and the southern part of Germany, the Italian version of the oratorio continued to find favor. An example is provided by *La Conversione di Sant'Agostino,* one of about ten oratorios by Johann Adolph Hasse (1699–1783), composed for the Dresden court; Hasse, one of the foremost operatic composers (in the style of Naples) of his time, served there as chapelmaster. Recitatives and arias in da capo form constitute the bulk of that work, and choral writing is minimal (see *HAM,* No. 281).

Three works of Bach are inaccurately referred to as oratorios. The so-called *Christmas Oratorio,* composed in 1734, consists of six cantatas, each designed for one of the six Sundays preceding and following Christmas. In conventional cantata form, they include choruses, recitatives, arias, and chorales—64 numbers in all, of which Bach adapted about one fifth from his earlier sacred or secular cantatas. Our previous observations about Bach's cantatas apply in full measure to this set of six, and some of Bach's most jubilant settings—notably the closing chorale No. 64, set with extended orchestral interludes and accompanying figurations—are found here. But it is a falsification of Bach's intention to consider this a unified work and to attempt to perform it as a unit in a concert context.

The *Easter Oratorio,* composed about 1736, deserves the oratorio label even less; it is actually a single cantata of 11 numbers on a Resurrection text, but containing music that had first appeared in two secular cantatas a year or two earlier. As for the work often referred to as the *Ascension Oratorio*, it is a resetting of Cantata No. 11, *Lobet Gott in seinen Reichen (Praise God in His Kingdom)*, again consisting of 11 numbers arranged in the usual fashion. Bach's reputation will not be adversely affected if the term "oratorio" is dropped and these works are properly identified.

Handel

Of quite another nature are about two dozen oratorios by Handel. After his major activity as a composer of operas in London showed signs of coming to an end, about 1739, Handel returned to the form that had occupied him intermittently since 1708. The exact number of works is given by different writers as anywhere from 18 to 29—depending on whether the Passions, the works on secular texts (which otherwise conform to the pattern), the several versions of certain oratorios, and the odes are included or not.

Handel's texts, all but the first two in English, are drawn largely from three sources. The majority represent paraphrases of or are based on scriptural texts dealing with events or individuals; of this nature are *Esther, Deborah, Saul, Israel in Egypt, Joshua, Samson, Solomon, Jephtha*, and several others. A second group is formed by those whose texts deal with mythological figures, of which *Hercules, Semele*, and *Acis and Galatea* are representative. A few are allegorical in nature, including *L'Allegro* and *The Triumph of Time and Truth*. And one stands alone: *Messiah*, with a text embracing both the Old and New Testaments, is less a dramatic narrative than an expression of meditative devotion. Handel was not always fortunate in his choice of librettists; unfelicitous poetry and undramatic structure appear often, and the public failure of many of Handel's oratorios may be attributed to his acceptance of texts that were unworthy of his musical genius and that failed to inspire his best work.

Among Handel's major achievements was the creation of a new kind of oratorio, one written for the concert hall rather than the church. In the process he enlarged the scope and appeal of its textual material, its expressive elements, and its forms, particularly in the new position he gave to the choir. Other composers, notably Carissimi, had employed choirs in their oratorios, of course, using them largely as foils for the ubiquitous recitatives and arias that carried the main weight. It remained for Handel to broaden the function of the choir so that it could express the reaction of the people to a dramatic event, take part in the action (as in *Solomon* and *Judas Maccabeus*), provide a reflective commentary (as in *Messiah*), and even carry forward the narrative by means of choral recitative (as in *Israel in Egypt*). The greatest difference between the oratorio as developed by Handel and earlier oratorios—especially those by Italian composers—lies in the new role given to the choir.

The choral writing is not the only distinguishing feature of the Handel oratorios, however. Equally important, from the standpoint of dramatic development, is the apt delineation of character Handel accomplished in the arias given

"The Oratorio." Satirical engraving by William Hogarth.

to the principal figures. In the oratorios on biblical subjects, the principals often come to personify their people, to become symbols of the peoples' strengths and virtues; such treatment is especially evident in *Saul, Samson,* and *Joshua.* The chief figures are often given two or three nearly consecutive arias that reflect various aspects of their characters; Handel began this practice as early as *Athalia* (1733), took it to a high point in *Saul* (1738), and continued it to the end of his oratorio writing. Depicting harshness or brutality with angular phrases separated by short pauses, showing vacillation with halting rhythm, suggesting strength with a melody based on triadic outlines—thus Handel drew lifelike pictures of his heroes.

One detail of Handel's treatment reflects the practice of Italian composers and recalls the close relationship that had existed between the oratorio and opera in the seventeenth century. Following the Italian operatic tradition of employing *castrati* for the sake of their vocal power and virtuosity, he set the roles of many of his most masculine heroes for male alto. As early as the *St. John Passion* of 1704 and continuing for forty years, Handel maintained that tradition. For example, Pilate in the *Passion*, the soldiers Sisara and Barak in *Deborah* (1733), the high priest Joad in *Athalia* (1733), David in *Joseph* (1743), Micah in *Samson* (1743), and King Cyrus in *Belshazzar* (1745) were all designed for male altos. This fact alone may militate against frequent modern performances of these oratorios.

In Handel's oratorios the orchestra too rose to a preeminent position. From his very first oratorio *La Resurrezione*, written about 1708 while still in Italy, he treated the orchestra as an essential element of dramatic expression. The merely decorative type of overture and the internal sinfonie in the oratorio gave way to colorful and virtuosic forms, often in several contrasting sections and often embracing the elements of the concerto. Sometimes, as in *Saul*, the overture is a suite of four movements, with its themes later suggested or quoted in the following choruses. The accompaniments to the choruses and arias generally enhance the moods of the vocal parts, and in effect stimulate the listener to imagine the scenic elements that are of course not present on the concert stage. Trumpets, horns, and bassoons are often used to set the tone of various scenes, and special effects are provided by harp (in *Esther*), mandolin (in *Alexander Balus*), and trombones and bassoons in several works. Handel was obviously alive to color contrasts and made full use of all available instruments to write scores that are brilliant and effective.

The eighteenth century knew nothing of copyright law, of course; self-borrowing and outright plagiarism were accepted and even respectable musical practices, and Handel (like Bach and virtually all other composers of the time) often borrowed existing music—especially his own. *Esther* (1733), the first of his English oratorios, makes liberal use of numbers drawn from the set of Chandos Anthems, from the second of his Passions (1716), and from other works as well. Several later oratorios reveal similar reappearances of works composed earlier in other contexts; the most extreme example is probably *Israel in Egypt* (1738), in which almost half of the numbers represent borrowings from Kerll, Stradella, and lesser-known composers. The borrowings continued to the very end of his career, for the second revision (1757) of the allegorical oratorio *The Triumph of Time and Truth* is based on his second Italian work in the form (1708). The later version includes several arias and choruses from various anthems, operas, and other works Handel had composed in the intervening years. In virtually every case, however, he transformed, expanded, or improved on the original—whether his own music or that of others—and successfully adapted it to its new context.

These general observations about the similarities in Handel's oratorios are not intended to suggest that major differences between one oratorio and another do not exist. The proportion of recitatives, arias, and choruses; the number of main characters; the method of emphasizing certain dramatic events at the expense of others—such details vary widely. *Deborah* (1733), for example, is filled with large choral numbers and contains only two short recitatives, with a consequent absence of the dramatic narrative on which the form depends. *Susannah* (1748), by contrast, is operatic in tone and relies mainly on a large proportion of arias for its effect. In other works, faced with an indifferent or uninspired text, Handel reacted in kind; the occasional routine or undistinguished aria or chorus may be blamed on a faulty text.

Messiah (1742) is unlike the other oratorios on several counts. Its text deals with prophecies about the coming of Christ, with His birth, His message of redemption, and His Crucifixion. Essentially, however, it is a series of meditations on the significance of that redemption for the world. Its spirit raises it above churchly doctrine, and its appeal is to all humanity. Handel was equal to the task of setting that lofty message, and yet his means were often of the simplest. Traditional arias in bel canto style—some in da capo form and others not—reflect his sensitivity to the meaning of each text in their harmony and modulations. Recitatives are sometimes instrumentally accompanied and lose the last vestige of formal dryness; the first recitative, "Comfort Ye, My People," provides an eloquent example. The choruses range from brooding to triumphant in tone; a mixture of unisons, chordal textures, and imitative counterpoint provides the flexibility required by the wide-ranging text. And the intensity and jubilation that animate the "Hallelujah" chorus at the end of the second part of *Messiah* raise that chorus to the deservedly high place it has held in the affections of singers and audiences everywhere for more than two centuries.

8

Pre-Classical and
Classical Music
1725–1825

The monumental choral works of Bach and Handel are
virtually the last examples of the Baroque style; in fact, many of them were
composed after that style had been all but abandoned by other composers of
the time. The early eighteenth century had witnessed the rise of a system of
thought—the Enlightenment—that rejected much traditional authority, aristocratic privilege, empty formalism, and the outworn rituals of the church. Chief
among these new ideas were the enthronement of freedom in the arts, a com-
monsensical approach to social and scientific problems, a faith in the value of
human instincts and "natural" feelings, and a belief that the common man should
be exposed to as much culture and education as he could absorb.

The new movement soon became influential in many spheres of human activity,
especially in the arts. The emphasis on national differences was for a time
minimized, and the brotherhood of all humanity became an ideal. In music,
nationalistic style elements began to lose their appeal, and the use of universal
elements eventually resulted in a style that became somewhat general in all parts
of musical Europe. To the degree that the common man (that is, the man who
belonged to neither the nobility nor the clergy) became aware of cultural matters,
he became a supporter of the arts. Public concerts arose, and the new music
began to reflect his interests and cater to his taste, thus avoiding complications
of structure and texture. In short, much music of the time became simpler through
minimal use of counterpoint, became an object of pleasure and entertainment
that made no great demands on the listener. The distinction between secular
and sacred styles, which had greatly lessened in the Baroque period, tended
virtually to disappear, and the expressiveness of a piece of vocal music did not
depend on the nature of the text to which it was set.

This complex of developments gave rise to a style in the arts called the Rococo. An essential element of Rococo painting is surface decoration, in which the ornamental—motives, scrolls, and the like—becomes an end in itself. An architectural style developed similarly, and the parallel musical style is closely analogous in its use of highly ornamented melodies that dominate the rather simple harmonic structures that support them. Rococo music emerged primarily in France and in areas culturally allied to that country, and was often referred to as being in the *style galant*. By the middle of the eighteenth century, German composers had developed a slightly greater degree of sentimental expressiveness in their music, and the German version became known as the *empfindsamer Stil* ("sensitive style"). Eventually steps were taken to deepen the expressiveness of the music, to abandon the basso continuo and give more weight to the inner parts, to employ a degree of restraint and control, and to make the *form* of an utterance appropriate to its content. Toward the 1780s, these characteristics culminated in the Classical style, of which Haydn, Mozart, and Beethoven are the greatest exponents. Thus the works composed in the period roughly from 1725 to 1780 (except those of Bach and Handel) are often interchangeably referred to as in the *style galant* or *empfindsamer Stil*, or in the Rococo or pre-Classical style, depending on their country of origin and their expressive content. And the works composed from about 1780 to the death of Beethoven in 1827 are most often referred to as being in the Classical style.

Mass

Johann Adolph Hasse (1699–1783), one of the foremost operatic composers of the time, is identified primarily with Dresden, but his melodic gifts and expressive range are largely Italian. He composed about ten Masses and large quantities of other church music, all of it forgotten today. In his Masses, Hasse represented a school of composers whose works are characterized primarily by a tendency to ignore all relationships between textual meaning and musical setting; effectiveness in performance seems to have been the first criterion. Lighthearted tunes, sentimental melodies, and meaningless fugues are typical of that music. Kretzschmar observes that the "overall impression made by Masses of this school reminds one of the money changers in the Temple and of the basket-carrying housewives, intent on buying groceries, who on their way to the market drop by the Cathedral to pray a bit" (Kretzschmar, *Führer durch den Konzertsaal*, II, 162).

Early eighteenth-century works of Salzburg composers at first show traces of Venetian influences; antiphonal writing, sonorous chordal passages, and a festive air are typical. Johann Eberlin (1702–1762) was among the first Salzburg composers to adopt dramatic recitative in the manner of operatic composers at Naples. Anton Adlgasser (1729–1777), Mozart's predecessor as court organist at Salzburg, represents a group of composers in whose Masses the influence of instrumentally conceived forms is to be observed. And Michael Haydn (1737–

1806), a younger brother of the great Franz Joseph and a friend of Mozart's, sometimes brought to his Masses a mixture of plainsong, modal writing, and the use of cantus firmi—and superimposed these elements on a mid-eighteenth-century harmonic background. But he also wrote Masses that are thoroughly in the style of their time, with no echoes of Renaissance or Baroque style; his *Missa Sancti Hieronimi* (*Mass of St. Jerome*), first performed in 1777, is a representative example.

In Vienna an even greater amalgamation of styles was at hand. The contrapuntal works of Johann Joseph Fux were still influential in the 1750s; so were those of Antonio Caldara with their mixture of Venetian and Neapolitan styles, to which Caldara's lyric gifts gave an individual flavor. The "official" Masses of Johann Reutter (1708–1772), chapelmaster of St. Stephen's Cathedral when Haydn began his service as a choirboy there, were part of the regular repertoire; their brilliant orchestral effects (sometimes at the expense of the text) became an element of Viennese style. Thus when Haydn began to compose Masses, he was faced with a style that had its roots largely in Italy. Neapolitan operatic effects, Venetian antiphony with alternations of choir, soloists, and orchestra in short passages, contrapuntal writing, and elements of Rococo display were all parts of that style. Out of these parts Haydn gradually forged a style that became truly representative of the Classical period.

Haydn

Franz Joseph Haydn (1732–1809), born in Rohrau in Austria, spent eight years (from 1740) in the choir of St. Stephen's, after which he earned a precarious musical livelihood in Vienna for about eight years more. In 1761 he was engaged as second chapelmaster (promoted to first in 1766) to the fabulously wealthy Esterházy family, in whose service he remained until 1790. Thereafter he became a pensioner of the Esterházys until his death. During most of his professional life he was kept busy at the Esterházy estates, some distance from Vienna; except for short visits to that city, he was thrown largely on his own resources and removed from close contact with other musicians of his stature. But he nevertheless remained aware of contemporary developments. His choral works include twelve or more Masses, three oratorios, a Passion setting, various secular cantatas, and about twenty miscellaneous and smaller works such as Te Deums and Offertories. Various publishers numbered Haydn's Masses not in accord with their order of composition. The best-known English edition, by Novello, carries the following numbers:

Approximate order of composition	Date	Novello No.
1. *Missa brevis*	c. 1750	11
2. *Great Organ Mass*	1766	12
3. *St. Cecilia Mass*	1769–73	5
4. *St. Nicholas Mass*	1772	7
5. *Little Organ Mass*	c. 1775	8

Approximate order of composition	Date	Novello No.
6. *Mariazell Mass*	1782	15
7. *Mass in Wartime*	1796	2
8. *Heiligmesse*	1796	1
9. *Nelson Mass*	1798	3
10. *Theresa Mass*	1799	16
11. *Creation Mass*	1801	4
12. *Wind-band Mass*	1802	6

(An early Mass in G major, published in 1957 under Haydn's name, is considered by several authorities to be of doubtful authenticity.)

Haydn's first Mass, a *Missa brevis* in F major, composed about 1750, is set for two soprano soloists, four-part choir, two violins, organ, and bass. Unlike the English short Mass, the *brevis* designation in this case refers to the fact that in a Mass of this type successive phrases of the text (especially of the longer Gloria and Credo movements) are generally set simultaneously, certain doctrinal statements are sometimes omitted, instrumental introductions and interludes rarely occur, and the practice of repeating text phrases for reasons of musical balance is largely absent. Haydn's first Mass reflects style elements that were to recur in later works—notably the recapitulation of the Kyrie music in the concluding *Dona nobis pacem*. The words are supplicatory, but it is quite in keeping with Haydn's optimistic spirit that the music should be cheerful in tone. A prayer was bound to be answered, hence there seemed little need for a gloomy setting.

No. 2, the *Great Organ Mass* of 1766, differs from the first in requiring four soloists, choir, and a larger orchestra including two English horns, trumpets, horns, strings, and organ. Brilliant writing for the soloists in the style of a Neapolitan opera, corresponding brilliance in the organ part, and elaborate treatment in other components of the Mass are typical. No. 3, called the *St. Cecilia*, is perhaps the longest of Haydn's Masses. Composed on the model of the Italian cantata Mass, with its various movements divided into arias, choral numbers, ensemble quartets, etc., it again requires four soloists, a four-voice choir, and an enlarged orchestra. Passages for the solo voices often emerge from the choral sections, a device derived in part from Masses by Venetian composers. Coloratura arias are sometimes preceded by recitatives, quite in the manner of the opera. The loose relationship between text and music and the repetition of text words and phrases on musical, not liturgical, grounds are evidence that purely musical considerations were beginning to take precedence over liturgical ones.

No. 4, the *St. Nicholas*, and No. 5, the *Little Organ Mass*, both from the early 1770s, are of the *brevis* type and have a full share of eloquent melodies. Several passages in these Masses attest that Haydn remained sensitive to textual meaning in spite of his concern with musical rather than textual matters.

No. 6, the Mass composed for the monastery at Mariazell in 1782, retains the smaller framework—but still requires about forty minutes in performance. Here Haydn settled upon an expressive feature he had occasionally employed earlier:

an ensemble of the four solo voices instead of an array of separate arias. The resultant lessening of purely virtuosic effects is more than compensated for by the subtle shades of expressiveness now demanded of the solo quartet. A few solo arias are still present, and a few choral passages revert to the *brevis* technique of introducing several text phrases simultaneously. Thus the *Mariazell Mass* represents a transitional stage in Haydn's stylistic development. He had temporarily reached a stylistic impasse; fourteen years were to elapse before he returned to the composition of Masses.

Among the causes of his long absence from the field was the set of reforms instituted by Emperor Joseph II, who ascended to the Austrian throne on the death of his mother Maria Theresa in 1780. Very quickly Joseph instituted a series of reforms dedicated to strengthening the centralized state, weakening the power of the nobility, and—of special interest here—liberalizing church government, closing many monasteries, abolishing many sacred orders, and simplifying the liturgy. For almost a decade composers lacked an incentive for composing church music. Joseph died in 1790 and was succeeded by his brother Leopold II; even though the latter reigned only two years, he was successful in restoring most of the old privileges, after which church music soon regained its old place. Many composers returned to the sacred field, now employing all the expressive resources and instrumental devices they had meanwhile been cultivating in the secular field. The distinction between secular and sacred music was further weakened, and musical considerations became more dominant over liturgical requirements than ever before. Optimism prevailed, mysticism had virtually no place, and sacred music anchored itself firmly in this world rather than in the next. Such is the nature of Haydn's six late Masses, composed between 1796 and 1802.

All of them are set for four soloists, a four-voice choir, and orchestra; the instrumentation of the latter ranges from trumpets, timpani, and strings in No. 9 (the *Nelson Mass*) to the full Classical complement of flutes, oboes, clarinets, bassoons, horns, trumpets, timpani, and strings in No. 12, nicknamed the *Harmoniemesse* ("Wind-band" Mass) because of the emphasis given to the wind instruments (which traditionally supplied the harmony in long-held tones in the eighteenth-century orchestra). Some texts in this series of Masses are set in contrasting sections with changes of tempo and key where the text suggests; others, notably some in the *Nelson Mass*, are cast into separate movements resembling the parts of a cantata Mass. And Haydn's practice of avoiding solo arias and substituting ensemble passages that grow out of or merge with the choral writing, seen occasionally in the earlier Masses, here becomes a stylistic feature.

Several of the six Masses contain individual movements of profound and serious treatment, in spite of the basically joyful tone that is characteristic of all of them. For example, in the Agnus Dei of No. 7, *Mass in Wartime,* Haydn introduces a fanfarelike passage in which trumpets and timpani are featured; the expressive intention may well have been to draw a sharp contrast between the sense of the text ("Grant us peace") and the idea of war. (Beethoven was to treat that passage in related fashion in his *Missa solemnis* of 1823.) In these late Masses the kind of thematic and harmonic thinking that led to the large instrumental forms became ever more apparent; a single example from the *Nelson Mass* will suffice.

The Kyrie of that Mass, in D minor, begins with a fifteen-measure orchestral introduction, after which the first *Kyrie eleison* is set for choir in chordal style. A short section for soprano soloist introduces a quasi-codetta (meas. 33), which is followed by the *Christe eleison* for the soloist with a few choral interjections (two of them on the word *Kyrie*), this passage being largely in F major. Then follows an extensive development beginning in F major (meas. 54–98) in imitative style and dealing with manipulations of the *Kyrie* motive. A complete recapitulation of the first *Kyrie eleison* then appears (meas. 99–115), but to this a florid soprano-solo passage has been added (see Example 46). Measure 116 introduces

EXAMPLE 46   Haydn, *Nelson Mass*

a second short development for choir and solo voices, largely on the dominant of D minor, followed by a short codetta. An extensive coda (meas. 143–60) in two sections, one on the submediant and the other on the tonic of D minor, ends the movement. Thus the whole closely resembles a movement in sonata-form with introduction, first theme (*Kyrie*, D minor, meas. 16), second theme (*Christe*, F major, meas. 39), development of first-theme motives (F major, meas. 54), recapitulation of first theme (*Kyrie*, D minor, meas. 99), second development in place of second-theme recapitulation (meas. 116), and coda (meas. 143).

The Gloria, set in three separate sections, is an example of modified symmetry, with thematic material from the first section appearing again in the third—in both cases in D major—and with the second section in a contrasting key (B flat) and tempo (adagio). In other movements of Haydn's late Masses similar instrumentally derived forms may be found. It becomes obvious that Haydn, in company with many other composers of the late eighteenth century, transcended the requirements of continuous nonsymmetrical prose texts and set them in accord with principles that were based on aesthetic rather than liturgical thinking.

Mozart

Wolfgang Amadeus Mozart (1756–1791) was born in Salzburg. Between his sixth and twenty-third birthdays he spent more than ten years away from home, being taken to Paris, London, Munich, Milan, Mannheim, and elsewhere by one of his parents—first as a child prodigy and later as an accomplished performer. Composing incessantly, exposed to all the styles that western Europe had to offer, Mozart remembered and synthesized, bringing his own style to the highest level of perfection—the essence of Classicism. A broad range of expressiveness, formal balance, and perfection of detail are components of that style. At least eighteen Masses, one Requiem Mass, and almost fifty miscellaneous works are included in his music written for the church.

Mozart's eighteen Masses represent two main types, half of them of the *Missa brevis* class. Since the *Missa brevis* is designed for use on a normal Sunday, the instrumental accompaniment is generally reduced to a minimum. Mozart usually set such Masses for an orchestra of two violins, with cello, bass, and organ on the continuo. (Conforming to the traditional practice at the Salzburg Cathedral, he did not include violas if the Mass was intended for that church.) The vocal forces usually consist of soloists and a four-voice choir, with solo passages brief and emerging out of the choral texture, as was the custom of the time. If extended solo or ensemble settings appear, they are most likely to be in the quieter movements—the Benedictus and Agnus Dei. Even though the longer texts are set as single movements, Mozart generally divides the Agnus Dei into two separated sections, composing the final *Dona nobis pacem* as an independent movement.

The *Missa brevis* in D major, K. 194 (186h), composed in 1774, is representative of all Mozart's Masses of this class. (The numbers in parentheses in these references represent a revision of the original Köchel numbers, made by Alfred Einstein in the third edition, published in 1937.) The brief compass of the work makes it necessary for Mozart to eliminate or drastically shorten the traditional fugues that end the longer movements; thus the *Amen* of the Gloria consists of only 11 measures in contrapuntal style, and that of the Credo only 22 measures partly imitative and partly chordal. Concise writing which, with the exception of three or four passages, is set in fast tempos adds to the brevity of the work—thus conforming to the wishes of Mozart's employer, the Archbishop Colloredo, who was impatient with elaborate or lengthy Masses.

The other Mass type represented in Mozart's work was characterized by extended treatment and elaborate accompaniments, and was designed for church festivals or other solemn occasions—hence the name *Missa solemnis*. Of the *solemnis* type are such works as the C major *Dominicus Mass*, K. 66 of 1769, the C major *Trinitatis Mass*, K. 167 of 1773, the *Coronation Mass*, K. 317 of 1779 (also in C major), several others without nicknames, and an incomplete C minor Mass, K. 427 (417a) of 1782–83. The *Coronation Mass* is both typical of this group and among the best known of Mozart's Masses.

The Mass is written for four-voice choir and orchestra, with solo voices occasionally emerging from the choral texture, which is predominantly chordal; only occasionally are bits of imitation and other contrapuntal devices found, primarily in the passages for solo ensemble. A major distinction between this Mass and those of the *brevis* type is the greater degree of solemnity and the sharper contrasts; the somewhat perfunctory formula writing that characterizes the short Masses is missing. In a few passages, notably in the Gloria, text phrases are sometimes overlapped, as in the *brevis* type, and instrumental introductions and interludes are kept to a minimum. In other respects, however, the *Coronation Mass* is true to the *solemnis* type.

Principles of organization found most usually in instrumental music are present in the Masses of Mozart, as they were in those of Haydn and in much church music of the Classical period in general. An example is seen notably in the *Coronation* Kyrie, where the melodic line given to the alto soloist in slow tempo is transferred to the Agnus Dei, first for the solo quartet and then for the choir, there set in fast tempo in counterpoint (see Example 47); thus a degree of thematic unity is provided in the Mass. Other movements approach instrumental forms—notably quasi-rondos in the Credo and Benedictus, and a type of sonata-form without a true development in the Gloria. Throughout this Mass, as well as in many of the others, the rich figuration supplied by the strings and the supporting harmonies in the winds provide a sonorous and colorful background for the voice parts.

The unfinished C minor Mass stands apart as one of Mozart's most profound and majestic compositions. It owes its origin to a vow Mozart made late in 1782 before his impending marriage to Constanze Weber; but in the spring of 1783, when the Mozarts returned to Salzburg from Vienna, the Mass was unfinished, and subsequently he had no occasion to complete it. In its present state the Mass includes the Kyrie, Gloria, Sanctus, Benedictus, and two parts of the Credo: one large section from the beginning through *descendit de coelis*, and the other from *Et incarnatus est* through *Et homo factus est*. Thus the Agnus Dei is missing completely, along with about half the Credo; further, inner orchestral parts in a few passages were left unfinished, notably in the *Incarnatus*. The Mass contains solos for two sopranos and tenor; its choral requirements vary from four-voice choir to double choir of eight voices; and the orchestra is expanded to include horns, trumpets, and three trombones in addition to the instruments usual in Mozart's larger Masses.

The existing portions make clear Mozart's intention to write a cantata Mass, such as the division of the Gloria into seven distinct movements and the separation of the *Incarnatus* from the first large portion of the Credo. The work was written at a time when Mozart had just become acquainted with the music of Bach; contrapuntal studies occupied much of his time, so that the Mass has an

EXAMPLE 47   Mozart, *Coronation Mass*

(a)

(b)

(Orch. omitted)

air of Baroque power and earnestness. The massive choral style of Handel, too, casts its shadow, especially in portions of the Gloria, and strong touches of Neapolitan coloratura writing in the soprano solos and melodic brilliance in general add other ingredients to the basic *solemnis* style. Yet all those disparate elements are brought together under the influence of Mozart's creative imagination. One may call attention to the source of this or that element in the Mass, but the expressiveness of the work as a whole is Mozart's own accomplishment.

The relationship between the sense of the text and the music is close throughout, yet the wide range of the emotional content is a cause for wonderment. For example, the Kyrie is based on a melancholy, pulsating figure in the orchestra (see Example 48); the Gloria, by contrast, is jubilant, dramatic, and mournful

EXAMPLE 48   Mozart, *C minor Mass*, Kyrie

in turn, with one of the literature's most heartfelt and poignant moments in the *Qui tollis*. A dotted rhythmic figure moving inexorably through long passages pervades the whole; above that figure the lines of the double chorus move slowly (see Example 49). Based largely on stepwise progressions or segments of the chromatic scale, they suggest deep anguish; in the words of Alfred Einstein, the

EXAMPLE 49   Mozart, *C minor Mass, Qui tollis*

movement is "quite evidently conceived as a representation of the Saviour, making His way under whiplashes, and bearing the burden of the Cross, toward Golgotha" (Einstein, *Mozart, His Character, His Work,* p. 348).

The *Et incarnatus est* is set as a soprano solo of surpassing beauty, filled with virtuosic passages in the manner of Neapolitan opera, even including a cadenza in which oboe, flute, and bassoon provide obbligato voices. The choral movements, finally, contain touches reminiscent of Handel—notably the short fanfares that accompany the beginnings of the Gloria and Credo; the spirit of Bach is reflected in the fugal writing of the *Osanna,* the dramatic tone of the *Qui tollis,* and the broad rhythmic sweep of entire movements. But all such influences are absorbed, fused, and synthesized; one recognizes the sources even as one marvels at the way Mozart has assimilated them.

Mozart, perhaps more than any composer before him, brought the Mass text into agreement with the requirements of musical form. Words or short phrases of the text are sometimes repeated or overlapped; occasionally a few measures of accompaniment intervene between one text phrase and the next; subtle changes of key, texture, and melodic contour are judiciously arranged to provide variety and contrast. The result is a series of musical forms in which balance, proportion, unity, and contrast are all provided, with musical considerations occasionally outweighing the liturgical in Mozart's mind.

Beethoven

The contributions of Ludwig van Beethoven (1770–1827) to the choral field include two Masses, an oratorio, several cantatas, two orchestral works with large choral sections or movements, and a few miscellaneous works. Born in Bonn, Beethoven moved to Vienna in 1792 and made that city his permanent home. The accounts of his life, his personal problems, the strong will with which he overcame those problems, and his position as one of the greatest of all composers are too widely known to require retelling here. Beethoven was primarily a composer of instrumental music; his relatively few choral works most often resulted from commissions; only rarely (as in the Mass, Op. 123, and the choral finale of the Ninth Symphony) do they reflect an inner need to write for voices.

The Mass in C major, Op. 86, was composed in 1807. Commissioned by Prince Nicholas Esterházy, it was not well received at its first incomplete performance (in the castle at Eisenstadt, with Beethoven conducting), and the composer suffered severe embarrassment. It is set for four soloists, four-voice choir, and orchestra with organ. As in many other Masses of the time, the solo voices emerge out of the choral group, are given relatively short solo or ensemble passages— sometimes accompanied by the choir—and at no point rise to the level of separate arias. While each movement may contain sections contrasting in tempo, meter, and tonality, the sections are connected and the Mass is cast in standard form. The texture of the Mass changes continually: a few measures in chordal style are interrupted by short passages for one or more soloists, often in imitative writing, which are followed by a phrase or two in mixed style, and so on. A few passages, especially in the Gloria and Benedictus, contain sections in which the ensemble texture is interrupted or accompanied by brief choral interjections; fugal writing is confined to two or three passages, notably the ends of the Credo and *Osanna*, and even there persists for only a few measures. The whole thus represents a fluid, ever-changing texture, with the solo voices used essentially to provide flashes of color—additions, as it were, to Beethoven's palette.

As in his instrumental works, Beethoven employs dynamics to enhance expressive details, not merely in a traditional way or to provide routine contrasts. Sudden changes in volume from loud to soft, or the reverse, accompany individual words or phrases; for example, in the Gloria, *benedicimus te* (*ff*) is followed by *adoramus te* (*p*); and in the Credo, *resurrectionem* (*f*) by *mortuorum* (*p*). Significantly, the Kyrie, Credo, and Agnus Dei begin quietly (*p* or *pp*), and the latter ends with a return of the quiet phrase with which the Kyrie began. The subjective approach throughout the C major Mass reveals the extent to which Beethoven freed himself from formulas and set the Mass in accordance with its meaning to him. It is an essentially personal document; the fact that Beethoven wished it to be published with a German text in addition to the Latin suggests that he conceived of a life for this work outside the liturgical framework—that is, as a work for the concert stage.

The Mass in D major, Op. 123, usually called the *Missa solemnis*, owes its origin to Beethoven's wish to honor his friend and patron the Archduke Rudolph by composing a Mass for his enthronement as Archbishop of Olmütz in 1820. The work was begun early in 1819 but was not completed until 1823, three years after the ceremony for which it was intended. Set for four soloists, a four-voice choir, full orchestra of symphonic dimensions, and organ, the Mass became an enormous work requiring almost two hours of performance time—thus far exceeding the limits of a church service. Transcending liturgical requirements both in size and content, the Mass is concerned more with ethical than dogmatic matters; it stands as an expression of Beethoven's reverence and faith, and in this sense embodies a religious feeling perhaps stronger than that seen in many more traditional settings.

Possibly no work in the literature reveals a closer interpenetration of soloistic, choral, and orchestral forces than the D major Mass. While the forms of the various movements cannot be classified as sonata-form, rondo, etc., what may be called "symphonic thinking" is present on virtually every page. Short motives as well as long melodies provide the basic material; the motives are developed, the melodies are expanded and recapitulated, later sections of a movement are often derived from an earlier, and the vocal lines often progress independently of the instrumental. In short, the work represents a symphonic setting of the text, and all its forces share equally in its dramatic evolution.

The Kyrie, in one large three-section form (the *Christe* constituting the middle section) is based largely on five motives and melodic figures, set variously for orchestra or voices (see Example 50a–e). These motives are developed, transposed, and used to establish melodic unity in this large movement. Similarly, the Gloria contains eight sections contrasting in tempo, key, and meter, but

EXAMPLE 50   Beethoven, *Missa solemnis*

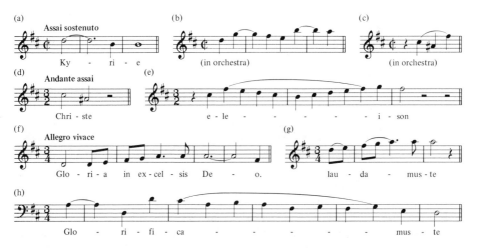

unified by the presence of several motives and phrases of which the three most prominent are given in Example 50f–h. As in the Kyrie, the successive text phrases are set in an ever-changing texture; a choral passage will contain a few measures set for a solo voice, or vice versa, and the orchestra will amplify, support, or work independently of the voices.

The Credo, in keeping with its longer and more varied text, contains sections ranging even more widely in tone and tempo, with sections from *allegro molto* to *grave*, as the sense of the text suggests. Of particular significance is the section on the phrase *Et incarnatus est;* here the quartet of soloists accompanied only by a few strings and winds presents the words in a kind of harmonized recitative style. Although the passage is short, its effect is profound. A few measures later, on the text *Crucifixus*, but now for choir and a larger number of instruments, a somewhat similar treatment occurs with the same magical effect.

The Sanctus and Benedictus together constitute one large movement, again divided into contrasting sections; but now the textural variety is increased. The orchestral writing is particularly rich in the first section and resembles that of a symphonic slow movement. After a dramatic transition, orchestra and choir together burst into a brilliant fugue on *Pleni sunt coeli . . . osanna*. The fugue, ending abruptly, leads directly into the Benedictus, which begins with a quiet orchestral passage marked "Praeludium" and proceeds into a long section for solo violin and orchestra. Gradually the solo voices enter with quiet melodies, occasionally augmented by a few phrases for the choir. The mood is quiet and pastoral throughout; even the final phrase on *osanna* is restrained and ends quietly.

The Agnus Dei is unique in both form and content. Its first section, in slow tempo, consists of orchestral introduction and interludes, long solo passages, and only two or three short choral phrases. The second section, contrasting in tempo and meter and carrying the inscription, "Prayer for inner and outer peace," is concerned entirely with a development of the melodies on the phrase *dona nobis pacem*, set mainly for the choir. Then, abruptly and as if from a distance, comes a brief warlike fanfare for trumpets with timpani in the background; gradually other instruments enter as the fanfare is repeated, and in two short recitatives over an orchestral tremolo, alto and tenor soloists shout in anguish to make themselves heard: *Agnus Dei, miserere nobis.* The mood changes abruptly as the earlier tempo and texture are restored, and the choir, in mixed contrapuntal and chordal textures, dominates the movement, which proceeds in tumultuous fashion. The final measures, however, are again quiet and set with only a few instruments doubling the voices; but interrupting the prayer for peace, *dona nobis pacem*, comes a brief reminder in an exposed passage for timpani of the anguish expressed in the warlike scene.

The use of extreme contrasts is a notable feature of Beethoven's instrumental music; here it is employed dramatically to underline the meaning of the text. In any prayer for peace, the opposite state (war or other major turmoil) is necessarily present in the supplicant's mind. Beethoven presents both these states clearly, gives a tone of utmost urgency to the prayer, and suggests the consequences—in the shape of the military fanfares—should the prayer not be answered. Significantly, as if to provide assurance, in the following section (from meas. 216) Beethoven introduces a phrase derived from Handel's *Messiah* (on the text "And He shall reign forever"), a work he knew and admired.

Several other features reveal Beethoven's close attention to textual meaning, but also his concern with musical rather than liturgical requirements. The sharply contrasting dynamics seen occasionally in the C major Mass are strongly in evidence here. Among such contrasts are the following: in the Gloria, the passage in measure 319, *quoniam tu solus* (*ff*) *sanctus* (*p*); in the Credo, measure 31, *visibilium omnium* (*ff*) *et invisibilium* (*p*); measure 227, *judicare vivos* (*ff*) *et mortuos* (*p*). Repetition of single words or entire phrases purely for reasons of expression, emphasis, or musical form also abound; the reiteration of the word *credo* in one voice while other voices continue with the text is typical (see Example 51). In the Gloria, in a passage extending from measure 296 to 303, the word *o* is added before the phrase *miserere nobis* because the musical phrase demands it. Similarly, at the end of the Gloria, after the final *Amen*, an extended coda recapitulates the first phrase, *Gloria in excelsis Deo*, with many repetitions—contrary to liturgical practice but necessary to round off the musical form.

Two final points in connection with the Credo may be taken as suggesting the nature of Beethoven's religious faith. After the phrase *cujus regni non erit finis* ("whose reign shall have no end") beginning in measure 241, the word *non* is repeated several times as if to emphasize the fact that the Kingdom of God shall indeed be eternal. The section immediately following (from meas. 264) is concerned with several doctrinal statements; Beethoven's attitude toward them may be inferred from the fact that he set that lengthy 43-word paragraph with overlappings almost in the manner of a *Missa brevis*, in a passage that requires scarcely one minute in performance; whereas the final five words of the text,

EXAMPLE 51   Beethoven, *Missa solemnis*

et vitam venturi saeculi. Amen ("and the life of the world to come. Amen"),
are then repeated and elaborated in an optimistic passage requiring more than
seven minutes. One senses here a statement of Beethoven's inmost beliefs and
hopes; that statement, applied to the text of the Mass, results in one of Beethoven's masterworks and one of the enduring monuments of western music.

Requiem Mass

The *Missa pro defunctis* (Mass for the Dead), generally known as the Requiem
Mass, has not been discussed at length earlier in these pages—largely because
its treatment by composers in the sixteenth century did not differ materially from
that given the normal Mass. Therefore, a brief review of the Requiem is in order
here as an introduction to the profound settings by eighteenth- and nineteenth-century composers.

The Requiem Mass differs from the normal type in that certain items otherwise grouped with chants of the Proper are given invariable texts and are combined with chants of the Ordinary, omitting the joyful Gloria and Credo. Thus musical settings of the form include Introit, Kyrie, Gradual, Sequence, Offertory, Sanctus with Benedictus, Agnus Dei, and Communion (see Appendix 2b). The form of the Requiem Mass remained somewhat fluid through much of the seventeenth century; liturgical practices often differed from one region to another, and settings of the Sequence, *Dies irae* ("Day of Wrath"), were not regularly included in composed Requiem Masses until late in the sixteenth century.

The majority of composers who wrote Masses also turned to the Requiem, including Palestrina, Lasso, Morales, and Victoria. The practice of alternating plainsong sections (intoned by the priest) with contrapuntal or chordal sections (sung by the choir) is typical especially in settings of chants of the Proper—most notably in the Sequence. In a Requiem by Giuseppe Pitoni (1657–1743), composed about 1688, that practice was abandoned and the entire text was set for choir in a mixture of styles: the texts of the Ordinary in a manner that recalled the style of late–sixteenth-century composers, and those of the Proper in a style derived from seventeenth-century opera. And a setting by Francesco Cavalli (1602–1676), one of the most important composers of Venetian opera, is among the first in which the text of the Sequence is set in the agitated, dramatic fashion that became customary in the eighteenth and nineteenth centuries.

Before that time the Requiem had been composed in accord with its full title, Mass for the Dead, and its function as a prayer for the repose of the soul had been reflected in the musical treatment it received; thus the *Dies irae*, with its emphasis on the terrors of the Last Judgment, played a minor part in earlier settings. The influence of opera on sacred music in the seventeenth century, however, gradually led to a new appreciation of the dramatic possibilities inherent in that text. Many phrases suggested violent or extreme treatment: day of wrath, Heaven and earth burning in ashes, the trumpet sounding through earth's sepulchers, King of majesty, the wicked doomed to flames—such striking images evoked corresponding musical treatment, and the *Dies irae* most often became a vehicle for sensational and sometimes extravagant music.

Finally, and parallel to developments in the normal Mass, the Requiem too was generally set with orchestral accompaniment in a style that often reflected the increasing use of secular elements in the sacred field. Settings by Giovanni Battista Bassani (c. 1657–1716), Antonio Lotti (c. 1667–1740), and Francesco Durante (1684–1755) are notable among the many works that illustrate this phase of the Requiem's development.

Two settings each by Johann Adolph Hasse (1699–1783) and Niccolo Jomelli (1714–1774) share a level of musical quality characteristic of many Requiem Masses of the time; the nature of the text, with its reminder of man's mortality, moved composers in a way that did not permit perfunctory treatment. Even though sentimentality sometimes prevailed (as in the settings by Hasse), a basic seriousness of tone and dignity of expression—seen especially in the Requiem by Michael Haydn, composed in 1771—pervade these works and distinguish them from the routine normal Masses of the time.

A page from a facsimile of the autograph score of Mozart's Requiem.

Mozart

The Requiem Mass, K. 626, by Mozart is the outstanding Classical example of dignified and exalted expressiveness. It was commissioned in July, 1791, by a Count Walsegg, who sent his steward to Mozart to arrange the details. Already in a state of declining health, Mozart apparently feared that the stranger was indeed a messenger of death. Romantic legend has it that the composer felt he was writing his own Requiem and that he worked feverishly to bring it to completion. The facts, however, reveal that in that same month Mozart composed *Die Zauberflöte (The Magic Flute)*, in August his last opera, *La Clemenza di Tito (The Clemency of Titus)*, and in early October his A major Clarinet Concerto, K. 622. Meanwhile he made a trip to Prague for a September performance of *Tito* and returned to Vienna to conduct the first performance (September 30) of *Die Zauberflöte*. Only then was he able to return to concentrated work on the Requiem, but at his death on December 5 the work was still unfinished, to be completed by Mozart's friend and pupil, Franz Xaver Süssmayr.

The extent of Süssmayr's collaboration was a subject of controversy during much of the nineteenth century. According to the most recent findings, the Requiem may be ascribed as follows:

1. Introit. Completely by Mozart.
2. Kyrie (without Gradual). Completely by Mozart.
3. Sequence. Vocal parts, figured bass, and sketches for the orchestration by Mozart, but the last section, *Lacrimosa*, was carried only through the ninth

measure. Süssmayr completed that section and orchestrated the whole on the basis of the sketches.

4. Offertory. As in the Sequence.
5. Sanctus. First part sketched by Mozart, completed and orchestrated by Süssmayr.
6. Benedictus. Measures 1–18 and 28–50, with the first part orchestrated, by Mozart. The rest, including a few final measures and the *Osanna* (based on the *Osanna* in the *Sanctus*) by Süssmayr.
7. Agnus Dei. Largely by Mozart; the extent of Süssmayr's contribution unknown.
8. Communion. All by Süssmayr, who employed the *Te decet* of the first movement for the *Lux eterna* and the fugue from the Kyrie for the text *Cum sanctis tuis in aeternum.* Thus the first and last movements end with the same music.

The work is set for four soloists, four-voice choir, an orchestra consisting of two basset horns (a type of tenor clarinet), two bassoons, two trumpets, three trombones, timpani, strings, and organ with continuo; significantly, the customary flutes, oboes, and clarinets are omitted, presumably to invest the orchestra with a darker tone color than usual.

Mozart had long since freed himself from reliance on models of musical style; all the influences to which he had been subjected were now thoroughly assimilated and refined. The forms in the Requiem are essentially those he had inherited, yet within them he achieved an expressiveness that brings the interpenetration of textual significance and evocative music to a new high level. Mozart's position toward the liturgy may be sensed here. In the Introit, for example, on the text *Te decet hymnus* ("A hymn becometh thee, O Lord"), a soprano soloist begins a melody derived from an old chorale tune, "My Soul Exalts the Lord." Yet only a few measures later, on *exaudi orationem meam* ("hear my prayer"), the jagged orchestral accompaniment seems to suggest defiance rather than supplication. Elsewhere, in sections of the Sequence, he attempts to assuage the pain of death by writing in a style that at times recalls plainsong, as if to suggest that the old musical language of the Church, sanctified by centuries, still had the power to heal. The Kyrie is a double fugue (one theme on *Kyrie eleison*, the other on *Christe eleison*), in a style that has a certain resemblance to the objective style of the late Baroque. Several sections of the Sequence are relatively short and concentrated, notably the *Rex tremendae majestatis;* yet even within its 22 measures Mozart draws a vivid contrast between the majesty of God and the powerlessness of human supplicants. Similar examples of sensitive—even metaphysical—treatment of text phrases abound in other movements.

In the years after Mozart's death the Requiem quickly assumed a dominant position in the literature. Within a few decades it had entered the repertoire of churches or concert groups in Italy, Russia, Germany, Sweden, France, Argentina, and other countries, and is today still one of the most highly regarded works in the literature.

Cherubini

Of completely different nature are two settings of the Requiem by Luigi Cherubini (1760–1842). Born in Florence, Cherubini spent two years in London (1784–86) and made several later visits to England, but his career developed mainly in France between 1788 and 1842. Highly esteemed as a composer of operas, he was also active in the field of sacred composition; he became associated with the Paris Conservatory in 1795, rising to the post of director in 1822. On a visit to Vienna he became acquainted with Beethoven, who considered Cherubini the finest of operatic composers and who was influenced especially by his choral writing.

Cherubini's first Requiem (1817), in C minor, is set for four-voice choir and large orchestra, with no soloists. In spite of its considerable length (more than fifty minutes), it has fewer separate movements than usual. The Introit and Kyrie are combined into one movement, as are the Sanctus and Benedictus (here following the Medieval practice), and the Agnus Dei and Communion. Further, the Sequence is cast as one enormous movement without change of tempo or meter from the initial *Dies irae* to *Lacrimosa dies illa*, with only the last two of its twenty stanzas set in a slower tempo. The Offertory is also set as a single long movement. The resulting amplitude and broad sweep of these movements give the Requiem much of its dramatic power and strength.

Unlike many other settings, Cherubini's is bathed in gloom and resignation. Much of the music is quiet (*p* or *pp*), but it is often marked by sharp accents (see Example 52a). Only occasionally does Cherubini sustain a loud dynamic level across a long passage, notably in the *Tuba mirum* and *Rex tremendae* sections of the Sequence. He makes much use of slowly descending chromatic lines,

EXAMPLE 52   Cherubini, *C minor Requiem*

contrasting passages in which the harmony is virtually static, and others in which short rhythmic motives lend an air of foreboding. And the texture of the vocal parts is fluid and ever changing. Often one voice is set opposite the other three (see Example 52b); at other times a solid chordal texture is maintained; at still others long passages of imitative and even fugal writing occur. Such variety, coupled with harmonic subtleties and imaginative settings of individual text phrases, combine to make this a work worthy of being restored to its former position in the repertoire.

Cherubini's second Requiem (1836), in D minor, may be discussed here even though it lies outside the chronological boundaries of this chapter. It is set for three-part men's choir and large orchestra. In omitting women's voices, Cherubini followed a tradition that extends back (in opera) to the early 1600s and that is represented in a Requiem setting by Giovanni Asola printed in Venice about 1586. He may have been more directly influenced, however, by the opposition of the then Archbishop of Paris, who objected to women's voices in the church. Although the D minor Requiem has many points in common with its prede-cessor—including even thematic and structural similarities—it has as many individual qualities.

First, the emotional bleakness characteristic of the earlier setting is often relieved in this one. There are moments of joy at the prospect of redemption, the Sanctus is full of festiveness, and the final prayer for perpetual light is imbued with an optimistic spirit. Second, the orchestra plays a role virtually independent of the choir; at times it reaches symphonic breadth in its development of themes and motives, while at other times it retreats entirely to give way to extended passages for unaccompanied voices. Finally, the element of contrast is employed more strikingly here—in thematic material, expressive type, and dynamic range alike. In a sense more subjective than its great predecessor, and with perhaps more variety of dramatic and instrumental color, it is a work of equal quality.

Oratorio

Haydn

Haydn's first oratorio, *Il Ritorno di Tobia (The Return of Tobias)* was composed about 1774 and first performed in Vienna in the following year. It is written for four soloists, four-voice choir, and a standard orchestra to which two trom-bones are added and in which English horns replace the clarinets. For a perfor-mance in 1784, the work was revised to add two choruses to the three in the original version. In deference to the conservative style favored by "official" Vienna, Haydn avoided the use of operatic elements in the oratorio; several of the arias approach sonata-form instead of the customary da capo pattern, the recitatives are expressive rather than merely narrative, and the choruses (with inserted solo passages) make full use of such dramatic elements as the text provides.

Haydn made two extended visits to England in 1791–92 and again in 1794–95. On the first of the visits he was present at a massive choral concert given at Westminster Abbey in memory of Handel; the sheer size of the choral forces employed (tradition has it that almost a thousand singers took part) made a lasting impression on the composer. That impression was strengthened some two years later, when Haydn heard a massed choir of children's voices (reputedly four thousand) sing a hymn at St. Paul's Cathedral. These experiences undoubtedly made him receptive to the idea of composing an oratorio on the Handelian model. A text on the Creation was available, assembled from the Book of Genesis and Milton's *Paradise Lost;* Haydn brought it from London, his friend Baron van Swieten arranged and translated the text into German, and in 1798 *Die Schöpfung* (*The Creation*) received its first performance.

The Creation is written for five soloists, four-voice choir, and a standard orchestra augmented by contrabassoon and three trombones. The traditional part of the Evangelist is here divided between three soloists representing the arch-angels Gabriel, Uriel, and Raphael; Adam and Eve, the only other characters to appear in the oratorio, are sung by the two remaining soloists.

The work begins with an orchestral representation of Chaos, using thematic fragments that emerge out of a dark and continually shifting harmonic back-ground, with abrupt dynamic changes and sharp accents that confuse the sense of forward motion. The Narrator and choir then introduce the first four verses of Genesis; on the word [Let there be] "light," a sudden fortissimo on a C major chord dispels the darkness and crystallizes the form and the harmony (see Example 53). The way is thus prepared for an account of other details of the Creation, set in a variety of arias, ensembles, and choruses.

EXAMPLE 53   Haydn, *Die Schöpfung*

(Tr.: "And God said: Let there be light, and there was light!")

Haydn's many decades of activity in the symphonic field are wonderfully reflected in the orchestral writing of the oratorio. The instrumental introductions and accompaniments recall his symphonies in their brilliance, variety, and textures, which range from the simplest homophony to the most involved counterpoint. And always, whether the text is a description of a tempest or a hymn of praise to the Creator, the orchestral writing is unfailingly appropriate. *The Creation* abounds with delightful descriptive passages. The soprano aria No. 15, for Gabriel, describes the emergence of the eagle, lark, and nightingale, and is a masterpiece of melodic writing with frequent coloratura touches. And the bass recitative No. 21, given to Raphael, is particularly noteworthy for its orchestral illustrations: a unison trill suggests the roaring lion, scale passages describe the leaping tiger; the noble steed is depicted by an angular running figure, a horde of insects by a string tremolo; and on an undulating chromatic line, in slow tempo, *in langen Zügen kriecht am Boden das Gewürm* ("in long dimension creeps the sinuous worm").

The greatest musical weight is carried by the choruses that end the three parts of the oratorio. A brilliant mixture of solid chordal writing, imitative and sometimes fugal texture, and soloistic passagework recaptures the spirit—if not the style—of Handel. The dramatic and lyric qualities of *The Creation* made it an immediate success at its first performance, and these qualities have ensured the continuation of its popularity to the present day.

Shortly after completing *The Creation* Haydn set to work on another oratorio, *Die Jahreszeiten (The Seasons)*. Its text is based on a poem by James Thomson, to the final section of which van Swieten added a few verses by two minor German and Austrian poets. Each of its four parts is named for one of the seasons, beginning with spring. Unlike the text of *The Creation*, however, Thomson's poem is primarily lyric and descriptive; the beauties of nature are described in detail, dramatic elements play little part in it, and the role of the poet is primarily that of a sympathetic observer. Haydn maintained this idyllic quality in a lyrical score of great charm. *The Seasons* is set for bass (Simon, a farmer), soprano (Hanne, his daughter), and tenor (Lucas, a young countryman), four-voice choir (of hunters and country people), and an orchestra of symphonic size.

The work begins with an orchestral introduction depicting the gradual transformation of winter into spring; this long movement, essentially in sonata-form, ends with a recitative in which all three soloists are introduced in turn as they welcome spring's arrival. Then follows a gentle and bucolic chorus in which the country folk greet the new season. Once this optimistic and purposely naive tone has been set, the various scenes of the text follow in an array of recitatives and arias, four choruses, and ensembles with or without choir; the whole totals 39 separate numbers.

As in *The Creation*, Haydn's mastery of the symphonic idiom is everywhere apparent in *The Seasons'* orchestral accompaniment, which is invariably colorful, wide-ranging, and appropriate to the sense of the text. Descriptive moments abound, the summer storm (No. 17) being the most extended. Haydn's treatment of the wind instruments is especially noteworthy; piquant or eloquent or ornamental obbligato wind passages help to establish the happy tone that prevails virtually throughout *The Seasons*.

Beethoven

In March, 1803, within a space of two weeks, Beethoven set to music a poem by the Viennese poet Franz Huber, based on the events that took place in the Garden of Gethsemane. Entitled *Christus am Oelberge (Christ on the Mount of Olives),* Op. 85, the oratorio was performed in April of the same year. It includes parts for three soloists (Jesus, Seraph, and Peter), four-voice choir, and large orchestra.

Beethoven set the text, which is often sentimental in tone, in a series of recitatives, arias, and ensembles, with three brief choral numbers and one final and imposing chorus of angels, *Welten singen Dank und Ehre* (sung to the text "Hallelujah . . . to God's almighty Son" in the English version). The arias and ensembles often approach operatic style, contain a few florid cadenzas, and reflect the melodramatic nature of the text. The strength of this rarely performed work lies in its imposing orchestral introduction with recitative, and in its majestic final chorus.

Other Works

Haydn

In 1785 Haydn received from Cadiz, Spain, a request to compose a series of instrumental pieces, to be performed during the Good Friday service commemorating the Seven Words of Christ on the Cross. His setting took the form of an introduction, seven slow movements, and a final movement called *Terremoto (Earthquake),* all written for orchestra. The work was completed and published in 1787; Haydn himself subsequently made two arrangements of the composition, one for string quartet and one for piano. A few years later another arrangement, with text and choral parts added, was made by an obscure musician in Passau, Germany. Haydn heard a performance of it there in 1794, found the idea of an added choir attractive, and prepared his own choral version for four soloists, four-voice choir, and orchestra. First performed in 1796 under the title *Die sieben Worte des Erlösers am Kreuze (The Seven Words of Our Savior on the Cross),* this version is one of Haydn's most expressive works.

Haydn's text was compiled by Baron van Swieten, who selected relevant verses from both the Old and New Testaments. The text for the chorus in each movement provides either a meditation on the corresponding Word or an elaboration of its sentiment, each Word except the fifth appearing as an unaccompanied phrase in choral declamation before the beginning of the corresponding choral movement (the text of the Words is below). The nondramatic and contemplative character of the texts required corresponding musical treatment; the seven Adagios, with the slow introduction and the orchestral intermezzo (the latter added by Haydn before the fifth Word in the choral version) constitute a work of great reverence and repose. The individual movements are set largely in mixed chordal and imitative style, with further contrasts of solo and choral writing. Haydn's choice of key for each Word is appropriate to the text, the Words themselves providing the overall unity that the tonalities do not supply. Here are the Words and the keys in which they are set (the text of the choruses is omitted):

(Introduction: D minor)

1: B flat major.
   Vater, vergieb ihnen, denn sie wissen nicht was sie tun ("Father, forgive them, for they know not what they do"). Luke 23:34.
2: C minor and major.
   Fürwahr, ich sage es dir: heute wirst du bei mir im Paradise sein ("Verily I say unto you: this day shalt thou be with me in Paradise"). Luke 23:43.
3: E major.
   Frau, hier siehe deinen Sohn, und du, siehe deine Mutter ("Woman, behold thy son; son, behold thy mother"). John 19:26–27.
4: F minor.
   Mein Gott, mein Gott, warum hast du mich verlassen? ("My God, my God, why hast thou forsaken me?"). Matthew 27:46.

(Intermezzo: A minor)

5: A major.
   Ach, mich dürstet ("I thirst"). John 19:28.
6: G minor and major.
   Es ist vollbracht ("It is finished"). John 19:30.
7: E flat major.
   Vater, in deine Hände empfehle ich meinem Geist ("Father, into thy hands I commend my spirit"). Luke 23:46.

(Earthquake: C minor).

The problem of adding texts to preexisting music was solved in highly successful fashion, with only a few details of orchestration differing in the two versions. Many of the orchestral lines are of course doubled in the voices, but changes of octave and rhythmic figuration, repeated notes in the vocal parts against sustained notes in the orchestra—such devices give the texted lines a life of their own (see Example 54). The solemn brooding tone of many passages gives way to one of faith and hope of salvation, and the sheer beauty of the music overwhelms the listener.

Mozart

Mozart wrote about 34 miscellaneous works for choir, from a short motet on English words, *God Is Our Refuge*, K. 20, composed in London in 1765 when he was eight, to the sublime *Ave verum corpus* (*Hail, True Body*), K. 618, another

EXAMPLE 54   Haydn, *Die sieben Worte*

(Tr.: "Be not overcome by evil, but overcome [evil with good].")

motet written in Vienna in 1791, six months before his death. The works—most of which require orchestral accompaniment—include seven Kyries, six Offertories, four antiphons, four litanies, and two vesper settings, the remainder being single works on various texts. Every year from 1765 to 1781 is represented by one or more of these compositions, the whole thus reflecting all the periods and style changes of Mozart's music. Several of them are worthy of individual attention.

Of the four settings of the litany, one (K. 243, written in 1776) is outstanding. The litany in the Roman Catholic Church is a series of supplications sung originally as plainsong in responsorial style. It customarily begins with the Kyrie, continues with a series of short sentences such as "Father in heaven, have mercy upon us; God of light, have mercy upon us" (the second phrase being identical in each sentence), and ends with the Agnus Dei. In choral settings such as Mozart's the responsorial element is discarded, however. Mozart's setting of 1776 calls for four soloists, four-voice choir, orchestra with organ and continuo, and is cast in ten movements. Rich contrapuntal writing, including a double fugue in the eighth movement, is balanced by passages in chordal style; brilliant arias, some with elaborate instrumental obbligatos, add a festive air; and the detailed orchestral writing enhances the sense of the text throughout. In several movements Mozart's later style is foreshadowed. The chromaticism and pulsating accompaniment especially of No. 3, *Verbum caro* (*The Word Becomes Flesh*), and the limpid ornamented melodies of No. 8, *Agnus Dei,* are recaptured in such works as the great C minor Mass and the Requiem.

On an even higher level stand the two settings of the Office of Vespers, the Roman Catholic sunset service. Both approach the C minor Mass of 1782–83 in dramatic power, fervor, and sheer melodiousness. The two settings (K. 321 and K. 339, 1779 and 1780) both include the five Psalms CIX, CX, CXI, CXII, CXVI

(110, 111, 112, 113, 117) and the Magnificat, and both are set for four soloists, four-voice choir, and orchestra.

The Vespers of 1779 reveals the extent to which Mozart had cast aside the traditional church music style of passages in counterpoint here, thin chordal texture there, a fugal ending on each "amen," and so on. Contrasts of tonality mark the six movements, set in C, E minor, B flat, F, A, and C, respectively. Textural variety is everywhere apparent: a short passage for one or more soloists gives way to choral declamation or solid chordal writing; passages in imitative style are followed by others in free counterpoint; an eloquent movement for soprano soloist, with elaborate coloratura passages, stands next to the majestic Magnificat with Handelian overtones. And everywhere one finds the expressive power, melodic beauty, and formal perfection that mark the mature style of Mozart. The Vespers of 1780 provides even more dramatic contrasts of tonality and texture, and the expressive melodies reach new heights of charm and beauty. Both settings represent Mozart at his very finest; they rank with the C minor Mass and the Requiem, and deserve to be more widely known.

Beethoven

In December, 1808, Beethoven organized a benefit concert at which his Fifth and Sixth Symphonies, his G major Piano Concerto, and portions of his C major Mass received their first public performances. For that occasion, and to provide an elaborate ending that drew together all the musical forces involved, Beethoven quickly composed a work for piano solo, choir and orchestra, known today as the Choral Fantasy, Op. 80. A lengthy and quasi-improvisatory introduction for piano alone is followed by a set of variations for orchestra; then the voices enter with a choral setting of a song Beethoven had composed fifteen years earlier. The Fantasy is an enjoyable piece of no great musical weight, but certain thematic materials and a few choral passages anticipate effects that appear in the fourth movement of his Ninth Symphony (Op. 125, 1824).

The choral finale of that symphony represents the climax of the emotional content of the three earlier orchestral movements; as such it can scarcely be considered separately. The first movement depicts a state of anxiety and strife; the scherzo is filled with driving self-will; the adagio transcends the joy of the finale to suggest serenity and divine repose. The finale, then, on a text selected from Schiller's *Ode to Joy,* presents the central idea of the symphony: universal joy and the brotherhood of all humanity, achieved through divine guidance.

Schiller's poem contains eight eight-line stanzas, each followed by its own four-line refrain. Beethoven selected only the first three stanzas and the refrains to the first, third, and fourth. The three text stanzas and the fourth refrain are subsequently set as variations of the principal theme, but the first and third refrains are given themes of their own and present the culminating sentiment of the work. The complexity of the movement's structure conceals the simplicity of its expressive purpose; for that reason a short outline may be helpful.

Fourth movement: Symphony No. 9, Beethoven

Meas.	Tempo	
1	Presto	D minor. Orchestral recitative as introduction.
30		Themes of first three movements pass in review, and theme of fourth movement is anticipated.
92	Allegro assai	D major. Main theme followed by three variations (meas. 116, 140, 164) and transition.
208	Presto	Recitative, baritone soloist, similar to meas. 1–29.
237	Allegro assai	D major. Baritone soloist and choir, first stanza (see Example 55a). The theme is in effect Variation 4 of meas. 92–115.
269		Variation 5. Three soloists and choir, second stanza.
297		Variation 6. Two soloists and choir, third stanza.
331	Allegro assai vivace	B flat. Variation 7, for orchestra alone.
367		Variation 8. Tenor and choir, fourth refrain.
431		Fugue for orchestra alone, on theme from meas. 237.
543		D major. Variation 9. Choir on return of first stanza.
595	Andante maestoso	G major. Choir, first refrain, on a new theme (see Example 55b).
627		G minor. Choir, third refrain, on another new theme (see Example 55c).
655	Allegro energico	D major. Variation 10. Choir, first stanza and first refrain combined, on themes from meas. 237 and 595.
730		Transition. Choir on third refrain, followed by first refrain.
763	Allegro ma non tanto	D major. Four soloists and choir, first stanza; modification of theme from meas. 237, with two interpolated sections, *poco adagio* (meas. 810 and 832), in which theme is further developed.
851	Prestissimo	Choir, first refrain; theme is a compressed version of meas. 595.
904		Choir, portion of first stanza; further development of theme from meas. 595. Movement ends in meas. 940.

In the recitative beginning in measure 208, Beethoven's text reads, *O Freunde, nicht mehr diese Töne! Sondern lasst uns angenehmere anstimmen, und freudenvollere* ("O friends, no more these tones; let us sing instead more joyful ones"). The reference to the earlier movements is clear and emphasizes the unified purpose of the symphony. When "man in man but hails a brother" and when the world "shall look upward [for] there must his mansion be"—the sections of Schiller's text that Beethoven emphasized—then shall joy be found: these sentiments are the cornerstone of the ethical philosophy and prophetic vision that are clearly revealed in the Ninth Symphony. Scarcely any other musical work contains a conception of such grandeur.

EXAMPLE 55   Beethoven, *Symphony No. 9*

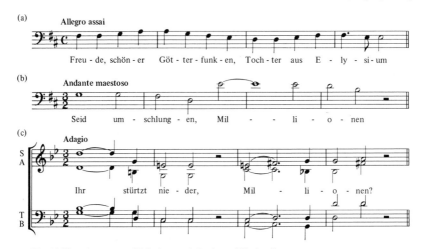

(Tr.: (a) "Joy, thou source of light immortal, daughter of Elysium."
      (b) "Embrace, ye millions!"
      (c) "Why bow down, ye millions?")

9

Early Romantic Music
1825–1860

The early nineteenth century was marked by a change in the relative strengths of two creative attitudes that have been present in the composition of virtually all music. One attitude gives rise to proportion, the ideals of restraint and balance, a conservative approach to matters of structure, and an objective, perhaps impersonal, manner of dealing with the musical material; when that attitude dominates in a composer's work or an historical period, the resulting music is said to be Classical. The other attitude is characterized by rhapsodic or unrestrained utterance, an experimental or even radical approach to form, a subjective or extremely personal involvement with the musical material, and the desire to seek out new means of expression; to the music composed under such influences the term Romantic is usually applied. Obviously the attitudes are not mutually exclusive, nor do they exist in isolation to any extent; elements of Romanticism may be traced in the music of the most conservative composers; conversely, the most highly original and subjective music depends on balance and proportion for much of its expressive validity.

The Romantic attitude, in one of its periodic alternations with the Classical, emerged even in some of Beethoven's works (witness the subjective treatment of portions of his *Missa solemnis*), and rose to a dominant position in the second quarter of the nineteenth century. Many German poets and writers were among those who led the way in the search for a new kind of subject matter; stories from mythology, tales based on superstition and the supernatural, and legends of remote or exotic lands—such subjects provided new material for composers. Musical forms both larger and smaller than earlier forms (and often more loosely assembled) became customary—a Schubert song and a Mahler symphony representing the two extremes of length. A range of styles from the naive and simple to the grandiose and colossal marked Romantic music, with stylistic differentiation between one composer and another, between one genre and another, more characteristic of Romantic music than that of any preceding period.

Thus the Romantic period is characterized by great amounts of highly expressive and colorful music—and much that is merely gigantic or novel; by music that often reflects contradictory impulses in its composers; by music that is tightly integrated as well as by some that consists of series of episodes loosely strung together. In the face of the opportunity to explore new subject matters and new instrumental tone colors, to experiment with ever-widening concepts of harmony, and to expand or compress musical forms, the major composers turned most often to the fields in which these opportunities could most immediately be realized—to instrumental music and opera. As a result, there was a rise of interest in secular matters in the nineteenth century and a corresponding fall in the quantity of choral masterpieces.

Mass

Schubert

In the music of Franz Schubert (1797–1828) several of the style elements that were to mark the early Romantic period were well established almost before that period was under way. Born in Vienna, Schubert became a member of the Imperial Chapel in his eleventh year after having received instruction in piano and violin; he never became a virtuoso performer, however, his consuming activity throughout his short life being composition. His works number almost a thousand, ranging from songs to symphonies; among them are six Masses, more than thirty small choral works on sacred texts, and a large number of short secular pieces for choir—some with piano accompaniment and many for voices alone.

The first four Masses, composed between 1814 and 1816, are not among Schubert's major works. Although he came from a Roman Catholic family, he was apparently not an ardent churchgoer; little evidence exists that he was more inspired by the words of the Mass than by any other text. All four Masses are composed for several soloists, mixed choir, and orchestra; they are of virtually uniform length (25–30 minutes each), are conventional in style and structure, and reveal in many passages the melodiousness that is Schubert's outstanding characteristic. Many commentators, however, have found these youthful Masses perfunctory in treatment; anyone hearing them will doubtless agree.

The fifth Mass, in the Romantic key of A flat and composed at intervals between 1819 and 1822, is a masterpiece of lyricism. About twice as long as any of the earlier Masses, it contains a full share of the harmonic subtleties that characterize Schubert's mature works. A mood of quiet trust animates the Kyrie; dynamic levels of p and pp prevail throughout, only briefly interrupted by a few mild accents.

The Gloria is divided into several connected sections set in various keys. The movement begins and ends in E major, illustrating the tendency of many early nineteenth-century composers to employ tonalities a major or minor third above or below the main key of a work. (In this case, E major is the enharmonic equivalent of F flat major. Schubert employed such key relationships on many occasions, following the lead of Beethoven, who had introduced them near the beginning of the century.) The Credo begins and ends in C major; its middle section, containing the *Incarnatus* and the *Crucifixus*, is based on A flat. A few passages in the third part are thematically related to or similar to those in the first part; thus a semblance of a three-part form is at hand, but in every case Schubert modifies the harmony or melodic material and a true recapitulation does not occur.

The Sanctus is distinguished especially by the variety of harmonic color revealed in its beginning measures. The single word *Sanctus* is shouted *fortissimo* three times by the full choir and orchestra—once each on F sharp minor, E flat minor, and C minor, each cry separated from the next by a few measures of pulsating orchestral accompaniment—before the movement settles down to its expected F major. Thereafter the piece progresses quietly, but the closing *Osanna* has the character of a dance movement. Returning finally to A flat, the Benedictus consists of simple harmonies over a staccato bass line, with the text set for an ensemble of three soloists and the choir—the two groups being heard first alternately and then together—to form a seven-voice texture (the solo bass is omitted).

The Agnus Dei begins in F minor, touches on several adjoining keys, and eventually turns to A flat in its final section. The text again alternates between the ensemble of soloists and the choir, each group being given a short phrase or two before giving way to the other. The textures are mainly chordal with a minimum of counterpoint, and except for an occasional outburst on the words *Dona nobis pacem*, the movement is quiet and reposeful in tone.

Contrapuntal texture in the A flat Mass is confined largely to the end of the Gloria. In this case Schubert composed a section in fugal style, with the phrase *Cum sancto spiritu in gloria Dei Patris, Amen* treated at considerable length, especially its last word. The old notion that Schubert could not write counterpoint has long since been disproved, of course. Let any remaining skeptics examine the technical features of this fugue, observing the wealth of subtle imitations, unexpected phrase extensions, and the like. It was not technical skill in counterpoint that Schubert lacked, it was interest. The contrived manipulation of melodies that counterpoint requires was foreign to his temperament. Where spontaneous outpouring of sheer melodic beauty is concerned, Schubert is matchless; in fugal writing he is "correct" but little more.

His sixth Mass, in E flat, was composed in 1828, the last year of his life. It resembles the A flat Mass in its external framework, general texture, and length, but it is less reflective than its predecessor, for it contains passages of agitation and drama. The E flat Mass relies largely on the choir, fewer demands being made on the solo voices; and many of its most eloquent passages owe their effectiveness to the orchestra rather than to the voices.

The Kyrie, in modified three-part form, employs chordal texture throughout; a quiet accompaniment in the orchestra, moving smoothly or pulsatingly in turn, moves the melodious phrases forward. The Gloria, also in modified three-part form, adds an extended fugal coda-like part on *Cum sancto spiritu*. Many of the phrases in the first three parts are set in choral recitative or declamatory style and with a minimum of accompaniment; others begin imitatively with the same spare accompaniment, flashing arpeggios in the strings supplying occasional colorful accents. The middle part of the Gloria (*Qui tollis*) presents the phrases in a strangely halting fashion: each phrase is separated from the next by rests, while a few long-held tones provide the accompaniment (see Example 56). In the following third part (*Quoniam*) and the fugal fourth part, the earlier types of declamation reappear.

EXAMPLE 56   Schubert, *E flat Mass*, Gloria

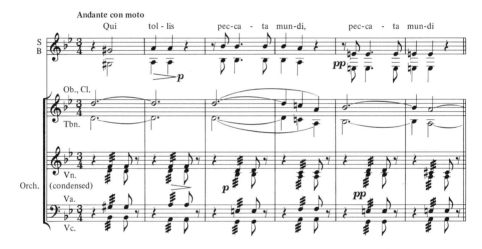

Like the Gloria, the three-part Credo also has an extended fugal section as a coda. Although the texture is mainly chordal, more passages in imitative style occur than elsewhere in Schubert's Masses. The middle part, in A flat and on the text *Et incarnatus*, is set as an expressive series of melodies given to the tenor soloist, later joined by soprano and second tenor soloists. This section is directed toward the Infant in the cradle; the effect is that of a soothing lullaby. Then with an abrupt change to A flat minor and on the heels of a diminuendo, the choir presents the *Crucifixus* in a kind of choral declamation accompanied by broken rhythms in the strings (see Example 57). The volume increases to an *fff* level as more instruments are added, then subsides again; in the midst of this eerie passage a phrase from the *Incarnatus*, sung by the three soloists, is inserted. Schubert presents here, side by side, the Infant Jesus and the Christ on the Cross. The effect is overwhelming. The final sections of the Credo return to the style of the first section and are based in part on its themes.

EXAMPLE 57   Schubert, *E flat Mass*, Credo

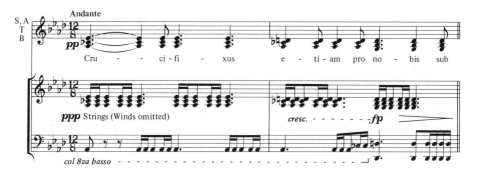

The Sanctus and Benedictus resemble the corresponding movements of the
A flat Mass; the same mixed textures are employed, and a single *Osanna* serves
both movements. The Agnus Dei is slow and is largely in fugal style with
interspersed episodes in which chordal textures dominate. The closing section,
Dona nobis pacem, is chordal, light, and uncomplicated, but near the end
Schubert brings back 23 measures of the fugal Agnus Dei, now in fast tempo.

Schubert's role as the harbinger of the Romantic period is revealed in his
treatment of the text in his late Masses: in a highly nonliturgical manner, he
omits several of the text phrases and adds others in passages where they are out
of context. In the Credo of the A flat and E flat Masses, for example, the second
phrase of the *Patrem omnipotentem* is missing, as are the sentences concerned
with the genesis of Christ, belief in one church, and belief in the resurrection
of the dead. On the other hand, words or phrases are added out of context: the
word *credo* many times, for example, even when the liturgical text does not
specify it. And in one place in both Credos, Schubert neatly telescopes two
phrases: *Confiteor unum baptisma in remissionem peccatorum. [Et expecto resur-
rectionem] mortuorum* by omitting the phrase in brackets—to the detriment of
the grammatical sense.

Without speculating about Schubert's religious beliefs, we may conclude that
considerations of musical form and phrasing, of expressive balance, and of melodic
expansion lay uppermost in his mind; liturgical scrupulousness took a minor place.
Schubert writes most expressively in the *Incarnatus*, the *Crucifixus*, and the Agnus
Dei; elsewhere he does not hesitate to use the liturgical text merely as a point
of departure for his musical planning. Thus his approach to the Mass text is a
subjective and nonliturgical one, an approach that will be characteristic in the
forthcoming Romantic period.

Rossini

After a long and successful career as a composer primarily of comic operas,
Gioacchino Rossini (1792–1868) turned to the Mass text in 1863 to compose his

Petite Messe solenelle (*Little Solemn Mass*). Written originally for four soloists, four-voice choir, with harmonium and two pianos providing the accompaniment, the Mass was later revised to include parts for full orchestra. In that form, and requiring about ninety minutes of performance time, there seems little reason for Rossini to have called the work a "petite Messe"; nevertheless, the term is generally applied to this full-scale setting.

The Mass is distinguished by excellence of contrapuntal writing and even complete fugues—features not often found in the music of composers of comic opera. Further, it contains two numbers not found in more traditional settings: before the Agnus Dei a hymn is inserted on the text *O salutaris hostia* (*O saving Victim*), normally employed in the Office of Lauds on certain occasions after Pentecost; and a *preludio religioso* for instruments alone is inserted before the Sanctus to serve as an Offertory.

The longer items of the Mass text (Gloria and Credo) are divided into several sections each, while the Sanctus and Benedictus are combined into one. Certain of the sections are set as long arias, notably the *Domine Deus* (for tenor) and the *Quoniam* (for bass) of the Gloria, and the *Crucifixus* (for soprano) of the Credo. In many of the choral numbers, such as the unaccompanied Sanctus, passages for one or more soloists emerge out of the choral texture, thus adding to the expressive variety and vocal color of the setting. Dignity and reverence are characteristic of Rossini's Mass, along with melodic beauty. Possibly too long for a traditional church service, the work is well adapted to concert performance and deserves more attention than it generally receives today.

Liszt

The fabulous career of Franz Liszt (1811–1886) as one of the greatest piano virtuosos of all time was paralleled by his activity as a prolific and innovative composer. Born in Hungary, Liszt became a true cosmopolite, living for extended periods in Paris, Weimar, Rome, and Budapest, and making extensive concert tours to all parts of western Europe. Of his compositions and arrangements, numbering more than seven hundred items, some sixty are in the field of choral music; four Masses, two oratorios, and several psalm settings are among the most important of the latter.

In the second quarter of the nineteenth century a group of musicians primarily at Munich and headed by Johann Aiblinger (1779–1867) reacted against the orchestrally accompanied Mass in which elements indirectly derived from the opera were included. They sought to restore the principles and techniques of the sixteenth century, and many minor composers among them wrote Masses in imitation of the Palestrina style. Later organized under the name of *Cäcilienverein* (St. Cecilia Association), they gradually gained a measure of support among composers generally. Independently of them, Liszt was animated by similar ideas; in 1848 he composed a Mass for men's voices and organ to express his adherence to the reform principles of the Association, using quasi-plainsong themes in a kind of harmonized declamation. In much of the Mass the accompaniment does little more than support the vocal lines and can be omitted. But in certain places Liszt made full use of the harmonic developments of his time, especially in regard to expressive dissonance. Thus there resulted an unusual mixture of modally inflected melodies set against advanced tonal harmonies.

About 1855, in preparation for the dedication of a cathedral in Gran, Hungary, Liszt turned to the Mass text again: the so-called *Gran Mass* resulted and was performed there in 1856. The reform principles of the Cecilians are not reflected in this work, however, for the *Gran Mass* is an elaborate setting for four soloists, four-voice choir (often divided into eight parts), large orchestra, and organ, that requires well over an hour to perform. The Mass is first of all characterized by the use of theme transformation—the device that Liszt employed so consistently in his symphonies and symphonic poems. Several themes recur in various movements, suitably altered in melodic shape, tempo, and harmony to conform to the corresponding texts. Three such themes are given in Example 58; out of them

EXAMPLE 58   Liszt, *Gran Mass*

Liszt derives much of the Mass's vocal, choral, and orchestral material. The themes themselves, or motives derived from them, reappear in later movements to provide an element of unity—the theme of Example 58b appearing in all movements after the Kyrie, for example. Most often, however, they are developed or transformed primarily in the orchestra; the vocal lines are generally treated chordally in a rich variety of harmonies.

Appropriate sections of the text—the middle section of the Gloria (*Propter magnum gloriam tuam*) and the Credo (*Judicare vivos et mortuos*)—are set elaborately with tumultuous fanfares and brilliant orchestral passagework in the style made familiar by Berlioz in his Requiem Mass some years earlier (see below). Other passages are of the utmost refinement and delicacy, notably the Benedictus. The whole, with its many changes of meter and tempo, its wide-ranging harmonies, and its sharp contrasts of style and tone, represents a highly dramatic and subjective approach to the liturgical text.

In 1865 Liszt composed a third Mass, the *Missa choralis*, this time in conformity with the principles of the Cecilians. (A fourth Mass, the *Krönungsmesse* [*Corona-*

tion Mass] of 1867, using a mixture of plainsong and themes with a Hungarian cast, has not survived.) The *Missa choralis* is for four-voice choir, with an organ accompaniment that can be omitted, for it does no more than double the voice parts. The term "choralis" refers to the use of plainsong (compare the German *einstimmiger Chorgesang*, which is equivalent to the English "Gregorian chant"); and Liszt either derived his themes from chant melodies or else composed them in the style of the earlier repertoire. In several cases, notably in the Credo at the words *credo* and *et resurrexit*, he used the melody with which Bach had introduced the Credo of his B minor Mass. In developing and harmonizing the themes, however, Liszt used the harmonic materials of his own time. Diminished chords, harmonic sequences, and remote modulations animate his harmonies; the result is a mixture of styles far removed from Liszt's characteristic manner.

Requiem Mass

From the period of the French Revolution and for a decade or two thereafter (about 1789 to 1810) music in France began to be afflicted with a kind of megalomania. Under the influence of patriotic fervor, minor poets turned to the writing of hymns to the people, odes to liberty, and other texts on timely topics; composers of equal stature set these texts in an elaborate manner with massed choirs and large orchestras augmented by military bands—music full of grandiose effects and empty pomp. The style soon decayed and a degree of aesthetic judgment returned, but echoes of the style were still current in the time of Hector Berlioz (1803–1869) and most likely had considerable influence on him. Berlioz possessed a vivid imagination, an unmatched sense for instrumental writing and orchestral color, an abiding interest in composing works that required many performers, and a characteristically unconstricted approach to traditional musical forms. Consequently, as we shall see, several of his larger works for voices do not fall easily into the conventional categories.

The work with which we are concerned at the moment, the *Grande Messe des Morts* or Requiem Mass, falls more closely into the traditional category in spite of its size. Composed in 1837, it is set for tenor soloist, choir of sopranos, tenors, and basses often divided into six parts (requiring altos only for two short passages in the Sanctus), and a large orchestra augmented by four separate brass bands. The text of the Requiem Mass is here set in ten movements; as seemed customary in the Romantic period, however, verses or stanzas are often recapitulated or repeated out of context and out of proper order—presumably to round out the musical forms of the respective sections. This treatment is sometimes accompanied by the repeated use of the same musical material; for example, two extended passages in the Agnus Dei (meas. 13–38 and 85–173) repeat the music first heard in the *Hostias* (meas. 1–21) and Introit (meas. 83–171)—with only such changes in the rhythmic figures as the respective texts require, and with a few changes in the distribution of the voice parts.

In most respects the Requiem is a work of great delicacy and refinement.

Particularly noteworthy are No. 1, the Introit and Kyrie; No. 3, *Quid sum miser;* No. 5, the unaccompanied six-voice *Quarens me;* No. 7, the Offertory; No. 8, *Hostias;* and portions of No. 10, the Agnus Dei. The Offertory is distinguished in particular by the economy of its melodic line; except for its last few cadential measures, this three-part chorus in octaves reiterates a two-note phrase, alternating A's and B flats, below which the orchestra spins a web of fugal writing.

The remaining numbers, however, give the work its reputation as a spectacular and monumentally dramatic composition. On the music for such phrases as *Tuba mirum, Judex ergo, Rex tremendae majestatis,* and *Lacrimosa dies illa,* Berlioz loosed his imagination, his tremendous gift for dramatic orchestral writing, and his penchant for large instrumental groups. The results are some of the most programmatic and gripping moments in all choral writing, moments that served as a model for later composers of the Requiem text (particularly Verdi, as we shall see in Chapter 10).

Berlioz's choral writing is essentially chordal; entire passages are based on

Leopold Damrosch conducting a performance of the Berlioz *Requiem* in the Seventh Regiment Armory in New York, 1881. Drawing by T. De Thulstrup.

EXAMPLE 59   Berlioz, *Requiem*

(Orch. omitted)

blocks of chords (see Example 59a), occasionally with an imitative or freely moving additional voice (Example 59b). Imitative writing, except in such passages, is relatively rare, and fugal writing occurs only in the Offertory and the *Hosanna*. In much of the work the main weight is given to the orchestra; symphonic textures with a wealth of involved figurations, many fanfares, solid blocks of overwhelming sonority, and Berlioz's mastery of orchestral color are everywhere apparent. Although a mixture of styles characterizes the work, an important element of unity is provided by its prevailing tone of melancholy balanced by hope, a tone that is present in even the more spectacular passages. The whole is one of Berlioz's great accomplishments, and it remains a masterpiece of dramatic writing.

Oratorio

As we have noted, the ever-growing strength of the Romantic movement was most apparent in instrumental music and opera. Several consequences of this shift of interest are reflected in the choral music of the mid-nineteenth century: some minor composers sought to remain within the confines of Classical style by setting choral texts with traditional or restrained orchestral accompaniments; others introduced elements of Romantic feeling into styles that departed only slightly from the Classical; and still others applied the vigor of their Romantic imaginations to the choral field and wrote compositions that bear little relationship to the earlier forms. Thus the period with which this chapter is concerned saw the emergence of a variety of old-fashioned works that have vanished from the repertoire (including those of such composers as Ludwig Spohr and Carl Loewe), along with hybrids that do not lend themselves to easy classification.

Mendelssohn

Among the first nineteenth-century oratorios worthy to be ranked with the great works of Haydn are the two composed by Felix Mendelssohn (1809–1847): *Paulus* (*St. Paul*) and *Elias* (*Elijah*); a third, *Christus*, remained incomplete at Mendelssohn's death. In his highly successful career as pianist, conductor, composer, administrator, and respected amateur of painting and literature, Mendelssohn was of great influence on his time. Traveling widely to many parts of Europe, he enjoyed the respect and friendship of cultural leaders everywhere, and his music was genuinely popular. His high standards and keen critical sense were applied to every segment of the musical world, and he was a major force in elevating the music of Bach to the high place it now holds.

Mendelssohn's first oratorio, *St. Paul*, was composed between 1832 and 1836. For three soloists, four-voice choir occasionally divided into eight, and large orchestra including organ, it is set in traditional manner in two parts and consists of 45 numbers of which about one-third are for choir. A large overture based on the chorale *Wachet auf!* (*Sleepers, Wake!*) begins the work; thereafter, in accordance with the biblical text, the music ranges from stormy and warlike to quiet and reposeful. Particularly noteworthy is the sequence of numbers (Nos. 12 to 21) in which the transformation of the intolerant Saul into the healing missionary Paul is depicted. Saul's vengeful spirit is expressed in a forceful aria based on angular melodic lines, "Consume Them All, Lord Sabaoth!" (see Example 60); this is followed by the quiet arioso, "But the Lord Is Mindful of His Own." The Voice of the Lord is then heard in a short chorus set in chordal style—quite in the fashion of the old Passion; and after an intervening triumphant chorus, a reflective chorale again on the text of *Sleepers, Wake!* continues the sequence of Paul's transformation. At its first performance (Düsseldorf, 1836) more than five hundred singers and instrumentalists took part, and the work was widely acclaimed. Many performances in Britain, Germany, and elsewhere took place in succeeding years, adding to Mendelssohn's reputation as one of the foremost composers of the time.

Next, Mendelssohn considered several oratorio texts, hoping to follow up the success of *St. Paul*, and finally settled on the story of Elijah, which he composed originally in German, although we invariably hear it in its English translation. Work proceeded steadily to about 1845, in spite of a host of professional engagements and administrative duties, and in 1846 *Elijah* was given its first performance in Birmingham. One of Mendelssohn's greatest achievements, it has remained among his most beloved works.

Elijah is composed for four soloists, a four-voice choir requiring several incidental solo singers, and orchestra. As in several of the forgotten oratorios of Carl Loewe (1796–1869), the work begins with a brief introduction in which the voice of Elijah is heard; then follow the overture itself and 43 vocal numbers. One of the outstanding features of the oratorio is the variety of forms and textures Mendelssohn employed to achieve his expressive purposes. Choruses, recitatives, and solo numbers are present in the expected fashion; but the subtle ways in

EXAMPLE 60   Mendelssohn, *St. Paul*

which they are combined and the constant changes of texture—from imitative to chordal, from declamatory to fugal—are evidence of Mendelssohn's great technical skill and creative imagination. An example is No. 16, "O Thou, Who Makest Thine Angels Spirits," which begins with a recitative, progresses to a fast chorus with women's and men's voices presented antiphonally, continues with a long section in counterpoint that terminates in a quasi-chorale passage, and ends with a short recitative and a brief phrase for chorus in unison.

The work is unified by Mendelssohn's mellifluous harmonic style and by the quality of the orchestral accompaniment. Whether fleeting, surging, calming, or overwhelming, the instrumental writing goes far to enhance the dramatic sense of the biblical text. Mendelssohn's ability to mirror in the music the emotional content of the text is here wonderfully revealed, as in the serenity of the trio for women's voices in No. 28, the famous "Lift Thine Eyes." The vocal melodies, too, contribute to the quality of the whole: from the limpid beauty of No. 31, "O Rest in the Lord," to the angular and chromatic No. 17, "Is Not His Word," the arias range widely in expressive type. And finally, two bits of musical reminiscence occur in the orchestra: No. 30, "Arise, Elijah" (meas. 8–10) contains a brief quotation from the accompaniment to No. 26, "It Is Enough" (meas. 46–48); and No. 33, "Night Falleth Around Me" (meas. 8, 9), quotes briefly from No. 1, "Holy, Lord" (meas. 10, 11). In both cases the musical references clarify or strengthen the new text.

Schumann

Oratorios based on secular texts had not been highly successful since the masterworks of Handel had appeared in the decades after 1730—*The Seasons* of Haydn being a notable exception. A century passed before a lasting secular-oratorio tradition was established; *Das Paradies und die Peri* (*Paradise and the Peri*) by Robert Schumann (1810–1856), composed in 1841–43 on a text drawn from *Lalla Rookh* by Thomas Moore was among the first successful nineteenth-century works in the field. The Peri is an angel expelled from Heaven; as a condition of her reinstatement she must descend to earth and return with "Heaven's dearest gift." Twice she fails; on her third attempt she returns with the tears of a repentant sinner and is readmitted amid sounds of angelic jubilation. On this slender story Schumann composed a work for six or eight soloists (the parts are interchangeable), choir, and orchestra.

Adhering to the old tradition, Schumann introduced a part for narrator (tenor soloist) to explain the action and occasionally to comment on it. But unlike the older practice, the narration is seldom set in recitative style. Most often it consists of a series of lyric melodies similar in style to the arias given to the Peri and to the other characters. In fact, lyricism is the predominant feature of the work—a lyricism that allows Schumann to express subtle nuances of feeling, often at the expense of drama. The choruses are largely in chordal style and consist of long passages set in fast-moving harmonies with little rhythmic differentiation between the voices. As in Schumann's art songs, the accompaniments serve to enhance the varied texts in magical fashion.

Berlioz

An abiding interest in dramatic expression marked the music of Hector Berlioz. When conventional forms and traditional techniques of composition stood in the way of that interest, he did not hesitate to abandon his musical heritage and strike out on new paths. In his choral music the result is a series of works that are derived from the forms employed by generations of earlier composers, yet depart widely from them. A case in point is *La Damnation de Faust*, completed in 1846 after many years of planning. Berlioz called the work a "dramatic legend in four parts"; it contains many scenic and stage directions ("The plains of Hungary," "Woods and meadows on the banks of the Elbe"; characters are directed to appear suddenly or to wander about the stage, for example), and it has been called a "concert opera" by some commentators, yet no evidence exists that the composer ever intended the work to be staged. *The Damnation of Faust* is here grouped with the oratorios for convenience and for the reason that it resembles an oratorio in being composed for four soloists, choir, and large orchestra, in its use of recitatives, arias, and choral numbers, and in its performance time, well over two hours.

Almost twenty years earlier, about 1828, Berlioz had composed *Huit scènes de Faust* (*Eight Scenes from Faust*) for soloists, choir, and orchestra as his Op. 1. *The Damnation of Faust* incorporates much of the music of the earlier version, with many additions to Goethe's text that the work of 1828 had lacked. Divided into twenty numbers (most of them consisting of several sections) arranged in four large parts, the work begins with Faust soliloquizing (tenor and orchestra); thereupon a "Peasant's Dance" is heard; the soliloquy is resumed, following which the well-known "Rakoczy March" is played by the orchestra. The second part proceeds similarly: long or short sections for one or another of the chief characters (mainly Mephistopheles and Marguerite) are interrupted or followed by an "Easter Hymn" (choir), a drinking scene (men's choir), a chorus of gnomes and sylphs, a dance of the sylphs (orchestra), and so on. The solo sections are largely of two types: one metrically free, in which the rhythms of the spoken word are mirrored; the other cast in metrical rhythms, with a series of nonrecurring phrases of irregular length moving from one cadence point to another. Only occasionally are formal arias or duets introduced, notably the duet in No. 13 between Marguerite and Faust; the latter offers perhaps the most lyrical moment in the work.

About a dozen sections or numbers are set as choruses. Except in the "Amen Chorus" in No. 6 (a parody set in fugal style), imitation and counterpoint are rarely used. Berlioz most often composes in chordal style or employs alternating pairs of voices in thirds or sixths. But whatever the setting, whether for choir or solo voices, the intensity and variety of the orchestral accompaniments are unfailing. Making virtuosic demands on the instrumentalists, writing with a keen sense for orchestral color, Berlioz here rises to the heights. Brilliance, delicacy, and overwhelming power are evoked by the work's orchestral sections—notably the "Rakoczy March" mentioned above, the "Dance of the Sylphs" (in No. 7), the "Minuet of the Will-of-the-Wisps" (in No. 12), and the "Ride to the Abyss" (in No. 19) which, although it contains a few vocal passages, is essentially an orchestral tour de force with few equals. *The Damnation of Faust*, in spite of a few arid pages, is one of the most eloquent as well as the most powerful of Berlioz's works.

Of completely different style and character is another quasi-oratorio by Berlioz, which the composer called a "sacred trilogy": *L'Enfance du Christ* (*The Childhood of Christ*), composed between 1850 and 1854. Berlioz turned his back on spectacular effects and grandiloquent expression and composed a work that is a model of delicacy and restraint. A narrator (tenor), three major soloists and three in minor roles, a choir, and a normal-sized orchestra suffice. The text, prepared by Berlioz himself, is divided into three parts—"Herod's Dream," "The Flight into Egypt," and "The Arrival at Saïs" (a city in Egypt in which the Holy Family found refuge).

Berlioz here sought to write in a naive fashion and to recapture the spirit of antiquity, in keeping with the subject. Melodic lines are sometimes given modal touches, and the recitatives are most often in the style of the seventeenth century. A few dramatic or exotic moments appear in the work—notably "Herod's Dream," composed in an operatic manner, and the "Procession of the Soothsayers," in which a recurring figure in the lower strings is set in 7/4 meter to provide an ominous note (see Example 61a). The great majority of the numbers are intimate in tone, however. Chief among them are a chorus in which shepherds bid farewell to the Holy Family (see Example 61b); a lengthy trio for two flutes and harp, performed for the spiritual refreshment of Mary and Joseph; and the closing unaccompanied recitative and chorus. Throughout the oratorio, the quiet tone of reverence and devotion is maintained.

EXAMPLE 61   Berlioz, *L'Enfance du Christ*

(Tr.: "You must go far from the stable where you were born.")   (Strings double the choral lines)

Liszt

From 1848 to 1861 Liszt served as director of the court music at Weimar, and renewed his interest in choral music. Two large oratorios were begun there and worked on periodically. The first, *Die Legende von der heiligen Elisabeth* (*The Legend of St. Elizabeth*), composed between 1857 and 1862, was planned for the celebrations held in connection with the 800th anniversary of the founding of the Wartburg, a huge fortress near Eisenach. A series of mural paintings, depicting scenes from the life of Elizabeth, was commissioned simultaneously, and the scenes in Liszt's work to some extent parallel those in the paintings. (The oratorio was first performed at Budapest in 1867, however.)

In *St. Elizabeth* Liszt made tentative use of melodic motives derived from folksong, church tunes, and plainsong; such motives are then transformed on occasion to fit the changed contexts. Vocal and choral forces (five soloists, an eight-voice choir, and a large orchestra are required) are used in restrained fashion, most of the expressive variety of the work being carried by the orchestra.

The second of Liszt's oratorios, *Christus*, composed in 1873, asks more of the choir than its predecessor does, as several of the choral numbers are unaccompanied. Liszt made considerable use of plainsong chants in *Christus*, chants that are later elaborated and altered in the choir, and employed as motives in the orchestra. Both *Christus* and *St. Elizabeth* were highly regarded in Liszt's time and were performed repeatedly, *St. Elizabeth* being staged annually in Vienna until about 1916.

Other Works

In earlier chapters we devoted separate sections to Te Deum, Magnificat, and Stabat Mater settings, because composers turned to them so frequently. From the middle of the eighteenth century, however, the total number of such settings declined markedly, and the major composers set them only rarely. In the present section, therefore, such texts are considered together with various other miscellaneous forms.

Te Deum

In 1832, inspired by a visit to Milan, Berlioz tentatively planned an orchestral work designed to commemorate Napoleon Bonaparte's victories in Lombardy and the triumphant return of the French armies to the homeland. The plan was not carried out, but Berlioz's *Te Deum* of 1849 embodied part of the earlier idea and some of the music he had written for it. A massive work resulted, requiring tenor soloist, three choirs, large orchestra, and organ. It is almost an hour in length, contains a rousing "Prelude" (No. 3 in the sequence of eight numbers!), and ends with a military "March for the Presentation of the Colors"—both for orchestra alone.

Berlioz's approach to the 29 stanzas of the traditional Te Deum is subjective in the extreme. The following table gives an outline of his procedure.

Berlioz, *Te Deum*

Movement	*Description*	*Text*
1	Hymn	Stanzas 1 and 2, sometimes alternately, sometimes simultaneously
2	Hymn	Stanzas 3–9, then 3–6, then 10–13, finally 4–6; the music for the three settings of Stanza 6 is similar, that for the other parallel settings is different
3	Prelude	For orchestra alone
4	Prayer	Stanzas 26 and 27, with portions of Stanza 21 inserted on an irregular basis
5	Hymn	Stanzas 14, 15, and 17 in various combinations; then Stanza 16 in an extended passage followed by Stanza 18; finally Stanzas 14, 15, and 18, with a setting of Stanza 14 to end
6	Prayer	Stanza 20, followed by Stanza 28
7	Hymn and Prayer	Stanzas 19 and 29, then Stanzas 22, 24, and 25 (Stanza 23 is not set); followed by Stanzas 19 and 24 simultaneously; finally Stanza 29 with phrases from 19 and 22 occasionally inserted
8	March	For orchestra alone

The three choirs are composed of soprano, tenor, and bass; alto, tenor, and bass; and soprano and alto (that is, a children's choir). Occasionally when two text stanzas are set simultaneously, as in No. 1, each of the two main choirs is assigned one text. In general, however, the various text stanzas or verses are distributed freely between the six voices of the first two choirs. The role of the third choir is somewhat restricted; in fact, Berlioz's note in the score indicates that that choir may be omitted, "although it greatly enhances the effect." It is employed only in the first, second, and seventh movements, most often in unison, and serves mainly to add yet another vocal color to the tonal mass. The choral writing is usually in chordal style, and the blocks of tone are often used antiphonally. Contrapuntal writing, a stylistic feature of the work, is especially prominent in No. 4, which is a delicate and restrained movement.

The variety of color Berlioz achieves in his purely instrumental compositions is present in the *Te Deum* in even greater measure, for the several vocal lines are contrasted or combined in unusual ways: tenors of the first choir with basses of the second and sopranos of the third, for example. And the rhythmic vitality of the climactic passages coupled with the sheer volume of sound produced by the orchestra and three choirs performing together is overwhelming. The *Te Deum* is a theater or concert work of the finest quality, suitable for festivals or commemorative occasions; its appropriateness as a church work is not relevant, for Berlioz was influenced by patriotic rather than religious motives.

Choral Symphony

Berlioz was a fervid admirer of Beethoven and was particularly receptive to the innovation of his Symphony No. 9. Embodying a choir in a symphony, as Beethoven had done, opened a whole new world of expressive possibilities to Berlioz. In typical fashion, however, he expanded on Beethoven's plan and conceived of a complete interpenetration of orchestral and vocal forces. The first result was *Roméo et Juliette*, a "dramatic symphony" (the composer's term) for three soloists, large orchestra, and choral forces that are divided at various times into five different groupings: semichoir of alto, tenor, and bass; two choirs each consisting of tenor and bass; and two choirs each of first and second soprano, tenor, and bass. Only in the final section of the work are as many as three groups used simultaneously, however. The composition was begun, completed, and performed in 1839, but was subsequently revised twice, in 1847 and again in 1857.

In its final form, *Roméo et Juliette* is divided into four large movements that correspond loosely to the four movements of a symphony. The first movement consists of an orchestral introduction, a choral prologue in several sections, and a scherzetto for voices and small orchestra. The entire story is sketched in narrative form in this first movement, predominantly in unaccompanied choral recitative; a few melodic bits, destined to form the main themes of the Ball and the Love Scene in subsequent movements, are also introduced here. With the dramatic outline and part of the forthcoming musical material having been thus presented, the way is prepared for the tone pictures that follow.

The second movement, for orchestra alone, begins slowly, its emotional content clearly suggested by the composer's heading: "Romeo alone; melancholy; concert and ball; grand festival at the house of the Capulets." In the third movement one hears a few phrases from the double choir of men's voices in the distance: the ball is over and the dancers are homeward bound. The rest of the movement, an eloquent orchestral piece, represents the love scene between Romeo and Juliet. The fourth movement is in several sections, beginning with the "Queen Mab" scherzo for orchestra alone. Then follow Juliet's cortege (orchestra and choir), Romeo at the tomb of Juliet (orchestra alone), and a finale of several sections, in which Friar Laurence's admonition to the Montagues and Capulets is prominent.

Thus the vocal sections are concentrated in the first and last movements of the symphony. In them the various parts—solo recitatives, choral declamations, antiphonal choral passages, etc.—are connected or intertwined so that a constant change of vocal color takes place. The writing for voices, whether solo or choral, is characterized in general by static melodic lines with many repeated tones on the same or adjacent pitches; only one or two extended passages assume an expressive lyric contour. Lyric melodies appear more often in the orchestral accompaniments or in the orchestral sections themselves—one of the finest of them the love scene that occupies much of the third movement. As in the majority of Berlioz's works, instrumental and choral alike, the variety of rhythmic treatment and instrumental color is among the outstandingly attractive features of *Roméo et Juliette.*

Among numerous other works in which choral writing is added to a symphonic framework, Mendelssohn's enjoyable *Lobgesang* (*Hymn of Praise*) must be mentioned. Called variously his Symphony No. 2, a symphony-cantata, or a sacred cantata, it was composed in 1840 as part of the celebration commemorating the 400th anniversary of the invention of printing. This work, unlike Berlioz's *Roméo et Juliette,* contains three connected movements (Maestoso-Allegro, Allegretto, Adagio) for orchestra alone, all the vocal writing being confined to the fourth movement. Its structure is that of a short symphony with a choral finale. Preceded by a fanfarelike introduction based on a chorale melody that occurs in several portions of the finale, the first movement is a standard sonata-form in Mendelssohn's most cheerful vein. The second movement, connected to the first but with return of the introductory material briefly intervening, is a fleet and charming piece in the general style of a scherzo, followed by the eloquent slow third movement with considerable figuration in the midst of soaring melodies.

The fourth movement, bearing the subtitle Cantata, constitutes the major part of the work. Divided into ten numbers (mostly connected), seven of which are choruses, it is scored for tenor and two soprano soloists, four-voice choir, and orchestra. A variety of vocal color is assured by frequent extended solo passages preceding or inserted in the choral numbers, and by both a chorale and a chorus in No. 8. As in virtually all Mendelssohn's choral works, contrapuntal texture is the most usual: imitation, free counterpoint, and fugal writing are present in abundance. Apart from a thematic connection to the first movement, the choral finale has nothing in common with the orchestral movements, rising far above them in expressiveness and intensity.

About 1854 Franz Liszt composed a program symphony based on the drama of Faust, in three movements titled "Faust," "Gretchen," (Marguerite), and "Mephistopheles." The original ending implied the triumph of the diabolical forces over idealism and love, which was contrary to Liszt's intention; in 1857, therefore, he added an epilogue for tenor soloist and men's choir. The text, from the final lines of Goethe's *Faust*, establishes the idea of redemption, and Faust is saved. The choral section is brief, composed in simple style—at first in unison and only later in chordal style—and eloquent in its appeal. The *Faust Symphony* is a monument to Liszt's idealism.

A somewhat similar work is Liszt's two-movement *Symphony to Dante's Divina Commedia*, composed in 1855–56. Here the program is based on the love of Paolo and Francesca, their damnation, and their eventual repentance. Again the choir—this time women's voices—performs the concluding section of the second movement, on the text of the Magnificat. Basically in two-part contrapuntal style and suggesting a vision of Heaven, the choral epilogue is serenely hopeful; again, as in the *Faust Symphony*, good has triumphed over evil.

10

Late Romantic Music
1860–1900

The last several chapters have indicated—often only by implication—that choral music was ever more influenced by orchestral music and the opera. The presence of choral movements in symphonies, of dramatic recitative and extreme emotions in oratorios, and of symphonic textures in many choral works of all types is representative of that trend. In the late nineteenth century, the use of operatic devices in choral music declined to a considerable extent, but the interpenetration of symphonic and choral styles became much deeper.

Virtually all the major composers of large choral works in the period after about 1860—Verdi and Fauré excepted—were first and foremost composers of instrumental music. It seems likely that such composers were more attracted to what may be called "instrumental thinking" than to its vocal counterpart—that the manipulation of musical material and the construction of large formal patterns were more important to them than the desire simply to set a text for voices and provide an adequate accompaniment. Thus in the works to be discussed in this chapter, the orchestral background to the textual setting becomes increasingly important in the total effect.

Mass

Bruckner

The Roman Catholic tradition in Austria found its most notable exponent in Anton Bruckner (1824–1896). After several years as a schoolteacher in various

164

Austrian towns, he received an appointment as organist at the Linz Cathedral in 1856. Twelve years later he moved to Vienna as teacher of organ and music theory at the Vienna Conservatory, where he remained until his retirement in 1891. He made concert tours to France, England, and Germany as an organist and was widely respected for the quality of his improvisations. Although he began composing in his thirteenth year and wrote a large number of works in the following decades, his first major work, a Mass in D minor, was not completed until 1864, when he was forty years old. It and two other Masses (E minor, 1866; F minor, 1867), a *Te Deum* (1881–83), and a setting of Psalm CL (150) (1892) are his principal contributions to the literature. Some fifty additional works on sacred texts and about as many more secular works for voices also exist.

The D minor Mass (a misnomer, as D major is the prevailing key in most of the movements) is set for four soloists, four-voice choir, and orchestra; the solo voices are not given extended arias, however, but are confined to relatively short phrases emerging out of the choral texture. Fugal writing is restricted largely to the *Amen* at the end of the Gloria, and several imitative passages occur at intervals throughout the Mass; in general, however, the writing is chordal, and long melodies are seldom found. In overall form the Mass looks to the past, with each of the movements a connected whole not divided into sections as in the eighteenth-century cantata Mass (Bach's B minor Mass had been divided into 25 sections, it may be recalled). And in conformity with liturgical requirements often neglected by Classical composers, the choral part of the Gloria begins with the second phrase, *Et in terra pax*, and the Credo similarly with *Patrem omni-potentem*—the first phrases being reserved for the Gregorian intonation sung by the officiating priest. Except in a few passages, text repetition is generally absent, each phrase being set but once.

In other respects, the Mass represents the music of Bruckner's own time. His affinity to the music of Richard Wagner is clearly seen in his use of leading motives, quite in the style of Wagner's music dramas. As in the Masses of Liszt, several such motives introduced early in the Mass appear occasionally in later movements, thus providing a cyclical form (see Example 62 for representative

EXAMPLE 62   Bruckner, *D minor Mass*, Kyrie

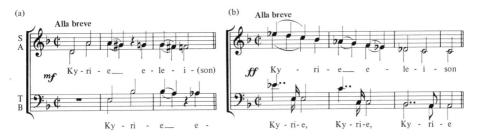

motives). Bruckner's harmonies are wide-ranging, and they modulate freely, often chromatically; indeed, chromatic melodic lines are common and give the composer ample opportunity to inflect the harmonies accordingly. Two further characteristics of Bruckner's style may be noted: the use of octave leaps in the melodic lines (see Examples 62b and 63); and the continuous rise and fall of the dynamic levels. Such elements, together with a fluid, colorful, and ever-changing orchestral accompaniment, contribute to the individuality of the D minor Mass among Bruckner's major works.

EXAMPLE 63   Bruckner, *D minor Mass*, Credo

The second Mass (1866), in E minor, is of completely different character. Here an eight-voice choir without soloists is accompanied by a wind band consisting of pairs of oboes, clarinets, bassoons, and trumpets, four horns, and three trombones. In many passages the voices sing alone, in others the wind parts double the choral lines, and in yet others the winds provide rhythmic pulsations under the choral writing; only in a few passages do the instruments have a thematic life of their own. The choir is used in various ways: sometimes divided between four men's and four women's voices, as in the opening of the Kyrie; at other times condensed into a four-voice group, either in chords or in unison; and at climactic moments rising to full eight-voice sonority.

Many extended imitative or even fugal passages occur—notably in the *Christe eleison*, portions of the Gloria, and the beginning of the Sanctus. In general, however, a chordal texture prevails; melodic lines are harmonically derived rather than lyric, but sometimes suggest plainsong in their contours. And as in the D minor Mass, the first phrases of the Gloria and Credo were not set by the composer—perhaps indicating that the E minor Mass too was designed for liturgical rather than concert use.

At intervals from the spring of 1867 to the fall of 1868, and interrupted by a serious mental breakdown, Bruckner worked at a third Mass. Completed in September, 1868, the Mass in F minor is set for four soloists, four-voice choir, and large orchestra. It is an extended setting, requiring more than an hour in performance time (about double the length of the E minor), and may be counted among those large Masses that are more at home in the concert hall than in the church. Yet it is filled with expressions of Bruckner's steadfast, heartfelt, and childlike religious faith.

The F minor Mass, like its two predecessors, is again cast in six large movements. But here each movement is divided into two or more connected sections (five in the case of the Gloria, eleven in the Credo) marked by changes in meter, tempo, or both. The thematic material in general consists of short phrases derived from melodic or rhythmic motives, often linked in chainlike fashion—notable exceptions being fugue themes in the two longer movements and one extended melody in the Benedictus. The choral texture is predominantly chordal, relieved on occasion by contrapuntal writing; but within that chordal texture Bruckner writes with high regard for changes in color. A single solo voice set against two or three choral voices, alternations between high and low voices, choral parts tightly compressed or widely separated—such devices ensure that a fluid and colorful choral sound is present at all times.

The orchestral writing here reaches symphonic dimensions. Motives different from those given to the choir are often introduced and developed in symphonic fashion. Recurring themes in the various movements give the Mass its unity; themes heard in the Gloria return in the Agnus Dei, for example, and brief recapitulations of earlier sections occur later in the Credo. Further, many ostinato figures (see Example 64) and extended scale passages in the string instruments give the Mass a high degree of rhythmic momentum and add to the power of the climactic moments.

EXAMPLE 64   Bruckner, *Mass in F minor*

With all the variety of harmonic, vocal, and instrumental color, with all the masterful employment of the material, and with all the dynamic and textural changes that characterize this Mass, one expressive feature stands out: the depth and extent of Bruckner's devotion to the Roman Catholic faith. For example, the *Crucifixus* and *Et incarnatus* in the Credo suggest a degree of compassion and involvement not found in more traditional settings. Near the end of the Credo, the fugal *Et vitam venturi saeculi* is interrupted eight times by fortissimo shouts on the word *Credo!,* and the movement itself ends with another such statement. A similarly dramatic affirmation of a composer's personal faith would be difficult to find elsewhere in the literature.

Requiem Mass

Verdi

Shortly after the death of Rossini in 1868, Giuseppe Verdi (1813–1901) proposed that several prominent Italian composers collaborate on a Requiem Mass in honor of Rossini, to be performed in Bologna. Verdi, at the height of his powers as perhaps the foremost opera composer of the century, contributed a setting of the Responsory, *Libera me.* The plan encountered administrative difficulties and was subsequently dropped.

In 1873 Alessandro Manzoni, one of Italy's outstanding novelists, died. Verdi, who had greatly respected the writer, composed a Requiem in his memory which included the Responsory he had written four years earlier. Scored for four soloists, four-voice choir (divided into eight in a few passages), and large orchestra, the *Manzoni Requiem* was first performed in 1874 and has kept a high place as one of the most dramatic and heartfelt settings in the literature. Several sections of the Sequence, *Dies irae*, are unmatched in expressing the terrors of the Last Judgment, and two or three of the solo arias are frankly operatic. These sections have incurred the occasional charge that the *Manzoni Requiem* is a sacrilegious treatment of the liturgical text, that it is an opera in ecclesiastical dress. Such charges, based on only a few spectacular passages, overlook the deep religious faith that underlies the work as a whole.

The Introit (*Requiem aeternam*), restrained and reverent, is in a symmetrical form (diagrammed A[ab]BA[ab]) with the middle part for choir unaccompanied. It leads without a break into the Kyrie, which is set for solo voices and choir in imitative style; a phrase first given to the soloists is then sung by the choir in halved note-values (see Examples 65a and b). The text phrases are intertwined, and the movement ends quietly.

EXAMPLE 65   Verdi, *Requiem*

With the greatest possible contrast the Sequence *Dies irae* follows. It is set as one large movement with thirteen connected sections, which differ greatly in tonality, tempo, and emotional content, the settings expressing in turn terror, majesty, supplication, and tenderness—all reflecting Verdi's deep personal involvement with the text. The musical treatment ranges from the serene *Recordare pie Jesu* (Stanza 9) through the powerful *Tuba mirum* (Stanza 3) with its imposing fanfare in the orchestra (probably suggested by Berlioz's similar treatment of that stanza in his setting), to the agonizing cries of *Dies irae* over tumultuous accompaniment (Stanza 1, twice recapitulated in Sections 5 and 11). But again the ending is quiet and trustful in tone.

The Offertory, *Domine Jesu*, is set in imitative texture as a five-part sectional and symmetrical movement for the four soloists, the form being diagrammed as ABCBA with three contrasting tempos. The prayerful tone that animates the text of the Offertory is wonderfully expressed in Verdi's flowing melodies and subdued orchestral accompaniment.

With the Sanctus, set for double choir in fugal style (see Example 66a), the tone changes to one of praise to God; again the music is in perfect accord, and an air of jubilation is suggested in the *Hosanna*, on the same theme (Example 66b). The Benedictus that follows employs a second modification of the theme, this time in the relative minor (Example 66c), but the treatment is imitative rather

EXAMPLE 66   Verdi, *Requiem*

(a) Allegro

San - ctus, San - ctus, San - ctus, Do - mi - nus De - us___ Sa - ba - oth

(b) Allegro

Ho - sa - na in ex - cel - sis, in ex - cel - sis

(c) Allegro

Be - ne - di - ctus qui ve - nit in no - (mine)

(d) Allegro risoluto

Li - be - ra me, Do - mi - ne, de mor - te ae - ter - na___

than fugal. The repetition of the *Hosanna* text at the end of the Benedictus departs from traditional treatment by being unlike the first *Hosanna*, in that it is set chordally, with antiphonal passages for the soloists and choir.

The Agnus Dei reveals a unique pattern in its three presentations of the text phrase. The first, in C major, is for soprano and mezzo-soprano soloists, in octaves and unaccompanied; the choir repeats that section, again in octaves but supported by a few instruments. The second phrase is virtually identical with the first, except that it is in C minor and is accompanied; in the harmonized choral refrain, only the last half is repeated and the accompaniment is a bit heavier. The third phrase, again for soloists and in C major, is followed by the choral refrain; but now the soloists add their voices to the choir and the accompaniment grows in complexity. After a few cadential measures, this reverent piece ends softly.

Then follows the Communion, *Lux aeterna*, set for three soloists. In part unaccompanied in contrapuntal texture, in part in a quasi-parlando style, and in part based on lyric melodies over a pulsating accompaniment, the movement expresses resignation and faith in magical fashion.

The final movement is the Responsory, part of the Absolution that concludes the burial service, on the text beginning *Libera me, Domine*. Set for soprano soloist and choir, it begins with a passage in which first the soloist and then the choir present a phrase in parlando fashion—on one pitch and without meter; the effect is one of awe. A moving arioso for soprano deepens the awe and suggests fear of the Last Judgment. At this point the Responsory text refers back to the Sequence, but on the text *Dies illa, dies irae, calamitatis et miseriae*. Verdi consequently recapitulates the music that accompanied the beginning of the Sequence, but the passage ends on a note of repose and leads directly into a return of the music of the Introit, now elaborated and sung without accompaniment. Then follows a fugal section on the text *Libera me* and on a theme derived by inversion from the fugal theme of the Sanctus (see Example 66d, and compare 66a–c). And finally, on a descending motive used sequentially in the orchestra and reminiscent of the motive with which the Introit began, and with a brief return of the parlando phrase in the soprano solo, the movement ends quietly.

This description of the *Manzoni Requiem* cannot do justice to its expressiveness, its eloquent melodies, and its wealth of musical inventiveness—all dedicated to setting the sacred text in appropriate fashion. Overwhelming power in some passages is balanced by the utmost delicacy and refinement in others, as the emotional content of the text suggests. The music at times approaches the programmatic, but Verdi's solution of the problems set by the text is profound.

Fauré

Of completely different style is the Requiem Mass composed by Gabriel Fauré (1845–1924) in 1887, dedicated to the memory of his father. Fauré's career as organist and teacher was centered primarily in Paris. While he enjoyed the respect of the relatively few who knew his music, he did not become a widely known composer outside France. Restraint and subtlety mark his music, as reticence and discretion marked his personal life. Yet Fauré's harmonic originality and resourcefulness assure him a modest place among the important composers of the late nineteenth century.

His setting of the Requiem Mass is composed for soprano and baritone soloists, four-voice choir, organ, and a small orchestra that includes harp but no oboes and relegates the violins to a decidedly minor role. They are not used in the first movement, appear only occasionally in later movements and then in unison or octaves with the divided violas, and are given only a few measures of what can be considered independent melody. As a consequence, a subdued and limited orchestral color is characteristic throughout the work.

The Introit and Kyrie are combined into one almost entirely chordal movement, with the orchestra mostly in unison—or at the most in three-part harmony. And a major contrasting event in this movement is a long passage for the choral tenors accompanied only by cellos and organ. The traditional second movement, on the text *Dies irae*, which looms so large in the Mozart, Berlioz, and Verdi settings, was not set by Fauré—possibly because he was unwilling or unable to write in the grandiose manner the text demands, a manner very foreign to the rest of the work.

The Offertory that follows is cast in a three-part form: choir without sopranos in the first part, an extended baritone solo (on the text *Hostias*) in the second, and an enlarged recapitulation of the beginning section—but now with sopranos added—in the third. The Sanctus, as third movement, is lightly scored for choir, sopranos alternating with men's voices in a series of restrained phrases; the altos sing only a single word, *Sanctus*, near the end of the movement, and the prevailing pianissimo is only once raised to a fortissimo on the phrase *Hosanna in excelsis*.

Gabriel Fauré, 1845–1924.

At this point, as the fourth movement, Fauré wrote a soprano solo on the text *Pie Jesu Domine*—the text taken from the last line of the Sequence. Accompanied by the organ (and with strings doubling the organ after the first two phrases), the solo voice sings the prayer of supplication simply and unpretentiously. The fifth movement combines the Agnus Dei and the Communion (*Lux aeterna*); since the text of the latter includes the phrase *Requiem aeternam*, Fauré is enabled to return briefly, near the end of the movement, to the music with which the work began.

The sixth movement, *Libera me*, forms the Responsory sung after the Absolution, and is here set for baritone soloist and choir. Briefly on the phrase *Dies irae* the terrors of the Last Judgment are suggested in a short section; but even here, in an agitated fortissimo passage, Fauré does not employ the full orchestra—omitting the woodwinds, harp, and timpani. The movement ends with a return of the first section, *Libera me*, now sung softly by the choir in octaves. For the final (seventh) movement, Fauré chose to set the text *In paradisum*, which in the liturgy constitutes the antiphon sung at the grave after the Absolution. A long eloquent melody is sung by the sopranos of the choir; near the end a few short phrases for the other voices are added, to bring the work to a quiet close.

The above description may reveal to what extent restraint and outward simplicity characterize the Fauré *Requiem*. It cannot, however, disclose the harmonic subtlety, expressive variety, and sheer beauty the work contains in full measure; adequate examples of the treatment would necessarily include entire pages of this clear and transparent score. Modulations to the mediant and submediant, root progressions up or down a whole step, some chromatic modulation—such devices form the basis of Fauré's harmonic practices. But they are employed with such imagination, coupled with melodies that are themselves harmonically derived, and appear in such varied contexts, that they add an expressive element of rare charm. Analysis alone is not enough to disclose the musical uniqueness of this setting; the work must be heard, and heard repeatedly, before its full quality can be appreciated.

Dvořák

Antonin Dvořák (1841–1904), perhaps the most important Czech composer of the nineteenth century, was active as a professional violist in Prague at the outset of his career, and as a teacher from about 1873 to his death—including three years as director of a conservatory in New York. Known principally for his many orchestral and chamber works, he also composed a *Stabat Mater*, a Requiem Mass, and many other large and small choral works.

The *Requiem* (1890), for four soloists, four-voice choir, and large orchestra, was composed as a kind of companion piece to his *Stabat Mater* (see below). It is a large and powerful setting, almost half again as long as Verdi's; it differs also in that Dvořák, with his vast experience as an instrumental composer, applied symphonic techniques to the music.

In the traditional manner, Dvořák combined the Introit and Kyrie in one large movement. He then departed from tradition, however, by inserting a setting of the Gradual (*Requiem aeternam*) as the second movement and, in the third, repeating many stanzas of the Sequence—sometimes out of their liturgical order.

It is likely that considerations of musical form took precedence over the liturgy in Dvořák's mind. Symphonic thinking is evident in his use of leading motives that are transformed and developed in many of the movements (see Examples 67a–c for the principal recurring motives). Further, other figures are used as bassi ostinati across extended sections (Examples 67d and e), above which a rich texture of melodic passages adds strength and independence to the orchestral accompaniment.

EXAMPLE 67   Dvořák, *Requiem*

The choral textures vary from simple chordal passages to large fugues, and Dvořák's mastery of vocal color is everywhere apparent. The solo passages reflect his sensitivity to textual nuances and his gift for lyric melody, one of his outstanding characteristics. Such elements, combined with a full-scale orchestral accompaniment that both supports and enhances the choral writing, result in a work that is powerful, expressive, and wonderfully moving.

A German Requiem

All the Requiem Masses mentioned up to this point have been settings of the Roman Catholic *Missa pro defunctis* (Mass for the Dead), and have more or less adhered to the liturgical form of that service. As such they commemorate the souls of the dead and offer prayers on their behalf. But the Requiem by Johannes Brahms has the implicit intention of providing consolation for the living. Named *Ein deutsches Requiem* (*A German Requiem*) by the composer, it grows out of the Protestant tradition and is unrelated to the Roman Catholic liturgy.

Brahms (1833–1897), born in Hamburg but associated primarily with Vienna during much of his professional life, owes his position as one of the great masters largely to his many instrumental compositions. But his music for voices is of equal importance; it includes a half-dozen large choral works, some sixty smaller ones, about two hundred songs, and many miscellaneous vocal works. Of these, the *Deutsches Requiem,* composed between 1857 and 1868, stands in the front rank.

The Requiem, in seven movements, is written for soprano and baritone soloists, four-voice choir, and standard orchestra. The text, selected by Brahms himself from Luther's German version of the Old and New Testaments, is skillfully arranged to show the composer's expressive intention. Its direction may be seen in the following selection of key phrases:

> Blessed are they that mourn, for they shall have comfort
> The righteous are in the hand of God
> How lovely is Thy dwelling place, O Lord
> Blessed are they that dwell within Thy house
> Ye are now sorrowful. . . . Yea, I will comfort you as one whom his own mother
>   comforteth
> Here on earth we have no resting place
> We shall all be changed at the sound of the trumpet
> Death shall be swallowed up in victory
> Worthy art Thou to be praised
> Blessed are the dead which die in the Lord

With a complete absence of sentimentality, Brahms succeeds in expressing comfort, suggesting the joys of Paradise, showing his faith in the righteousness of God, and imbuing the whole with an aura of acceptance and contentment. Strength and tenderness are present in equal measure, carried by eloquent melodies and rigorous counterpoint alike. Making full use of the expressive possibilities of thematic development and fugal writing, Brahms composed a work that is both tightly constructed and, above all, outstandingly lyrical.

Several of the movements are symmetrical within themselves, notably the first, fifth, and seventh. The third and sixth, namely those set for baritone soloist with the choir, contain large recapitulated sections but end with fugues, hence are not symmetrical. And the seventh, further, contains thematic material from the first movement, thus may be considered as contributing to the work's overall symmetry.

The choral treatment varies as the text requires. From unison or chordal writing through passages in tight imitation (see Examples 68a and b) to fully developed fugues, the ever-changing textures provide Brahms with the means of expressing every shade of textual meaning and emotional significance. The rich orchestral writing is similarly sensitive, with its symphonic development of themes and its expressive range from somberness to brilliance.

EXAMPLE 68   Brahms, *Ein deutsches Requiem*

(Tr.: "But yet the Lord's word endureth."
"The redeemed of the Lord.")

Oratorio

An increasing interest in choral singing on the part of musical amateurs had marked the late eighteenth and early nineteenth centuries—possibly the result of a growing attitude of secularism and of improved economic conditions among people of the middle class. That interest was particularly strong in countries where the Protestant faith flourished, notably in northern Germany and England but to a lesser degree elsewhere as well. To further that interest, many choral societies were formed in cities and towns alike, and composers of all levels of ability wrote large and small works to supply their needs. In time, many of these groups established choral festivals, commissioning composers to write for them and often offering prizes on a competitive basis.

Oratorios and cantatas were especially favored in such festivals, and many of these works were therefore composed. Among composers prominently represented in that literature, several names may be mentioned: the French Charles Gounod (1818–1893) and Camille Saint-Saëns (1835–1921); the Franco-Belgian César Franck (1822–1890); the German Max Bruch (1838–1920); the Irish Charles Villiers Stanford (1852–1924); and the English John Stainer (1840–1901) and

Charles Hubert Parry (1848–1918). Although their choral music was competent and individualistic, and many of their works enjoyed repeated performances in their time, virtually none of them have survived to the present day.

Elgar

One oratorio rose above this mass of music by virtue of its beauty, dramatic strength, and sincerity: *The Dream of Gerontius,* composed in 1900 by Sir Edward Elgar (1857–1934). It is set for mezzo-soprano, tenor, and bass soloists, four-voice choir (sometimes set as a semichoir, at other times divided into eight voices), and large orchestra. The text, by John Cardinal Newman, is concerned with Gerontius on the point of death and fearful of the Last Judgment, receiving the last rites of the Catholic Church, being led by his guardian angel past the demons of hell and the trials of Purgatory, and left awaiting salvation. Elgar, as a devout Roman Catholic, proved himself equal to the task of expressing the doubts, terrors, hope, and faith inherent in the text.

The work is constructed in two large parts, each consisting of several connected sections that generally contrast in mood, meter, tonality, and setting. Elgar's chief organizing principles are those of Wagner: the breakdown of the traditional division between recitative and aria, the use of a type of "endless melody" (see Example 69), and considerable use of leading motives that tend to unify the work. As a consequence, lyric melodies are relatively few; when used, they reveal the

EXAMPLE 69   Elgar, *The Dream of Gerontius*

(Orch. condensed)

composer's fondness for large intervals, melodic sequences, and rhythmic diversity. The orchestral writing, in its flexibility and variety of color, displays Elgar's masterful technique in orchestration. Choral textures, too, reveal his interest in vocal color: full choral sonority gives way to women's voices alone, to men's voices plus a semichoir, to the inner or outer voices heard separately, and so on. And always the poetry of the text is imaginatively reflected in the writing; few works of the period achieved so close a relationship between text and music. Although Elgar composed several other choral works—notably two oratorios, *The Apostles* (1903) and *The Kingdom* (1906), as well as a few cantatas—none compare to *The Dream of Gerontius*.

Parker

In the last quarter of the nineteenth century a group of American-born composers became active in New England, principally in Boston. Several, John Knowles Paine and George Chadwick among them, received much of their training in Germany. Returning to the United States, they brought with them the technical procedures and emotional content of German music and constituted in effect an outpost of late–nineteenth-century German Romanticism. Horatio Parker (1863–1919), a pupil of Chadwick's in Boston, also followed the pattern by studying in Munich; on his return, however, he first became professionally active in New York before moving back to Boston. Simultaneously he became professor of music at Yale University, a position he held until his death.

Of almost three dozen choral works composed by Parker between 1882 and 1919, including oratorios, cantatas, and choral songs, one oratorio composed in 1893 became widely known during the composer's lifetime, was performed several times at British festivals, and became the work for which his name is remembered today. This work, *Hora novissima* (*The Latest Hour*), is set for four soloists, four-voice choir (occasionally altered into two choirs), and orchestra on a Medieval Latin text. Divided into eleven numbers that include arias, ensemble numbers, and choruses, the work reflects Parker's talent for vocal and instrumental color, his excellent contrapuntal training, and his fondness for employing leading motives in the Wagnerian fashion. Parker's vocal lines reveal considerable use of melodic sequences that are often doubled in the orchestra; in his choral passages, imitative and fugal writing are the most usual. Somewhat conservative in form, traditional in treatment, and Brahmsian in flavor, *Hora novissima* nonetheless has a quality of eloquence all its own.

Cantata

The cantata was last discussed in Chapter 7, particularly in connection with the many chorale cantatas of Bach. In the decades after Bach's death (1750) a secular version of the form was often employed for a variety of purposes: to celebrate birthdays of kings or princes, to commemorate military victories, or to mark patriotic festivals. And although eminent names are represented in a list of cantata composers in the period about 1750 to 1825—Haydn and Beethoven among them—the cantata literature of the period is not distinguished by outstanding works.

In the nineteenth century the cantata often resembled an oratorio in all but size and dramatic scope. On a smaller scale, its form was similar to that of the oratorio—a series of recitatives and arias, ensemble numbers, and fugal or homophonic choruses—and it was generally accompanied by an orchestra. Because the cantata's form was so unstandardized, many works of the time were not called cantatas by their composers. For the same reason, on the other hand, the term was sometimes applied to works that in earlier centuries had been referred to simply by the first lines of their respective texts—notably the Stabat Mater and sometimes the Te Deum. Thus in the nineteenth century the term "cantata" covered a variety of forms set to a variety of texts.

Brahms

In 1869, shortly after the *Deutsches Requiem* appeared, Brahms published *Rinaldo*, a cantata for tenor soloist, four-part choir of men's voices, and orchestra, on a text by Goethe. The stylistic individuality that is usually so striking a characteristic of Brahms is not obvious in this minor work: reminders of Schubert, Schumann, and Mendelssohn are all present in the solo writing. The melodic phrases are sometimes folklike, sometimes expansive; the men's voices are handled both chordally and imitatively, and the orchestra occasionally departs from its discreet accompanying role to engage in full, sonorous passages.

Dvořák

A setting of the Stabat Mater, which Dvořák called "a religious cantata," was begun early in 1876 and completed in the following year, during a time when Dvořák had suffered the loss of three of his children. After its first performance in 1880, the work was performed repeatedly in Britain, the United States, and elsewhere, contributing to Dvořák's growing fame as a composer. It is set for four soloists, four-voice choir, and standard orchestra, and is divided into ten numbers distributed about equally between soloists, choir, and soloists plus choir.

As in many choral works of the nineteenth century, the hand of the instrumentally oriented composer is seen, with the text providing no more than a point of departure for the writing of numbers that are conceived from the standpoint of instrumental form. Dvořák does not hesitate to repeat words or entire lines out of context if the musical form requires such repetition. Furthermore, he sometimes gives precedence to the musical accentuation of a phrase rather than to the correct Latin accentuation of the words to which the phrase is set; this procedure results in several unfelicitous settings of individual words such as *judicii* and *virginum*.

In other respects, however, the reverence and sincerity of the music reflect Dvořák's simple religious faith. The text is set appropriately, with Dvořák's mastery of choral techniques—ranging from simple unisons to rich eight-voice writing—and his skill in handling the orchestra everywhere apparent. Although overshadowed by the Requiem Mass (written about ten years later), the *Stabat Mater* is a powerful composition with its full share of heartfelt writing.

Other Works

Brahms

Among Brahms' many choral works, there are five (all on German texts) that should be mentioned. The first, *Triumphlied* (*Song of Triumph*), for baritone soloist, two four-voice choirs, and large orchestra, is an occasional piece in celebration of the end of the Franco-Prussian War in 1871 and the founding of the German Empire. Based on biblical texts chosen by Brahms himself, the work resembles a Handel anthem in form, and a spirit of joy is expressed throughout.

The four remaining works are somewhat related in that each of them presents two conflicting ideas and a musical resolution of the conflict. The earliest, following shortly after the *Deutsches Requiem,* is the *Rhapsodie* (*Alto Rhapsody*) for alto soloist, four-voice men's choir, and orchestra, composed in 1870 on a text by Goethe. The brief text depicts a wanderer, moody and forsaken, who finds tranquility. Brahms' means are of the simplest: a series of poignant melodies given to the soloist, occasional chordal passages for the men's voices below the solo line, and a delicate and refined accompaniment (see Example 70). Less than two hundred measures in length and requiring only thirteen minutes in performance, this masterpiece succeeds in transforming a subjective text into a universal statement; the dissonant C minor of the beginning is magically changed during the course of the work to the optimistic C major of the conclusion.

In 1871 Brahms published his *Schicksalslied* (*Song of Destiny*), on a poem by Friedrich Hölderlin and composed for four-voice choir and orchestra. The first two stanzas of the short text describe heavenly bliss and divine repose; the final stanza draws a picture of humanity on earth hurled about by blind destiny and doomed to uncertainty. The first two parts of Brahms' setting contrast these two states in dramatic fashion. Spacious and quiet, an orchestral prelude in E flat introduces melodious choral phrases that suggest divine calm. Abruptly, with a change of meter and tempo, the contrasting third stanza is set in an agitated manner; angular choral melodies, sharp accents, and tumultuous orchestral writing express the lot of suffering humanity driven by fate to an unknown end. At this point Brahms goes beyond the mere contrast of the two ideas in the poem and adds a short third section: a transformation of the prelude with which the work began, but now in C major and with changed orchestration. The composer's intent is obvious: to recall the bliss and calm of the heavenly state and to end on a note of hope. A similar transformation, suggesting the change from darkness to light, is often implied in Brahms' instrumental works; here it serves to reveal how magically instrumental writing can be used to illustrate and comment on a text.

About ten years later, following the death of the painter Anselm Feuerbach,

EXAMPLE 70   Brahms, *Rhapsodie*

(Tr.: "But if from thy psalter, Father of love.")

with whom the composer felt spiritually allied, Brahms set a short poem by Friedrich Schiller, *Nänie* (*Elegy*), for choir and orchestra. Recalling the ancient Greek idea that death is the brother of sleep (an idea expressed also in John Donne's sonnet *Death, Be Not Proud*, in the line "Rest and sleep, which but thy picture be"), Schiller's poem contrasts the agony of death with the healing power of consolation; in his noble setting, Brahms emphasizes the consoling element. Cast in one extended three-part movement, *Nänie* is filled with long, flowing melodies against a detailed, harmonically rich, and expressive orchestral background.

In 1882 Brahms set a fragment of Goethe's *Iphigenie auf Taurus* for six-voice choir and large orchestra. Called *Gesang der Parzen* (*Song of the Fates*), it offers a decided contrast to *Nänie*. Goethe's fragment contrasts pictures of the relentless, pitiless Fates with helpless, resigned humanity. Brahms' setting is in part stormy, dispassionate, and suggestive of cruelty; in part moody and fearful. By introducing yet a third mood, one of sympathy, the composer provides a bridge between the opposites; the music suggests that the Fates will heed the cries of their victims and give them hope. A variety of chordal textures, pounding rhythms, and many twisted chromatic lines enable Brahms to set the forbidding text and invest it with a spirit of reconciliation.

Bruckner

The composition of his *Te Deum* occupied Bruckner intermittently from 1881 to 1883. Set for four soloists, four-voice choir, organ, and large orchestra, it was for many years the most widely performed of Bruckner's choral works. It is cast in five movements, the first embracing Stanzas 1–19, the fourth Stanzas 22–28; the second, third, and fifth movements are each concerned with only one of the remaining stanzas, that is, Stanzas 20, 21, and 29, respectively. When groups of stanzas are set, as in the first and fourth movements, Bruckner presents the texts straightforwardly with virtually no repetition of individual verses. Conversely, the settings of the single stanzas contain a number of verse repetitions and recapitulations. The last movement, concerned only with Stanza 29, is a long and elaborate setting: the first verse is in chordal style; the second and third verses are heard simultaneously in an elaborate fugue on two themes; and the last verse is again in chordal style.

As in his D minor and F minor Masses, Bruckner makes considerable use of leading motives. One motive in particular, appearing often in the first movement, reappears in the fourth and provides climactic passages in the fifth. Again as in the Masses, the *Te Deum* is a glowing metaphor of Bruckner's faith in its elaborate setting of the final stanza and its reiteration of significant words in other passages. And in power, brilliance, and sonority, few of his other works equal the *Te Deum*.

A setting of Psalm CL (150), composed in 1892 and the last of Bruckner's choral works, may be mentioned briefly for its general similarity to the *Te Deum*. Written for four-voice choir (sometimes divided into as many as nine voices), a brief soprano solo, and large orchestra, it presents the text in jubilant fashion and rises to enormous levels of sonority. Contrapuntal writing takes precedence over chordal writing in the Psalm, and a fugal section near the end is marked by an unusually angular theme of the type seen often in Bruckner's works (compare Example 63, page 166).

Verdi

Near the close of his career Verdi turned again to church music, and in 1898 published his *Quattro pezzi sacri* (*Four Sacred Pieces*); the last two of these, a *Stabat Mater* and a *Te Deum*, were composed between 1895 and 1897. The *Stabat Mater*, for mixed voices and orchestra, is an economical setting with no text repetition, in an eloquent and flexible harmonic style that allows Verdi to express all the nuances of the text.

The *Te Deum*, for double choir and large orchestra, Verdi's last composition, shows no decline of creative imagination in the 84-year-old composer. It begins with a fragment of Gregorian plainsong, taken from the traditional chant, and contains other thematic material that is similar to plainsong in contour and restraint. Unlike most other settings of the Te Deum, which emphasize the text's appropriateness to festive occasions, Verdi's places in the foreground the prayerful aspects of the text in its hope of deliverance from God's wrath. Thus, although it contains a full share of dramatic and overpowering passages, its essential tone is quiet and reverent.

Vocal textures include simple unisons, full eight-voice choral writing, involved eight-voice counterpoint, and antiphonal writing (for the two choirs and for all the men's voices set opposite the women's), in every case appropriate to the nature of the text. The sharp emotional and dynamic contrasts, both in the orchestral and the choral writing, are balanced by the thematic unity that is assured by the many transformations of the Gregorian themes, which are brought into the nineteenth century by their expressive harmonic treatment. Underlying the whole is Verdi's attitude toward the text, an attitude of reverence and poetic insight in equal measure.

Choral Symphony

For several decades after Beethoven had introduced a choir into the finale of his Symphony No. 9 and Berlioz had combined choir and orchestra in his dramatic symphony *Roméo et Juliette,* few composers followed along the new path marked out by these masters. The notable exceptions, Mendelssohn and Liszt, have been discussed (and the first symphony of Alexander Scriabin [1872–1915], written about 1895, may be mentioned). It remained for Gustav Mahler (1860–1911) to carry the new type forward and to make significant contributions to the literature of symphony with choir.

Mahler was born in Bohemia (now Czechoslovakia) and rose to fame as one of the finest opera conductors of all time; after a series of minor positions, he conducted in Prague, Budapest, Hamburg, Vienna, and, for a short time, New York. In addition to carrying out his conducting responsibilities, he composed nine symphonies (a tenth remained unfinished), three of them containing choral movements, as well as many songs and several miscellaneous works for voices and orchestra. The works that are of interest here are the Symphonies No. 2 (1894), No. 3 (1895–96), and No. 8 (1907).

The Second Symphony, called the "Resurrection" Symphony, uses in its last movement part of the *Resurrection Ode* by the German poet Friedrich Klopstock, to which the composer added a few lines of his own. Scored for soprano and alto soloists, four-voice choir, and large orchestra with an augmented brass section (parts of which play offstage during one movement), the symphony is concerned with the meaning of life. Three massive orchestral movements deal with Mahler's responses to the question; the fourth movement is an alto solo on the folk text "I am from God and will return to God, who will light my path to eternal life." The fifth movement is a large sonata-form with several themes derived from the third movement. In place of a true recapitulation, however, a new section for the choir, with soprano and alto solo passages, constitutes the culmination of the symphony and of Mahler's program. The vocal writing is at times chordal, at times imitative, expressing emotions of deep reverence, divine exaltation, and fierce joy. The work as a whole illustrates Mahler's intention to write music of such vast scope "that the whole world is actually mirrored therein." The glory of the Resurrection is one aspect of that preoccupation.

A very large orchestra is required for the Third Symphony. Dealing with certain aspects of nature, the symphony presents summer as the victory of life over the inert forces symbolized by winter; other aspects of the program concern the significance to mankind of flowers, animals, the power of love, and angelic purity. The massive first movement, some 45 minutes in length, is balanced by the five shorter movements that follow; an alto soloist on a text by Nietzsche appears in the fourth; alto soloist, boys' choir, and women's choir in the fifth; and the sixth movement is again for orchestra alone. The boys' choir sings primarily on the text "bimm, bamm"; the composer gives a detailed directive: "The tone is to imitate the sound of bells, the vowel to be lightly touched and the tone to be sustained by humming on the consonant." The three-voice women's choir, on the other hand, is given a German text concerned with "three angels who sang a sweet song." Colorful and varied orchestral writing of symphonic scope supports the vocal phrases, and the whole is a powerful and dramatic reflection of Mahler's programmatic purpose.

The Eighth Symphony is an enormous work requiring seven soloists, a boys' choir, two four-voice mixed choirs, and a huge orchestra including celesta, harmonium, piano, organ, two harps, and a greatly augmented wind section in addition to the usual instruments; the size of the work has led to its being called the "Symphony of a Thousand." Two texts are employed: the first part is a setting of a Medieval Latin hymn, *Veni creator spiritus* ("Come, Holy Spirit"); the second part sets in German the closing scene from Goethe's *Faust*. Both texts present a similar idea, namely man's longing for love, wisdom, guidance, and assurance; the Latin text reflects the viewpoint of the Church, the German text expresses the humanistic tradition. To this noble purpose Mahler devoted the full power of his creative imagination and his enormous technical skill; and to emphasize the unity of that purpose, Mahler employed themes from the first movement in the second also.

Part I of the symphony, a greatly modified sonata-form with many theme groups undergoing constant development and expansion, and containing a double fugue, corresponds roughly to the conventional symphonic first movement. Part II, cast in many contrasting and connected sections, in effect embraces the usual remaining movements—adagio, scherzo, and finale. The vocal parts, both solo and choral, are tightly integrated into the symphonic structure by engaging in the thematic manipulation; thus the concept of a choral work "accompanied" by orchestra has not the slightest validity here. Mahler in this work achieved the final synthesis between orchestra and voices; the Eighth is a choral symphony in every sense.

Space does not permit a detailed analysis of this stupendous work, nor could such an analysis reveal the wealth of beautiful, awe-inspiring, delicate, and colossal passages it contains. Here one can only call attention to the grandeur of the conception expressed in the music and the overwhelming technical mastery Mahler revealed in its pages. The sheer size of the Eighth Symphony and the demands it makes on singers and players alike contribute to the relatively few performances it receives. Although it has not attained a regular place in the performing repertoire, it takes a high position among the monuments of the literature, and it remains an eloquent testimonial to the power of the human imagination.

11

Music of the
Twentieth Century

The decades just before and after 1900 marked one of the major turning points in the evolution of musical styles. In many respects the time was closely analogous to the years around 1600, which marked the turn from the Renaissance period to the Baroque, from the dominance of the modal system to the gradual emergence of the system of major and minor scales, and from the pervading contrapuntal texture to that characterized by the use of basso continuo.

At the turn of the twentieth century, the various Romantic styles had reached the highest point of their development, and many composers reacted against the subjectivity and sentimental expressiveness that had characterized Romanticism in general and sought new means of expression. Several of them emerged with new styles that stressed objective and impersonal utterance. Furthermore, the increasing use of chromaticism in melody and harmony after about 1850 had opened the path to new systems of tonal organization, new harmonic procedures, and a new regard for dissonance as an expressive factor in music.

As in all similar periods in the history of the art, a time of stylistic individuality resulted; thus, large generalizations of the type that were valid in discussing the music of earlier periods cannot be made about music of the early twentieth century. Certain composers born in the late nineteenth century seemed unaffected by contemporary developments and continued to compose in the spirit of Romanticism well into the twentieth. Others began in that spirit, but soon adopted experimental attitudes and led the way to new means of expression. Eventually a few dominant figures emerged and exerted a major influence on the younger generation of composers—each in an individual way. Any discussion of the choral music written since about 1900 must reckon with many different approaches and solutions to the expressive problems of the time. Contemporary music represents not one style, but many.

Mass

In music designed for the church, an ever-increasing use of secular elements had marked much of the nineteenth century. A subjective approach to liturgical texts, the introduction of symphonic textures in the orchestral accompaniments of Masses, and a tendency to weight melodic materials with emotionally rich and sentimental expression—such elements had tended to distract the listener from the sense and purpose of the sacred words themselves. In 1903 the Vatican took notice of the problem, and Pope Pius X issued a *Motu proprio* that sought to establish principles governing the composition of music suitable for the Roman Catholic Church.

In that document the restoration of Gregorian chant and the "classic polyphony" of the sixteenth century was recommended. A liturgical text was always to be sung in Latin, and sung "as it is in the books, without alteration or inversion of the words, without undue repetition, without breaking syllables." The use of instruments was severely restricted; notably, "the employment of the piano is forbidden in church, as is also that of noisy or frivolous instruments such as drums, cymbals, bells, and the like," and wind instruments could be used only with special permission. Finally, the length of a Mass setting was to conform to the requirements of the liturgy, for "it is not lawful to keep the priest at the altar waiting on account of the chant or the music." (The entire *Motu proprio* is translated and reprinted in Slonimsky, *Music Since 1900*, pp. 523–29.)

Subsequently, in 1922, the Society of St. Gregory of America issued a list of compositions that violated the principles set forth in the *Motu proprio*. This so-called Black List includes many of the more popular hymnals, Masses, psalm settings, and the like; but it also disapproves, for American use, the religious compositions of Haydn, Mozart, Schubert, Rossini, and others—not because of their musical values, but because of "their purely liturgical unfitness according to the principles declared in the *Motu proprio*." And even though those principles have not been fully observed by all composers, many early–twentieth-century works on liturgical texts reveal a more dignified and appropriate style, a further decline in the use of theatrical effects, and a degree of restraint in the use of instruments.

On the other hand, the last ten years have seen the emergence of other trends that are radically altering the shape and sound of liturgical music. Decrees of the Vatican Council, taking effect late in 1964, permitted the use of vernacular languages, congregational participation in prayers, and the singing of hymns by non-Catholic composers such as Martin Luther and Samuel Wesley. The extent to which these liturgical reforms are observed varies from one diocese to another, often from one parish to another. Under the influence of the new freedom in the form of the service, the "folk mass" has often found a place. In this form, texts having sociological or contemporary interest are often inserted into the Mass, are sometimes composed in the style of rock music, and are accompanied by guitar, drums, tambourines, and other nontraditional instruments. The result is a degree of flexibility in the Roman Catholic service and—in some churches— the substitution of musical values quite different from those that had characterized sacred music through the centuries.

Vaughan Williams

Ralph Vaughan Williams (1872–1958), one of the foremost English composers of the twentieth century, wrote his Mass in G minor about 1922. Set for four soloists and eight-voice unaccompanied choir with organ ad libitum, it reveals the composer's adherence to the principles embodied in the *Motu proprio* (although Vaughan Williams was not a member of the Roman Catholic Church) and is designed for liturgical use, in that the first phrase of the Gloria and the Credo are to be intoned by the priest.

Throughout the Mass a variety of chordal, imitative, and mixed textures is characteristic, each texture always appropriate to the sense of the particular liturgical phrase, and word or phrase repetition is most generally confined to the Kyrie and the *Hosanna*. Often an antiphonal effect is introduced by setting the four solo voices against the choir or by dividing the choir into two opposing four-voice groups, the full eight-voice sonority most often reserved for climactic passages. The Mass shares the stylistic diversity that is often found in other choral works by Vaughan Williams: certain passages are as simple and direct as hymn tunes; others, with series of sixth chords, suggest fauxbourdon; and still others resemble a kind of choral declamation. Yet the effect of the whole is dignified and reserved.

Poulenc

A Mass in G major was composed in 1937 by Francis Poulenc (1899–1963), a French composer who made notable contributions to the choral field. Set for unaccompanied choir ranging from four to eight voices, this Mass omits the Credo. It reveals the influence of Stravinsky (see below) in its diversity of meters, which change frequently enough to suggest unmetrical rhythm. Extended passages are set with each measure having a different metrical signature: 5/4, 6/4, 7/4, 5/2, and so on; Poulenc's intention of retaining the unmetrical rhythm of the prose texts is obvious in such passages (see Example 71a). A variety of imitative and chordal textures is typical of the several movements; short phrases set in melismatic or declamatory style are equally characteristic. Many of the melodies are angular, sometimes to the extent of revealing octave displacement (see Example 71b). And the prevailing harmony is triadic but dissonant and with far-reaching modulations. Economically written, the Mass is a model of restraint, elegance, and impersonal expression.

EXAMPLE 71   Poulenc, *Mass in G*

Reprinted by special permission of copyright owner, Editions Salabert.

Kodály

Zoltán Kodály (1882–1967), an eminent Hungarian composer, is perhaps best known for his works on national themes and those that embody nationalistic folk idioms. His *Missa brevis* (1948), however, reflects the composer's Hungarian origin only faintly, for it is written in a straightforward though richly harmonic diatonic style that sometimes suggests the influence of plainsong. Kodály's original scoring was for mixed choir and organ, but he rewrote the accompaniment for orchestra in 1951. In both versions, the textures include contrapuntal and chordal writing employed in economical and dignified fashion.

Stravinsky

Quite different in structure and expressive effect is the Mass composed by Igor Stravinsky (1882–1971) in 1951 and set for four-voice choir (with each voice occasionally divided) and ten instruments—five woodwind and five brass; the specification of children's voices for the soprano and alto choral parts adds to the unusualness of the sound. The accompaniment serves several functions: at times supporting the voices, at others providing independent melodic lines, and occasionally supplying brief prologues or interludes in the several movements. A few passages for solo voices appear in the Gloria and Sanctus, and a few melismatic passages occur in the *Christe eleison* and the *Amen* of the Credo; virtually all the other choral writing is in the style of harmonized chant or choral declamation.

Stravinsky's long career as one of the world's foremost composers was marked by a great variety of changes of style, form, and expressive content, but rhythmic vitality and the considerable use of unmetrical rhythms remained characteristic of all his music. Thus in the Mass single measures of 2/4, 2/8, 3/8, etc., are inserted in an otherwise basically 4/4 context; this device enables Stravinsky to emphasize or minimize the importance of textual accents at will. In other passages in which a metrical rhythm prevails, the irregular placing of long and short tones as well as the use of syncopations allows him similar freedom in regard to textual accentuation (see Example 72). In view of Stravinsky's expressed purpose to "objectify" musical expression, to remove from it all traces of senti-

EXAMPLE 72   Stravinsky, *Mass*, Credo

mentality and Romantic accretions, one must assume that his shifting of textual accents (often resulting in distortions, as seen in Example 72) is part of that purpose. In any case, these accents contribute to the tone of austerity and impersonality that the Mass evokes.

Thompson

In the twentieth century the Mass has often been set to a translation of the liturgical text, and there are many English settings. An outstanding example is provided by the *Mass of the Holy Spirit*, written by Randall Thompson (b. 1899) in 1955–56. Thompson is well known for his faithful adherence to the tonal system and for the expressive quality of his many choral compositions. The Mass, in English except for the Kyrie, is set for unaccompanied four-voice choir, but it contains a few solo passages and occasionally requires eight choral parts. Its harmonic scheme is tonal throughout; A major and A minor are the predominant tonalities, with the *Glory Be to God* (Gloria) set in D major. The writing is direct, diatonic, and vocally attractive; the Mass is not burdened with a desire to be "original" for its own sake, and is proof that the expressive possibilities of the tonal system have not yet been exhausted.

Thompson makes full use of the relatively limited palette available to the composer of an unaccompanied choral work. A variety of textures and vocal styles—ranging from highly melismatic through antiphonal to involved poly-phonic—characterize the Mass. Fugues and canons occur in several movements, notably a three-voice canon in the *Christe eleison,* a four-voice canon in the *Blessed Is He* (Benedictus), and a two-voice canon with two free contrapuntal parts in the *Lamb of God* (Agnus Dei). Other movements are written primarily in chordal style. Expressive melodies abound throughout the Mass, and the sentiment of the translated text is everywhere appropriately reflected.

Walton

The *Missa brevis* by William Walton (b. 1902), among the best-known English composers of the twentieth century, was composed about 1966 for Coventry Cathedral, and thus follows the rite of the Church of England. The Kyrie remains in Greek, other texts are in English, but the Credo is omitted. The Mass is set for eight-voice choir and is accompanied (by the organ) only in the Gloria, which is set as the last movement. The choir is occasionally employed antiphonally, and the writing includes a few passages for solo voices. A high level of dissonance, characterized by the use of many intervals of the second, is maintained through extended passages, but this is relieved by other passages in triadic harmony or in unison. The result is a pungent, somewhat acrid, but eloquent setting.

Requiem

Britten

Among contemporary English composers, Benjamin Britten (b. 1913) holds a high position by virtue of the variety, high quality, and forceful expressiveness of his operas and choral works in particular. Several of the latter, notably the

Benjamin Britten, b. 1913.

charming *Ceremony of Carols* for women's voices and harp, and a cantata, *St. Nicolas,* have become well known; the cantata will be discussed below. Of greater significance is his *War Requiem,* composed in 1961. This is not a liturgical setting of the traditional text, however, for between sections of the Requiem Mass in Latin Britten has inserted several antiwar poems in English by Wilfred Owen. A soprano soloist, a boys' choir, and a four-voice mixed choir, arranged in various combinations, sing the text of the Requiem; the boys' choir is accompanied by an organ, the others by a large orchestra. The interpolated poems are given to tenor and baritone soloists, singing sometimes individually and sometimes together, and accompanied by a separate chamber orchestra.

The entire text of the Requiem Mass, including the final *Libera me* and *In Paradisum,* is presented in normal order, except that Stanzas 11, 14, and 20 of the *Dies irae* are omitted and Stanzas 1 and 2 are repeated between 17 and 18. The secular poems are interpolated at irregular intervals: one between the Introit and Kyrie, four within the *Dies irae,* one within the Offertory, and so on. The vocal or choral sections, supported by the accompanying organ and two orchestras, sometimes overlap, so that a great measure of continuity is assured. These complex forces are always imaginatively at the service of the secular and liturgical texts. A great variety of melodic types characterizes the vocal writing: the melodies in the choral sections of the Introit are based on only two tones—F sharp and C—heard in various configurations and imitative rhythmic patterns, for example, while harsh chordal writing and intricate polyphony (including some brief canons) are found elsewhere. Lyric, impassioned, and recitativelike melodies are given to the soloists as the texts require. And the powerful orchestral writing, often attaining symphonic scope, supplies enormous dramatic power. Britten's *War Requiem* is a tremendous achievement, and it has taken its place as one of the most successful large choral works of the twentieth century.

Psalm Settings

Musical settings of psalms had appeared frequently in the Romantic period, but most often they were by minor composers or were relatively small works overshadowed by the more important compositions of the time. In the twentieth century, however, composers have again become interested in the psalms as texts for large compositions, and several outstanding works have resulted. Four psalm settings, unlike in form and expressive content, may be discussed here as being representative of the stylistic variety that marks the music of the twentieth century.

Reger

Among the controversial composers of the time, the German Max Reger (1873–1916) is outstanding. In several hundred compositions in a great variety of forms, including some three dozen large choral works, Reger developed enormous contrapuntal facility, with a harmonic style characterized by wide, imaginative, and continual modulation. His music is filled with accidentals—symbols of his harmonic flexibility—and its expressive scope has won him both warm enthusiasts and bitter opponents.

A setting of Psalm xcix (100), composed about 1908–10 in Leipzig, is his most important choral work. Set in German for a four- to eight-voice choir, large orchestra, and organ, it is an elaborate composition requiring about thirty minutes to perform; since the Psalm text itself consists of five verses, with a reading time of about thirty seconds, one may gain an idea of the scale of Reger's setting. Two or three short choral phrases are set in chordal style, and a few measures are unaccompanied. In virtually every other passage the choir is constantly in contrapuntal motion: involved rhythmic figurations express a jubilant air, and fugal sections develop a massive sonority that is fully supported by the orchestral writing. These and still other devices result in a virtuosic work that contains only a few relaxed moments.

Kodály

In 1923 Kodály composed his *Psalmus Hungaricus* for tenor soloist, choir ranging from four to eight voices (with the recommendation that boys' voices reinforce or replace the women's voices in several passages), and standard orchestra with organ ad libitum. The text, set in Hungarian, is based on Psalm liv (55), but is a paraphrase rather than a translation. Made by Michael Vég, a sixteenth-century Hungarian poet and preacher, it contains many interpolations and exhortations, and concludes with a short epilogue in the poet's own words: "These words King David wrote in his Psalter, the fifty-fifth of his songs of praise; and for the faithful . . . I made from it this song." Reflecting certain aspects of Hungarian culture and history, to which Kodály was always sensitive, the *Psalmus*

Hungaricus transcends the biblical text and becomes a personal and historical document.

Cast in one large movement containing several contrasting sections, the work gives the main responsibility to the tenor soloist. The choir—in predominantly chordal texture with many changes of meter—is confined to five passages: three totaling 38 measures, which comment on the main text; a fourth (with solo) of 24 measures, which gives added weight to the soloist's text; and a fifth comprising 123 measures, which expresses supplication, vengeance, and faith, and which contains the poet's words in the epilogue. An orchestral introduction and several long passages for orchestra alone supply contrasting moments. The melodic lines in both the solo and choral parts are distinguished primarily by rhythmic vitality, many repeated tones, considerable use of melodic leaps in which intervals of fourths and fifths are prominent, and an absence of conventional lyric expression. The orchestral writing ranges from thin tremolos to full symphonic sonority; serving partly to accompany, partly to enhance the vocal writing, and partly to provide mood pictures that amplify the text, it adds a colorful and striking note. The *Psalmus Hungaricus* is a powerful and passionate setting, and it must be reckoned among Kodály's most expressive and successful works.

Stravinsky

In 1930, about twenty years before writing his Mass, Stravinsky had composed his *Symphonie des Psaumes* (*Symphony of Psalms*) for the fiftieth anniversary of the founding of the Boston Symphony Orchestra. The work is divided into three connected movements—prelude, fugue, and introduction and allegro, on texts (sung in Latin) from Psalm XXXVIII, Verses 13 and 14 (Psalm 39, Verses 12 and 13, King James version), Psalm XXXIX, Verses 2, 3, and 4 (Psalm 40, Verses 1–3), and all of Psalm CL (150), respectively. The work is scored for four-voice choir (with boys' voices preferred for soprano and alto) and a large orchestra that includes a harp and two pianos but omits clarinets, violins, and violas.

The texts of the three Psalms deal with prayer, testimony of faith, and praise, all very different in tone; the contrasts are mirrored in the three contrasting movements, but in Stravinsky's uniquely impersonal fashion. While the prayer of the first movement is appropriately restrained in its vocal lines (the first and last sections of the movement are based on melodies consisting largely of two tones heard in alternation), these lines are accompanied by agitated and percussive orchestral figures. And while the praise and jubilation of the third movement are reflected in the animated and colorful orchestral writing, the choir sings ostinato figures in slow tempo and a few unsymmetrical phrases cast in halting and interrupted rhythms—a strange way to praise the Lord. Such expressive paradoxes are found often in Stravinsky's works; they doubtless reflect his wish to avoid sentimentality and to throw new light on textual meanings. In that wish he succeeded admirably. And in his use of a harmonic system that marks a considerable expansion over nineteenth-century practices, he imbued the traditional texts with new poignancy, great dramatic tension, and expressive power. The *Symphony of Psalms* is one of the most important choral works of the twentieth century.

Dello Joio

A setting of Psalm L (51) by Norman Dello Joio (b. 1913) represents yet another type of setting. Composed in 1951 and entitled *A Psalm of David*, it is set for four-voice choir with piano or orchestral accompaniment, and is divided into three connected parts. A cantus firmus employed by Josquin in his setting of the same text about 1500 plays an important role in Dello Joio's version. The cantus firmus, an eight-note phrase with all but one tone on E and the other on F, appears systematically in each of the sections of the Psalm; it rises from time to time to successively higher pitch levels across seven degrees of the scale, with various rhythmic configurations. Other voices engage in imitations of the phrase, or sing free counterpoints developed from it, or merely provide chordal support. The accompaniment includes several brief interludes, as well as brilliant rhythmic figures that enhance the text. This revival of the cantus firmus device serves Dello Joio in unifying the composition, and enables him to write a colorful and expressive work.

Te Deum

As in the case of the Psalms, a number of outstanding settings of the Te Deum appeared in the twentieth century. Settings by Kodály, Vaughan Williams, and Persichetti, to be discussed here, are representative of the group—a group that also includes works by the English William Walton and Benjamin Britten and the German Ernst Pepping.

Kodály

The *Te Deum* composed by Kodály (1936) is set in Latin for four soloists, a mixed choir ranging from four to eight voices, and a standard orchestra with organ ad libitum. It consists of one large movement in several sections, with each section often built on a distinctive motive or figure that enhances the corresponding text: a brief running figure in one section, a rhythmic pattern in another, a slow moving melodic line in a third, and so on. A similar practice is to be observed in many of Kodály's other works.

The predominating texture in this setting is chordal, with the chords based on triadic harmony but containing many dissonances. Several stanzas are treated fugally, however, or are written in imitative counterpoint, and some are set as canons. Among them, Stanzas 6, 14, 15, and 29 are especially rich in contrapuntal writing, often set for the solo voices alone, or in combination with the choral voices; and Stanza 27, on the word *Miserere*, is set in a kind of rhythmic counterpoint that strengthens the solemnity of the text and gives rise to a feeling of awe. Significantly, the stanzas that are either prayerful or reflect the majesty of God are the ones so treated. Such an individualized approach to textual significance may be taken as strong evidence of Kodály's sensitivity to textual meaning. Overall, the work is varied, rhythmically alive, and appropriate to the sense of the text.

Vaughan Williams

In 1937, to celebrate the coronation of George VI of England, Vaughan Williams composed his *Festival Te Deum*. This work (not to be confused with an earlier *Te Deum in G*, composed in 1928 for the enthronement of the Archbishop of Canterbury) is set for four-voice choir and orchestra on the Anglican version of the text. Vaughan Williams here composed a straightforward setting, largely in chordal style but varied by the use of a few melismas and several passages for the choir in octaves. Only one stanza is somewhat extended: the last phrase of Stanza 21 ("in glory everlasting") is repeated several times—and is the only section of the text so treated. Vigorous melodic lines with a few modal touches supply a triumphant note; and, in keeping with the occasion for which the work was written, the *Te Deum* is festive throughout.

Persichetti

Among American composers who occupy a middle position—neither ultra-conservative nor wildly experimental—Vincent Persichetti (b. 1915) holds a prominent place. His short *Te Deum* (in English), composed about 1964, illustrates the attractive nature of his style, in which a wide variety of expressive dissonances marks the harmonic structure. Set for four-voice choir (sometimes expanded to eight) and standard orchestra, the *Te Deum* is primarily in chordal style occasionally varied by the use of unisons, imitative passages, and, in the case of Stanza 27 ("O Lord, have mercy upon us"), choral declamation. Text repetitions occur in Stanzas 2, 21, 27, and 29, but a recapitulation of Stanza 24 after 25 (with different music) marks the only other departure from the traditional text. Metrical changes are characteristic of several passages, possibly introduced to maintain the prose nature of the text through the use of asymmetrical phrases.

Other Sacred Text Settings

As we have seen, twentieth-century choral composers have been attracted by many sacred texts and have set them in any number of forms. A few outstanding works may be mentioned to illustrate the extent of this variety: an *Avodath Hakodesh* (1934), the Jewish Sabbath morning service, by Ernest Bloch (1880–1959); a *Magnificat* (1959) by Alan Hovhaness (b. 1911); a *St. Matthew Passion* (1950) by Ernst Pepping; *Litanies to the Black Virgin* (1936), a *Stabat*

Mater (1951), and an *Office for Holy Saturday* (1962) by Francis Poulenc; a *St. Luke Passion* (1963) by Randall Thompson; and a *Stabat Mater* (1937) by Karol Szymanowski (1882–1937). A few other works in this miscellaneous category deserve closer attention because of their unique qualities and general effectiveness.

Holst

The English composer Gustav Holst (1874–1934) had become interested in mysticism and philosophies of the East early in his career. This interest resulted in four groups of choral settings of *Hymns from the Rig Veda* for various combinations of voices and instruments, composed about 1908–12. A few years later he turned to the Acts of St. John in a translation of the Apocrypha, and in 1917 composed *The Hymn of Jesus* for two four-voice choirs, a semichoir (sopranos and altos), and a large orchestra including piano, organ, and celesta. The work is in two connected sections: a Prelude mainly for orchestra alone but containing two extended passages in which a few voices chant a Latin text in unmetrical fashion over a rhythmical accompaniment; and the Hymn proper, in English, in which the full vocal and instrumental forces are employed.

The choral parts are set largely in chordal style with only a few imitative passages. But antiphonal writing is equally characteristic, with text phrases divided between the two choirs. And the semichoir is confined largely to the word *Amen*, frequently interspersed between the choral phrases. Holst provides a great variety of vocal colors: the women's voices of both choirs are set opposite the men's in some passages; in others, full sonority is often provided by dividing the several vocal parts. Frequent unisons occur, and in one passage the choirs speak a phrase over a pulsating accompaniment. Throughout the work the orchestra enjoys an equal coloristic variety. Not a single measure uses the full ensemble, with every instrument playing; most often a few instruments from one section—strings, for example—are combined with a few from another—winds or percussion. A number of ostinato figures are employed: ponderous descending scale patterns, short rhythmic designs, arpeggios, and the like; and irregular meters such as 5/4 and 7/4 play important roles. The result is a colorful, exotic setting that does full justice to the text.

Vaughan Williams

A small work for alto soloist, women's choir, and orchestra was published by Vaughan Williams in 1932 with the title *Magnificat*. It is not suited to liturgical use, for it does not adhere to the traditional text. Set in English, it employs only a few lines from that text, along with other biblical verses, the text of the Sanctus, and part of an invocation to the Virgin Mary. As the work represents a hymn of praise to Mary, the title is in a sense justified. Characterized by alternations of solo and choral sections, with many unison passages in the latter, and by a light and discreet orchestral background in which a solo flute is featured, the *Magnificat* is an effective piece without being in the least pretentious.

Pinkham

Two works by the American composer Daniel Pinkham (b. 1923) are representative of a neo-Classical, transparent style that is thoroughly contemporary in its expressive dissonance and vital rhythmic quality. The smaller of the two, *Lamentations of Job,* is a Latin setting of a fragment from the Book of Job; published in 1966, it requires a four-voice choir, nine players of brass and percussion instruments, and one contrabass. The vocal texture is about equally divided between imitative and chordal, and the frequent use of one or two voices set above or antiphonally against the others gives an attractive variety of vocal color. Changes in meter are frequent; in one passage single measures of 4/4, 3/8, 7/8, 3/8, 2/4, 4/4, and 3/4 are heard in succession—and are justified by the textual accents and the voice leadings of the individual parts.

The larger of the two is a setting in English of the St. Mark Passion (Chapters 13–15), to which a number of texts from the Old Testament are added. The work is for four soloists, four-voice choir, and twelve instruments; three of the latter (harp, contrabass, and chamber organ) are reserved to accompany the voice of the Evangelist, the tenor soloist, who narrates the events of the Passion in the traditional manner. The part of the Evangelist is set largely in recitative style, but with melodic contours that conform to the angular and dissonant style of the other passages. In this work as in the *Lamentations,* melodic leaps of sevenths, diminished octaves, and ninths occur frequently in both vocal and instrumental lines, and many consecutive seconds in the latter add pungent dissonances. The dramatic moments of the story are treated with skill and imagination, and the effect of the whole is appropriately moving.

Oratorio

The oratorio in the twentieth century has undergone considerable modifications in structure and expressive function; only rarely has the composer of a contemporary oratorio adhered to the centuries-old pattern that included an array of separate numbers for soloists, ensemble, and choir, accompanied by an orchestra. In its place has come a variety of patterns that defy generalization; virtually every work has its own scheme of organization and approach to its text. This fact also explains the array of terms by which twentieth-century oratorios are described: dramatic psalm, staged oratorio, choral suite, and the like; or else the work is referred to only by its title and grouped with oratorios simply by virtue of its general nature and its size.

Schoenberg

About the time Edward Elgar had completed *The Dream of Gerontius* (1900), Arnold Schoenberg (1874–1951) in Vienna began his eleven-year task of composing a massive oratorio, *Gurrelieder* (*Songs of Gurre*). The work is set for five soloists, a speaker, an eight-voice mixed choir, three separate four-voice men's choirs, and a huge orchestra that rivals the group Mahler employed in his Eighth Symphony (Mahler was content with two harps, whereas Schoenberg required four, for example). Schoenberg's high place in twentieth-century music as the inventor of twelve-tone music (later called "serial music") has sometimes obscured the fact that he began his career in the late Romantic style; certain of his early works carried the methods and expressive devices of Wagner, Mahler, and Strauss to their logical conclusion. This oratorio is a case in point.

Based on verses reflecting events in thirteenth-century Danish history by the Danish poet Jens Jacobsen, *Gurrelieder* is in effect a long love poem divided into three unequal parts (I and III are each over a thousand measures in length, while Part II is barely a hundred). The work is equally unusual in its distribution of vocal forces. While the protagonist, King Waldemar the Conqueror (tenor soloist), appears throughout the work, other characters sung by soloists appear in one part only: two in Part I, two others and the speaker in Part III. The choral singing is confined to Part III, in which the three men's choirs are given three relatively brief passages and the mixed choir appears only in an extended section at the end of the work. The orchestral writing supplies a major share of the work's dramatic effectiveness, particularly the long prelude and several highly romantic interludes that serve to connect the various vocal scenes.

The soloists' melodies greatly resemble the "continuous narrative" found in Wagner's music dramas: a series of unsymmetrical phrases with harmonic cadences concealed, delayed, or elided lead forcefully from one dramatic climax to another. An interesting contrast is the long series of phrases (about 150 measures) given to a speaker near the end of Part III: Schoenberg indicated metrical rhythms but only approximate pitches in that part, which is spoken above an involved accompaniment. The effect is a dramatic heightening of the text, and contrasts greatly with the chordal section for the mixed choir that follows. Here, and throughout, the orchestral accompaniment is filled with recurring figures and suggestions of leading motives, which add a varied and colorful background. The dramatic impact of *Gurrelieder* is enormous; this massive work is one of the last outpourings of pure Romanticism, and marks the virtual end of the style.

Brief mention must be made of Schoenberg's unfinished oratorio *Jacobsleiter* (*Jacob's Ladder*), begun about 1917, worked on periodically, but not completed at the time of the composer's death in 1951. The work is reported to have been planned for a massive choir of several hundred voices plus an offstage choir, accompanied by a huge orchestra supplemented by four offstage orchestras. The existing fragments are distinguished in being perhaps Schoenberg's first use of a twelve-tone row. In his later years Schoenberg was quoted as considering *Jacobsleiter* among his most important projects. One can only speculate about what its final form would have been.

Honegger

Arthur Honegger (1892–1955), French by birth but Swiss by background, made several notable contributions to the choral field; chief among them are a dramatic psalm, *Le Roi David* (*King David*, 1921), and a "stage oratorio," *Jeanne d'Arc au bûcher* (*Joan of Arc at the Stake*, 1935). *King David*, based on Old Testament texts, was composed as incidental music to a play by René Morax. The success of the work at its early performances was so great that Honegger undertook to make the music available to concert audiences. In its final form, the addition of a part for a narrator, who speaks the biblical texts, provides the dramatic continuity necessarily missing in the earlier version. The accompaniment, originally scored for only a few instruments, was enlarged to the size of a standard orchestra, and a few musical passages were added. The concert setting includes, in addition, three soloists and a four-voice choir; it is divided into three parts consisting of 27 sections that range from a few measures to several minutes in length.

The dramatic story unfolds in a series of orchestral, vocal, and choral numbers of great pictorial effectiveness, rhythmic force, dissonant—sometimes polytonal—expressiveness, and lyric beauty. The narrator's text—a sentence or a paragraph or two at a time—is generally placed between the sections, but in a few passages the narrator speaks above the rhythmic accompaniment in the style of eighteenth-century melodrama.° And in one notable if brief passage in No. 12, the Witch of Endor intones her dire prophecy in similarly melodramatic fashion—with spine-chilling effect. The vocal solos are a deeply expressive combination of pure lyricism and a chantlike style. The choral passages are similarly varied: the choir is given passages in unison (sometimes for women's or men's voices alone), but most often it is set in a solid chordal style that develops great rhythmic momentum. And the choir comments on the action or plays the role of characters in the story—all of this in a highly effective manner.

Honegger's *Joan of Arc* is set for five soloists, four speaking parts, a four-part choir, a choir of children's voices, and large orchestra. Consisting of a prologue and eleven connected scenes, it is composed in a style somewhat similar to that of *King David*—except that the speaking parts are more numerous, more consistently employed, and more varied. The main characters, Joan and Father Dominic, are two of the four speakers. Although the parts for all four speakers are set most often in the style of melodrama above a rhythmical orchestral accompaniment, occasionally they sing, sometimes in French and sometimes in Medieval Latin. (Joan is given a few phrases to sing in one scene, but a note in the score says that if the performer is not a singer, the women of the choir are to hum the melody while Joan speaks the words.) The choir also speaks in numerous passages, either in imitative style or in a kind of choral chant. The purely vocal portions, both for the remaining soloists and for the choir, vary from simple childlike passages through passages of rare lyricism to rhythmically intense chordal sections. Supporting this vocal variety is the rich, detailed, and colorful orchestral accompaniment that enhances the dramatic impact of the pathetic story of Joan of Arc.

Walton

If ever a twentieth-century choral work reflected dramatic force and engendered excitement, that work is *Belshazzar's Feast*, composed in 1931 by William

Walton. Set for baritone soloist, mixed choir that often changes from four voices to eight or is separated into two choirs, large orchestra that includes an expanded percussion section, and two brass bands spatially separated from the orchestra, the work is based on Old Testament texts selected and arranged by Osbert Sitwell. One large movement that takes about 35 minutes to perform, it has no internal divisions to impede the enormous forward thrust of the work, although changes in tone, tempo, and meter occur frequently.

In this oratorio Walton succeeded in devising a choral idiom that is realistically adapted to the requirements of twentieth-century harmony. Whether embracing angular contours, dissonant intervals, or rapidly changing meters, the choral lines are eminently singable. The dramatic nature of the text and Walton's concern with its proper English accentuation are largely responsible for the frequent syncopations and irregular meters that are characteristic of the choral writing. Chordal and imitative textures play a large part, along with many effective melismatic passages that create an expressive thickening of the harmony. The baritone's four solos are mainly in free recitative style, unaccompanied and sung without meter to accommodate the natural accents of the text; an ensemble equivalent of that style—a kind of harmonized chant—occurs frequently in the choir.

Much of the effectiveness of *Belshazzar's Feast* may be attributed to the energetic, colorful, and virtuosic orchestral accompaniment. Passages based on ostinato figures—for one or two instruments, for larger sections of the orchestra, or for the total instrumental forces—add great variety to the orchestral color. In its forthrightness, originality, and sensitivity to its text, the work is outstanding.

Penderecki

In recent decades a young Polish composer, Krzysztof Penderecki (b. 1933), has contributed a number of highly original choral works to the repertoire, notably a short work, *Dimensionen der Zeit und der Stille (Dimensions of Time and Silence,* 1959–61), for a forty-voice mixed choir, groups of percussion instruments, and strings; a setting of the *Passio . . . secundum Lukam (Passion According to St. Luke,* 1965); and an oratorio, *Dies Irae,* 1967.

In addition to the familiar text of Luke 22–23, the *St. Luke Passion* contains verses from several psalms and the St. John Gospel, portions of two hymns, six stanzas from the Sequence Stabat Mater, and other sacred verses—all selected to amplify the traditional text and to supply appropriate commentary. The work is set for narrator, three soloists, a children's choir, a four-voice mixed choir occasionally divided into three separate groups, and a huge orchestra augmented by piano, organ, harp, harmonium, and many exotic percussion instruments. The orchestral writing is so complex that a table of additional notational symbols is required in the score: a symbol for playing the highest possible tone on the instrument, one for playing between the bridge and tailpiece on a string instrument; others for raising or lowering the pitch of a tone a quarter-step (or three quarters of a step) above (or below) its written pitch; still others for ignoring exact notated rhythmic values in a particular passage—such are the symbols.

CORI

A page from the score of Krzysztof Penderecki's *St. Luke Passion*.

We can scarcely speak of texture in the ordinary sense in this work, but we can describe a few of Penderecki's special effects. In a passage early in the work, six voice parts of the divided choirs enter on the same text syllable but at fractionally different time intervals and on pitches a half-step apart, from F sharp to B, and sustain that vocal cluster at the will of the conductor; in another passage, wailing effects ending with glissandi (upward sliding of the voice) are indicated. And again, in a twelve-voice division of the choirs, each of the twelve voice parts speaks a different word or phrase of the text, and repeats that element at will; simultaneously, each of ten cellos and each of eight contrabasses plays a different tone of the chromatic scale, sustains that tone during the time the choir is speaking, then executes a glissando to the highest tone on the instrument and plays in tremolo fashion. Similar tone clusters can be found in the brass section, organ, and other instruments.

Effects such as these are combined or alternated with many others; and although each effect or passage is connected to the next, one gains little sense of a prevailing rhythmic pulse in the work, or a sense of a tonal center. The materials of music—tone, pitch, interval, accent, etc.—are manipulated in such novel ways that a new set of expressive criteria must be created to evaluate the results. Shouting, murmuring, sighing, and humming are combined with singing; tone clusters, ostinato patterns, sharp dissonant chords, and mere noises dominate the accompaniment. Yet the impression made by the work as a whole is anything but chaotic; the length and dynamic level of every effect is carefully planned to serve a particular purpose—the expressive rendering of the text. Penderecki, by avoiding the usual uses of melody, harmony, and rhythm, may well have contributed to a new expressive system. The extent to which he has succeeded cannot yet be determined.

The oratorio *Dies Irae* is textually not related to the Sequence of that name in the Requiem Mass. Part of Penderecki's text is from the Psalms and elsewhere in the Old Testament, sung in Latin; part is from *The Eumenides* by Aeschylus, sung in Greek; and the remainder is several short poems or verse fragments mostly by contemporary Polish poets, translated and sung in Latin. The work is written in memory of the victims of Nazism who lost their lives in the gas chambers at Auschwitz. It is set for three soloists, mixed choir, and huge orchestra (again with an unusually large percussion section), and it is divided into three movements: "Lament," "Apocalypse," and "Apotheosis." All the vocal and instrumental effects described above are present in the *Dies Irae* also, with the addition of whispering, whistling, and shrieking in the choral parts. And if drama and poignancy are the chief impressions gained from hearing the *St. Luke Passion*, anguish and horror are reflected in the *Dies Irae*. A more fitting musical memorial to the victims of Auschwitz can scarcely be conceived.

Dimensions, the earliest of the Penderecki works, is included here even though it can scarcely be called an oratorio, the forty-voice choir lacking any text. In *Dimensions* the choir is accompanied by an orchestra of 16 string and 39 percussion instruments, plus celesta, harp, and piano. As one might expect, the percussion instruments play a dominant role in the work. All the novel effects of the two larger works are here in abundance also, with an even greater array of rhythmic patterns and devices. The choir is confined to whistling, humming, hissing (on the sounds represented by *s*, *sh*, and *z*); and in several passages to articulating the consonants *g*, *t*, *k*, *b*, and *d* "without the preceding and following vowels," and doing this in eight-voice "counterpoint" so that no two groups perform the same sound at any given time. As if this were not enough, instead of indicating a specified number of measures for each combination of these effects, Penderecki indicates time intervals ranging from 4 to 30 seconds during which the effect is to be sustained. As in his other works, dynamic changes are carefully indicated and a basic though not obvious rhythmic pulse underlies this fifteen-minute composition. *Dimensions* is in effect an essay in sounds, noises, pitches, and rhythms; from these its expressive qualities must be determined.

Cantata and Related Forms

In the twentieth century, the cantata has experienced even more changes of definition, alterations of structure, and modification of function than the oratorio. This century has also seen the rise of a number of works for soloists and choir, often with instrumental accompaniment—works of no classification, identified only by their titles. Consequently, while several of the works to be mentioned or discussed in this section are called cantatas by their composers, others are not. It should be pointed out that throughout its lifetime of three and a half centuries, the cantata has been characterized by singular freedom from formal rigidity; much of the time the term has meant no more than a "sung piece." The continued flexibility of the form into the twentieth century may thus be taken as one of its characteristics.

Pierné

Among many cantatas that carried on the Romantic tradition, *La Croisade des enfants* (*The Children's Crusade*, 1902) by Gabriel Pierné (1863–1937) may be singled out for its melodic charm and vigorous choruses. Pierné, a prominent French conductor and organist in Paris, called the work a "musical legend." Set for five soloists (one of them the narrator), children's choir, mixed choir, and standard orchestra, the cantata contains a rich mixture of solos, ensembles, and lively choruses. Pierné succeeded admirably in suggesting the various "scenes" called for in Marcel Schwob's poem—a sun-drenched highway, the arrival at the shore, a terrifying storm at sea—and showed great skill in manipulating his large forces. The choirs are often divided into eight or more parts over a fast-moving orchestral accompaniment; solo voices are heard alone, in ensembles, or in counterpoint with the choirs. Pierné's treatment minimizes the sentimentality inherent in the text, and the total effect is one of strength and faith.

Bartók

Among the relatively few choral works by Béla Bartók (1883–1945) is his *Cantata Profana* (*Secular Cantata*). An outstanding pianist and the most prominent Hungarian composer of the century, Bartók was also a tireless student of the folk music of eastern European and Mediterranean countries. The *Cantata Profana*, composed in 1930, bears the subtitle "The Giant Stags" and is based on a Romanian folk tale. The text, written in Hungarian by Bartók himself, tells of the nine sons of an old man; in the story they are magically turned into stags, roam the forests freely, and resist all parental attempts to return them to their home. The work is set for tenor and baritone soloists, two four-voice choirs, and large orchestra. Several commentators see in this work a reflection of Bartók's reaction to the dictatorship of the Hungarian government of the time; others see it as symbolizing the revolt of a younger freedom-seeking generation against the confining influence of its parents.

The text is set in narrative fashion in one continuous flow, richly varied by changes of texture and meter. The magical transformation of the sons into stags is passed over matter-of-factly, in the best folklore manner; but the following passages, concerned with the appeal of the father (baritone soloist) to his eldest son (now the largest of the stags, tenor soloist), are set in poignant fashion and eloquently express the human problems involved. Bartók's richly embellished harmonies depart widely from triadic consonances, yet are basically tonal, with several recurring figures in the bass and melodic lines in the choral parts that strongly suggest the key of D major.

Orff

In 1935–36 *Carmina Burana* (*Songs of Beuern*), a "scenic cantata" embodying a unique style was composed by Carl Orff (b. 1895), a respected German educator and composer. Selecting about 25 poems from a collection found in the Benedictine Monastery at Beuern in Bavaria, Orff set them for three soloists, a small group of boys' voices, two four-voice choirs often divided into small and large choirs, and a large orchestra including two pianos and expanded percussion section. Most of the poems, secular in content and written by the wandering minstrels and goliards of the Middle Ages, are in the vulgar Latin of the time, the others being in a Medieval German dialect. Orff arranged the poems in three parts or movements concerned respectively with springtime, activities in the tavern, and the court of Love. A prologue, addressed to "Fortune, Empress of the World," appears again as a closing number, and two short dances for orchestra alone appear in Part I.

The style of *Carmina Burana* is notable for the emphasis placed on rhythm, for its harmonic simplicity, for the complete absence of counterpoint in any form, and for the deliberate avoidance of any trace of thematic development. Orff's melodies are usually based on short recurring rhythmic figures, are almost invariably diatonic, and often reflect the simplicity of folksong; only in two or three of the solo phrases is a degree of impassioned expression required. The choral writing is entirely chordal or in unisons, thirds, or octaves; such textures, often embodying phrases of irregular length or phrases characterized by quick changes of meter and many syncopations, drive forward relentlessly to climactic points and give the work tremendous vitality. Contrasts are provided by a few quieter moments, by great variety in the disposition of the vocal and choral lines, and by occasional antiphonal writing. Underlying the whole is the colorful and animated orchestral accompaniment, filled with short rhythmic patterns and sharp accents. *Carmina Burana's* expressions of lovesickness, abandon, and youthful exuberance, and its sheer originality of style have contributed to its enormous popularity from the time it was composed.

Two of Orff's later works on Latin texts are *Catulli Carmina* (*Songs of Catullus,* 1942) and *Trionfo di Afrodite* (*The Triumph of Aphrodite,* 1950), the latter also called a scenic cantata and sometimes given a staged presentation. Both works continue the style introduced so successfully in *Carmina Burana,* and, in addition, the *Afrodite* includes an extended passage for soloist and choir speaking in rhythm over an accompaniment provided by percussion instruments. But lacking the advantage of novelty enjoyed by *Carmina Burana,* they have not gained a comparable place in the repertoire.

Prokofiev

In 1938 Serge Prokofiev (1891–1953) completed the musical score for a Russian motion picture based on the victory of Alexander Nevsky, a thirteenth-century Russian prince, over the Knights of the Teutonic Order. Shortly thereafter he arranged the music as a cantata, dividing it into seven scenes that reflect episodes in the historical account ("Russia under the Mongolian Yoke," "The Crusaders in Pskov," "The Battle on the Ice," and so on), and set it for mezzo-soprano soloist, four-voice choir, and large orchestra. Bearing the title *Alexander Nevsky,* it has taken its place among Prokofiev's best-known choral works. It is representative of the period in the composer's stylistic development when he abandoned an acrid, dissonant style in favor of lyrical expression, clearly defined tonality, and simplicity of form. But the rhythmic vitality and colorful orchestral writing always characteristic of Prokofiev's compositions are very much present here. *Alexander Nevsky* remains an enjoyable work, of special interest for the expressive variety of its orchestral writing.

Foss

Lukas Foss (b. 1922), an American citizen though of German birth, composed his secular cantata *The Prairie,* based on a poem by Carl Sandburg, about 1942. For four soloists, four-voice choir, and orchestra, it is divided into seven numbers set variously for soloist, ensemble, and choir in different combinations. Its harmonic style is basically tonal, characterized by many modulations; ostinato figures in the bass and frequent changes of meter occur in a texture that is about equally divided between chordal and contrapuntal writing. *The Prairie* was followed in 1952 by *A Parable of Death,* based on verses by Rainer Maria Rilke and scored for narrator, tenor soloist, choir, and orchestra. The influence of Hindemith, one of Foss's teachers, may be detected in the work; but a gift for lyric melody (somewhat lacking in *The Prairie*) is equally evident.

Webern

Of Arnold Schoenberg's many pupils, none applied the twelve-tone system more consistently than the Viennese composer Anton von Webern (1883–1945). Among Webern's few choral works are one entitled *Das Augenlicht* (*The Light of the Eye,* 1935) and two called simply Cantata (No. 1, 1940; No. 2, 1943), all set to German texts by Hildegard Jone. The Cantata No. 2, requiring two soloists and a small orchestra (only one each of the usual woodwinds and brasses, a few percussion instruments, harp, and strings) in addition to a four-voice choir, may be singled out as most representative of Webern's mature style.

The Cantata is divided into six short movements, of which three require only one of the soloists; one is set for women's voices and soprano soloist, one for full choir with soprano, and only the last movement is for choir alone. As in the majority of Webern's other works, the melodic lines are extremely angular, with a constant use of octave displacement: a fragment such as B, B flat, and D sharp, say, will be set with the B flat an octave lower than its neighbors. Consequently, instead of intervals of a half-step and an augmented third appearing between the respective tones, intervals of a diminished octave and an augmented tenth are found. Canonic and less rigorous imitative writing are likewise characteristic of Webern's style, and are copiously employed in the three choral movements. Further, the orchestral accompaniment makes use of the thinnest of textures and suggests the pointillistic technique of Seurat and other late–nineteenth-century painters; a melodic line in the orchestra may be passed from one instrument to another, each instrument contributing a tone or two to the melody. And finally, the work is characterized by many changes of meter, with consecutive measures often designated 3/8, 2/8, 4/4, 2/2, 5/4, 4/8, and so on. The result is a highly expressive and unique style—unique at the time it was introduced. Since that time the Webern version of the twelve-tone style has influenced many other composers; and serial style, which evolved from the earlier technique, is still in frequent use.

Britten

Benjamin Britten is one of the many composers who has not adopted serial style, but has preferred to remain within the framework of the expanded tonal system. His cantata *St. Nicolas,* for tenor soloist, four-voice choir, and small orchestra including two pianos and organ, was composed in 1948 and eloquently reflects his conservative harmonic style. The cantata is set in nine movements, each movement after the Introduction being concerned with one episode in the Saint's life. The music is descriptive on occasion, notably in the fourth movement, which tells of a storm at sea on the Saint's journey to Palestine. Other passages are prayerful, melancholy, or jubilant in accord with the changing text. The choral writing enhances all these changes in exemplary fashion by its alternation of chordal, unison, and contrapuntal passages (see Example 73), and the coloristic variety provided by frequent passages for men's or women's voices alone. The solo passages include some in recitative, others in highly dramatic and expressively lyric style. And the orchestral accompaniment, often rhythmic in effect, is well designed to support and amplify the vocal parts.

EXAMPLE 73   Britten, *St. Nicolas*

Hun - ger holds   our   hor - ses' reins

Vaughan Williams

In 1953 Vaughan Williams composed *Hodie* (*This Day*), a Christmas cantata on a text derived from a variety of sources including portions of the Gospels of Matthew and Luke, a few phrases from the Office of Vespers, and verses by Milton and other poets. The cantata is set for three soloists, four-voice choir, and large orchestra; its scope and length (about forty minutes) bring it close to an oratorio in size. The work is divided into sixteen parts or movements, two of which are unaccompanied chorales. The diverse nature of the texts, some of which are openly sentimental and others deeply symbolic, is reflected in the variety of solo, choral, and instrumental writing. Yet unity of expression is assured by the solidity and clear expressiveness of the music.

Stravinsky

Having taken a negative view of twelve-tone writing after its introduction in the 1920s, Stravinsky eventually turned to its later version, serial composition, and modified it to meet his own expressive purposes. Several choral works illustrate Stravinsky's gradual absorption of serial writing into his music, among them a cantata on Medieval poems, set in English (1951–52); a *Canticum sacrum* (*Sacred Song*) in honor of St. Mark, set in Latin (1955); a large work entitled *Threni, id est Lamentationes Jeremiae prophetae* (*Dirges, that is, Lamentations of the Prophet Jeremiah*), set in Latin (1957–58); and another English cantata, *A Sermon, a Narrative, and a Prayer* (1961).

The second of those works, *Canticum sacrum*, about seventeen minutes in length, is set for tenor and baritone soloists, four-voice choir, and an orchestra consisting of the standard wind instruments, harp, organ, violas, and basses; violins and cellos are omitted (as were the violins and violas in the *Symphony of Psalms*), perhaps to provide a more austere tone color. After a brief Dedication, sung by choral tenors and basses on the text "To the city of Venice, in praise of its patron saint, the blessed Mark the Apostle," five movements follow. The last of the five is essentially a retrograde (backward) version of the first, the fourth bears a textural similarity to the second, and the middle movement is divided into three parts of which the first and third are similar in emotional content. Thus the work is highly symmetrical; Dika Newlin (in Jacobs, ed., *Choral Music*) calls attention to the five golden domes of St. Mark's Cathedral and the overall symmetry of that magnificent structure, and finds a parallel in the form of the *Canticum sacrum*.

Stravinsky's texts include verses from the Gospels, the Psalms, and other books of the Bible. The first movement begins: "Go ye into the world and preach"; the last movement: "And they went forth and preached"; the middle part is concerned with faith, hope, and charity—but presented in reverse order. It seems obvious that the beginning and ending texts suggested the retrograde form of the last movement. Serial writing appears to some extent in the outer movements, where it is combined with hints of polytonality. And serial style is basic to the three inner movements, where a twelve-tone row provides the chief melodic and harmonic material. The orchestral writing here begins to take on elements of Webern's pointillistic style, but always combined with Stravinsky's unique rhythmic thrust.

In the last of the works mentioned above, *A Sermon, a Narrative, and a Prayer*, serial writing dominates throughout. Set for alto and tenor soloists, speaker, four-voice choir (often in eight voices), and large orchestra, it is divided into three movements. The text of the *Sermon* consists of a few verses from St. Paul's Epistles to the Romans and the Hebrews; the *Narrative* deals with the story of the martyred Stephen, found in the Acts of the Apostles 6–7; and the *Prayer* is by Thomas Dekker, an Elizabethan poet. These diverse texts are unified by the elements of strong faith and reconciliation with God's will; thus this work is another in which Stravinsky's religious feeling is expressed.

The work is characterized by a great variety of textures, colors, sonorities, and meters; a few examples must suffice, for a complete account of the varied instrumental and vocal combinations would require almost a measure-by-measure description. In the *Sermon*, a short passage for choir in contrapuntal texture (see Example 74) gives way to a brief tenor solo followed by a spoken phrase for the choir, but the last two words of the phrase are sung; the accompaniments in these passages include one for trombones, another for horns, and a third for strings playing in tremolo fashion. The *Narrative* includes several passages for the Speaker, sometimes set as normal speech and at other times as a rhythmic incantation over instrumental accompaniment. Choral writing is largely contra-puntal, sometimes with the soloists joining in and sometimes without. This diverse array of vocal textures is supported by an incredible variety of rhythmic figures, angular melodic passages with frequent octave displacements, and instrumental sonorities, all based on forms of the tone row out of which all the harmonic and melodic materials of the work are constructed. The imaginative variety of tone colors is achieved by using virtually every possible instrumental combination except one: the full orchestra is never employed.

EXAMPLE 74   Stravinsky, *A Sermon, a Narrative, and a Prayer*

EXAMPLE 74   Stravinsky, *A Sermon, a Narrative, and a Prayer*

Barber

Written in a more conventional style, one of the choral works by the American Samuel Barber (b. 1910) may be mentioned. *Prayers of Kierkegaard* (1953–54), set for soprano soloist with brief passages for alto and tenor soloists ad libitum, mixed choir, and orchestra, is based on prayers in the writings of the nineteenth-century Danish philosopher Søren Kierkegaard. The four prayers are cast in four connected and contrasting sections, the first beginning with an extended passage for men's voices unaccompanied, in plainsong style, and continuing with a choral passage in mixed chordal and imitative style. The second section, following directly, is an expressive solo for soprano. In the third, for choir largely in chordal style, the choir is divided into halves that occasionally sing antiphonally. The fourth section is largely for orchestra alone, the choir entering in only the last 26 measures. The accompaniment is largely tonal and in traditional orchestral texture, but with its full share of expressive dissonance and forceful rhythms.

Other Forms

In addition to choral works that may be roughly grouped with the traditional forms, twentieth-century composers have written hundreds of works that cannot easily be classified. Some are settings of short poems, and might be called "choral songs." Others are settings of two or more texts selected to express a particular

Carl Orff, b. 1895.

emotion or to reflect a particular point of view; the term "occasional pieces" is appropriate. And a few large works, because of their diversity of content and novelty of form, resist any classification at all. In this section, we can select only a few representative compositions of these various types. It is unfortunate but inevitable that many other equally representative and notable works must remain unmentioned.

Milhaud

Darius Milhaud (b. 1892), one of the most prolific of contemporary composers, is French by birth and training, but spent many years as a teacher in the United States; his choral activity is reflected in about three dozen works in many forms. Early in his career, and as an expression of his opposition to the tenets of Impressionism, he adopted a style of writing in which two or more tonalities are present simultaneously. Pursuing this polytonal style rigorously and systematically, he developed a high degree of acrid dissonance. In later years Milhaud retreated somewhat from his inexorable polytonality and restored a measure of lyricism and consonant expression to his music.

As a representative of his early style we may mention *Les Choéphores* (roughly, *The Libation Bearers*), composed in 1916. It is the second of three works designed to provide incidental music for a French translation of the *Orestes* trilogy by Aeschylus, *Agamemnon* being the first and *Les Euménides* being the third. *Les Choéphores* is set for three soloists, mixed choir, and large orchestra, and is divided into seven movements. An avoidance of counterpoint characterizes the work; unisons and passages in octaves dominate the choral writing, and the rhythmic impetus is carried chiefly by the orchestra. But in the fourth and fifth movements, pure rhythm reigns supreme throughout all the forces, and pitch disappears completely. A soloist speaks her lines in rhythm, and the choir is limited to short phrases or individual sounds ("ah," "o," "ha," "sss,")—all of this to the sole accompaniment of percussion instruments. In the earlier and later movements, where pitch is employed, polytonality provides a high level of dissonance; there are frequent long passages in which the keys of E flat and A, or C and E, appear simultaneously; occasionally two keys a half-step apart (F and G flat, for example) are used together; and such stridently dissonant passages are contrasted with others in which a single tonality dominates but in which frequent modulations take place. The end result is a powerful, expressive, and demanding work, which is oddly well suited to its Classical dramatic text.

Vaughan Williams

The use of voices as pure color is seen in concentrated fashion in Vaughan Williams's suite *Flos campi* (*The Flower of the Field,* 1925), set for four-voice choir occasionally divided, solo viola, and small orchestra. In the score each of the six movements is prefaced by a verse or two from The Song of Solomon. The text, however, plays no part in the work, for the choir is confined to singing vowel sounds ("ah," "oh") and to humming; Vaughan Williams is precise in his directions to the choir: they are to perform "with closed lips," "with partly closed lips," and so on. The solo viola is given a large share of the thematic responsibility, but the choir—despite its accompanying role—enhances the orchestral sound with its own very special colors.

Hanson

As a representative of a school of conservative American composers who unashamedly espouse neo-Romantic expression, Howard Hanson (b. 1896) takes a prominent place. Long active as a teacher, administrator, and conductor, Hanson has contributed several choral works to the repertoire, of which his one-movement *Lament for Beowulf* is among the best known. Composed in 1925 to a portion of the Anglo-Saxon epic, the work is set for four-voice choir and orchestra. The choral parts are most often in chordal style in a variety of meters, occasionally alternating with imitative writing. In the orchestra, long-sustained harmonies are often used, animated by frequent vigorous rhythmic figures or supported by a recurring tone in the bass; in one passage a single low B flat is reiterated across 39 measures in slow tempo, while the harmonies above shift freely. In keeping with the sense of the text, a mood of somberness prevails.

Lambert

One work by the short-lived English composer Constant Lambert (1905–1951) may be mentioned for its effective use of jazz idioms and its general rhythmic appeal. *The Rio Grande*, a setting of a poem by Sacheverell Sitwell, was composed in 1929 for mixed choir with an incidental solo for alto, piano solo, and a small orchestra of brass, strings, and five percussion players for a battery of seventeen instruments. The piano part rises to virtuosic heights with several cadenzas, and the percussion instruments supply a great variety of rhythmic effects. The orchestra provides a colorful and animated accompaniment for the choir, which sings basically in chordal style with a number of syncopations and irregular rhythms. *The Rio Grande* is an enjoyable and brilliant work that deserves to be restored to the repertoire.

Thompson

Three contrasting works by Randall Thompson illustrate qualities of expressiveness, adherence to tonal writing, and mastery of vocal idioms similar to those in his *Mass of the Holy Spirit*. In addition, the earliest of the works, *Americana* (1932), reveals a sense of humor, an ingredient that is all too rare in choral music. *Americana*, a sequence of five choruses for mixed voices and piano, is based on items culled from the column of that name in *The American Mercury* magazine. An expression of fundamentalist religious sentiment, a prediction by a necromancer, a leaflet issued by a temperance organization, a story by a crime reporter (see Example 75), and an advertisement for a book of verses—such diverse items are set to music in a delightful way. Imitations of choral chanting, mock profundity, and parodied fugal writing are used to set the texts; the effect is thoroughly entertaining.

The second of the works, *The Peaceable Kingdom* (1936), on a text from the Book of Isaiah, is set for unaccompanied mixed choir in eight voices, and is divided into eight short choruses. The sometimes somber, sometimes jubilant text requires a corresponding variety of choral textures. These Thompson imaginatively provides with solid blocks of chordal writing, imitative and antiphonal sections, long chains of expressive melismas, and phrases set in choral recitative.

The third of the three works is *The Testament of Freedom* (1943), on texts selected from the writings of Thomas Jefferson. Set for four-voice choir of men's voices and accompanied by a standard orchestra, the work is divided into four movements. Chordal writing predominates here, along with several passages in unison or octaves for the voices alone; but one extended passage for the voices in the fourth movement is written in canon. Powerfully rhythmic and martial figures and a number of fanfarelike passages in the orchestra reflect the spirit of the times (the American Revolution and World War II) in which Jefferson and Thompson were writing. And the clear, forcefully harmonized accompaniment increases the vigor of the work. *The Testament of Freedom* deserves the favorable attention it has received ever since its first performance.

EXAMPLE 75   Thompson, *Americana*

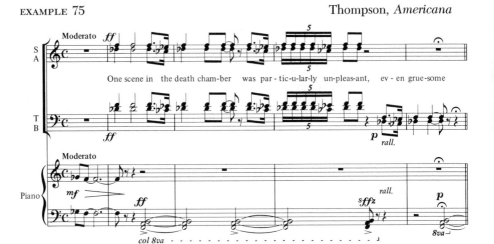

Dallapiccola

Offering a sharp contrast to the works of Thompson is *Canti di Prigionìa* (*Songs of Imprisonment*), composed by Luigi Dallapiccola (b. 1904), prominent Italian composer and pianist, in 1938–41. Born in a town near Trieste that was then part of the Austro-Hungarian Empire, Dallapiccola was influenced by German and Austrian musical developments early in his career and soon developed a marked affinity for the music of Schoenberg and his pupils, especially Webern. Thus one finds in his music the occasional use of the twelve-tone style—modified by his own temperament, however. The *Canti di Prigionìa* is set in three movements to words written by three eminent prisoners—Mary Stuart, Queen of Scots; Boethius, a fifth-century Roman philosopher; and Girolamo Savonarola, a fifteenth-century friar and reforming preacher in Florence—while awaiting execution in their respective prisons.

This 25-minute work is set for four-voice choir, two pianos, two harps, and about a dozen percussion instruments. In each of its three movements a fragment of the Gregorian chant associated with the Sequence *Dies irae* is introduced by the instruments; that phrase thus becomes a unifying theme for the entire work. The melodic material, both vocal and instrumental, is rich in chromaticism and occasionally suggests serial writing. But just as prominent are passages based on intervals of fourths and fifths, and others that are purely diatonic and set over rapidly moving harmonies. An even greater impact is made by the varied vocal colors and effects Dallapiccola has chosen to illustrate his poignant texts; choral chant, imitations of fauxbourdon, speaking, and humming are among the devices used. Above all is the emotional tension the work expresses. Including a range from whisperings of prayer to overwhelming cries of anguish, the *Canti di Prigionìa* is a masterful work.

Nono

Somewhat similar to the above work in emotional effect but widely different in style is *Il Canto sospeso* (*The Suspended Song*—with "suspended" having the grisly double meaning of "interrupted" and "hanging"), composed by the Italian Luigi Nono (b. 1924) about 1957. The work is set for three soloists, mixed choir, and large orchestra; its text is composed of excerpts from letters written by imprisoned participants in the Resistance movements of various countries—Bulgarians, Greeks, Poles, and Italians among them. This half-hour work is divided into nine movements, and is written in the serial style of Webern, but at times it goes even further in distributing a melody among several instruments or voices. Especially in the last movement, in which the choir is divided into ten parts, consecutive words and syllables of the text are set to single tones in different voices in a way that recalls the Medieval device of hocket (see Example 76).

EXAMPLE 76   Nono, *Il Canto sospeso*

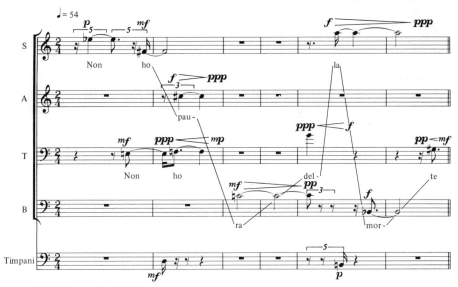

(Tr.: "I have no fear of death.")

Permission granted by Belwin-Mills Publishing Corp., agent for Ars Viva Verlag, B. Schott's Soehne of Mainz, Germany.

Throughout the work extreme angularity of melodic contour, caused often by octave displacement, is characteristic; intervals of minor ninths, major sevenths, and even augmented elevenths are found. Such intervals are often combined with extreme dynamic changes; for example, three consecutive eighth notes will be marked as follows: *f; ppp cresc f; f dim ppp.* The rhythmic complexity of the writing, finally, is equally extreme; it includes divisions of a beat into five or seven parts, with melodic fragments in the various voices entering on one or another of the subdivisions, and seldom the same subdivision in any two parts.

In this version of serial style a new choral idiom is at hand; its complete acceptance by all singers and listeners has not yet been determined.

Orchestral Works with Choir

Twentieth-century composers have had little interest in maintaining the century-old tradition of including a choir in an orchestral work, which Mahler brought to its expressive high point in his Eighth Symphony (1907). In their relatively few works of this type, the choir has most often been used merely to add another color to the orchestra. Claude Debussy in his *Trois Nocturnes* (1899) for orchestra was among the first to employ the choir for that purpose; the third Nocturne, entitled "Sirènes," includes a women's choir that hums and sings on open vowels to provide an eerie, quasi-wailing effect. Gustav Holst, in his massive orchestral suite *The Planets* (1916), made similar use of women's voices in the final section of the last movement, "Neptune." Only occasionally has a composer sought to give equal importance to the orchestral and choral forces; notable among such works are Vaughan Williams's *A Sea Symphony* (1905–10), and the *Folk-Song Symphony* (1939) by Roy Harris (b. 1898), in which traditional folk melodies make up the thematic material.

Special mention should be made of *Mass* by Leonard Bernstein (b. 1918), a work that combines the Latin Mass text with social commentary in English. Composed in 1971 for the opening of the Kennedy Center for the Performing Arts in Washington, D. C., the work includes soloists, choir, orchestra, onstage rock bands, a full company of dancers—and even the audience, which is invited to participate as a congregation in the traditional kiss of peace. Bernstein, eminent American composer, conductor, and pianist, identified *Mass* as "A Theater Piece for Singers, Players, and Dancers," but its central purpose is a reaffirmation of faith. One cannot easily classify this monumental work; it is neither operatic, choral, nor symphonic, but a masterful amalgamation of all three. Embracing a great variety of musical styles, filled with dramatic tension, containing both melodious and terrifying moments, it made an enormous impact on its listeners at the first performance. *Mass* is an "occasional work" in the best sense; written to dedicate a new concert hall and opera house, it fulfilled that purpose admirably.

Appendix 1

Glossary

This glossary includes terms that may be missing from a general musical vocabulary. As noted in the text, these terms are marked by asterisks when they are first used. A few other technical terms contained in this book have specific meanings in the field of musicology and can best be explained in their respective musical contexts; such terms are defined or exemplified at their first appearance in the foregoing chapters.

Cadence A formula consisting of a few tones (in a melodic context) or a few chords (in a harmonic context) at the end of a phrase, section, or movement that are designed to check the forward flow of the music. Cadences are analogous to punctuation marks in prose or poetry; hence they differ in their ability to impede or stop the progress of the music. Representative types are a full cadence (resembling a period or semicolon), half-cadence (comma), deceptive cadence (question mark), and so on. Through long periods of music history the full cadence—consisting of a series of chords on the fourth, fifth, and first degrees of the scale (indicated as "IV–V–I" or "subdominant–dominant–tonic")—has been the device used to bring a composition to a complete stop.

Canon A technique of composing in which one voice in a polyphonic texture is duplicated or imitated by the succeeding voices at a specified interval and a specified distance from the first voice. For example, each voice after the first may enter "at the interval of a fifth after two measures"—this being the "canon" or rule under which the piece is constructed. Canonic writing differs from imitative° writing in that it tends to be "strict" or exact and is carried out consistently through an extended passage. In formulating the self-imposed rules under which they construct canonic pieces, composers have been imaginative and resourceful. Sometimes the rule requires that every other voice be inverted (that is, with each interval set in the opposite direction—up or down—from the first voice), or be set in retrograde fashion (with the end of the melody set at the beginning), or be proportionately lengthened or shortened. Many other types of canons have been devised; in each case the "rule" is determined by the composer himself.

Chromatic, Chromaticism The terms refer to the use of tones not found in the major or minor scale (or the mode°) on which a section or an entire composition is based. In a piece based on the C major scale, for example, a tone such as F sharp, B flat, G sharp, or any other tone not integral to that scale, is an instance of chromatic usage. The ever-increasing use of chromaticism has marked music for many centuries; it reached a high point in Richard Wagner's music drama *Tristan und Isolde*. Chromaticism is basic to the twelve-tone music introduced by Arnold Schoenberg.

Circle-of-fifths An arrangement of the twelve major tonalities in a circle and in an order of ascending fifths (clockwise) or descending fifths (counterclockwise). Beginning with C at twelve o'clock, each tonality in a clockwise direction will be seen to contain one additional sharp in its signature; in a counterclockwise direction, one additional flat. Thus (clockwise), C, G, D, A, E, B, F sharp (enharmonically equivalent to G flat),

D flat, A flat, E flat, B flat, and F—with the return to C completing the circle. The same arrangement may be made to apply to minor scales, thus (clockwise), A minor, E minor, B minor, F-sharp minor, etc., and around to D minor.

Cross accent   An accent placed on a tone or chord that in its context would not carry one. For example, in a context of 4/4 meter, in which the first and third beats normally mark the primary and secondary accents, tones or chords on the second or fourth beats (or on subdivisions of any of the four) may be given accents for expressive reasons. A well-known example is seen in the Finale of Beethoven's Symphony No. 5, in the passage that marks the transition to the second theme; in that passage the accents are placed on the second and sixth eighth notes of each measure (that is, on subdivisions of the first and third beats).

Cross relation   A term denoting the use of two tones consecutively, one tone a component of the scale and the other an adjoining chromatic tone, but in different voices—for example, in a C major context, the use of an F in the alto, say, followed by an F sharp in the tenor. The term is most closely related to the modal system°; in that system a cross relation results from the simultaneous use of the normal form of the mode and the form as altered by *musica ficta.*° Since the late nineteenth century, with its ever-increasing use of chromaticism and the general weakening of tonality, the harmonic effect of a cross relation has been greatly minimized.

Imitation, imitative writing   A technique of composition based on the reappearance of a melodic phrase in a different voice or voices. In the subsequent appearance(s) the intervals, contour, and rhythmic shape of the original phrase may be imitated exactly or with slight modifications, on different pitch levels, and so on. Imitation when carried out rigorously and consistently may result in a canon°; when less consistently employed it serves to unify the section or composition in which it is used.

Linear   A term used to refer to the melodic or horizontal component of music, as opposed to the harmonic or vertical. It found widespread use in the early twentieth century, especially in connection with the contrapuntal style of Paul Hindemith, a style that was thought to emphasize the linear progression of its melodies at the expense of the harmonies that resulted from the melodic interaction; hence the term "linear counterpoint."

Mediant, mediant modulation   The term "mediant" refers to the third step of a scale or to the chord built on that step; and "mediant modulation," to a temporary shift from the central tonality of a piece to the tonality based on the mediant. Thus, in a C major context, a shift to E major or E minor would constitute a mediant modulation.

Melisma   A section of a vocal melody in which a single syllable of the text is carried by several tones; "melismatic style" is opposed to syllabic style, in which each text syllable is given its own tone.

Melodrama   A late–eighteenth-century style in which a spoken text was provided with a musical background. When applied consistently to an extended dramatic text, a form of presentation midway between a play and an opera resulted. In the nineteenth century the style was often applied to scenes within an opera (as in Beethoven's *Fidelio*), to entire poems (Richard Strauss's *Enoch Arden*), and so on.

Modal System   A system of tonal organization that dominated music (with many changes) from Classical Greek times through the sixteenth century and that still finds applications in music of the present day. The components of that system are the several modes, each of which consists of a scale fragment slightly more than an octave in extent and each having its individual arrangement of half- and whole-steps. The principal modes used in the Renaissance period may be reproduced on the piano by playing only the white keys: Dorian mode (beginning on D, with half-steps between 2–3 and 6–7), Phrygian (on E, half-steps between 1–2 and 5–6), Lydian (on F, half-steps between 4–5 and 7–8), and Mixolydian (on G, half-steps between 3–4 and 6–7). Two additional modes (Ionian on C, half-steps 3–4 and 7–8; and Aeolian on A, half-steps 2–3 and 5–6) were introduced later and were probably employed less often, but these two modes became the prototypes of present-day major and minor scales, respectively. And one remaining mode (Locrian on B, half-steps 1–2 and 4–5) represented little more than a theoretical possibility. Each mode existed in two forms: the "authentic form," as described here, and the "plagal form," beginning on the fifth step below and ascending to the fifth step above. To the second form of each mode the prefix *hypo* ("below") was applied—thus, Dorian and Hypodorian, Phrygian and Hypophrygian, Lydian and Hypolydian, and so on. It will be noted that each mode has a different arrangement of half- and whole-steps, and so each possesses a unique character and cadence-forming effect. The difference in sound between one mode and another is at least as great as the difference between a modern major and minor scale.

Modulation   The device of substituting one tonality or key center for another, on a temporary (transient) or relatively permanent basis, during the course of a composition.

Motive, motive manipulation   In a musical context, a motive is a short musical particle—melodic, harmonic, or rhythmic in character—that becomes a unifying element in a section or an entire composition. Ideally a motive has a distinctive shape (by way of interval, contour, or rhythmic pattern) that allows it to be immediately recognized on subsequent appearances. It may be abstracted from a longer theme, or may be one of several units out of which a theme is constructed. In either case, its "manipulation" is carried out by the use of repetition or reiteration, imitation, development (in which case new motives may result from the manipulation), and the like.

Musica ficta   The practice, primarily in the music of the Medieval and Renaissance periods, of altering a modal melodic contour in performance and contrary to the indicated notation; hence the affected tones were false (*musica falsa*) or fictitious (*musica ficta*). For example, in a melodic line consisting of A–B–A, under certain conditions a B flat would be performed in place of the B; or in a D–C–D fragment, a C sharp might replace the C. The practice represents a departure of performance practice from modal theory. And since in virtually every case the *musica ficta* brings the respective fragments closer to the sound of a major scale, its increasing use in time led to the decline of modal integrity; an approach to the tonal system of major and minor scales eventually resulted.

Psalm tone   A melodic formula several tones in length and consisting of an intonation, a reciting tone, and a cadence, employed in the chanting of plainsong psalms. Nine such formulas (one reflecting each of the eight church modes, the ninth a *tonus peregrinus* or "wandering tone") existed; in each case the melodic contours differed.

Rondeau   A term applied to a French poetic form current in the Medieval period, and later to the musical form in which the poem was set. The form consists of six or eight short lines, one or two of which were often repeated (by an audience) in the form of a refrain, with the others inserted or repeated between refrains. The diagram ABaAabAB (with the capital letters denoting the refrain) may be taken as representative.

Root position   The term refers to the position of a triad or chord when the tone on which the chord is constructed (the root) lies at the bottom of the chord. When the root is in any other position (for example, as the second, third, or fourth tone from the bottom), the chord is said to be "inverted."

SATB   Abbreviations that refer to the voices in a choir: soprano, alto, tenor, and bass, respectively. To this group the abbreviations M (mezzo-soprano) and Bar. (baritone) are sometimes added.

Sequence repetition   A practice in which a phrase or larger unit is repeated in sequential or systematic fashion; for example, each repetition may be a scale-step higher (or lower) than the previous one.

Sixth chord   A term that refers to a triad in the first inversion, with the root of the triad in the highest position—for example, the triad C-E-G written in the form E-G-C, in which case the interval between the outside tones is a sixth.

Tonal, tonal system   The system of tonal organization embracing the twelve major and twelve minor scales, together with the resulting keys or tonalities (G major, F minor, and the like), and the chords—tonic (I), subdominant (IV), and dominant (V)—that define those tonalities. The term is generally set opposite (often by implication) the modal° system.

Triad   The basic unit of harmony, in which chords are constructed by placing tones in vertical alignment, each tone at the interval of a third above the next lower one. A triad is a three-tone chord; a seventh chord consists of four tones (in which case the interval between the outside tones is a seventh), and so on.

Appendix 2a

The Ordinary of the Mass

Kyrie

Kyrie eleison, Christe eleison. Kyrie eleison.

Lord, have mercy upon us. Christ, have mercy upon us. Lord, have mercy upon us.

Gloria

Gloria in excelsis Deo. Et in terra pax hominibus bonae voluntatis. Laudamus te. Benedicimus te. Adoramus te. Glorificamus te. Gratias agimus tibi propter magnam gloriam tuam. Domine Deus, Rex coelestis, Deus Pater omnipotens. Domine Fili unigenite, Jesu Christe. Domine Deus, Agnus Dei, Filius Patris. Qui tollis peccata mundi, miserere nobis. Qui tollis peccata mundi, suscipe deprecationem nostram. Qui sedes ad dexteram Patris, miserere nobis. Quoniam tu solus sanctus. Tu solus Dominus. Tu solus Altissimus, Jesu Christe. Cum Sancto Spiritu, in gloria Dei Patris. Amen.

Glory be to God in the highest. And on earth peace to men of good will. We praise Thee. We bless Thee. We adore Thee. We glorify Thee. We give Thee thanks for Thy great glory. O Lord God, heavenly King, God the Father almighty. O Lord Jesus Christ, the only-begotten Son. Lord God, Lamb of God, Son of the Father. Who taketh away the sins of the world, have mercy upon us. Who taketh away the sins of the world, receive our prayer. Who sitteth at the right hand of the Father, have mercy upon us. For Thou alone art holy. Thou alone art Lord. Thou alone, O Jesus Christ, art most high. Together with the Holy Ghost, in the glory of God the Father. Amen.

Credo

Credo in unum Deum, Patrem omnipotentem, factorem coeli et terrae, visibilium omnium, et invisibilium. Et in unum Dominum Jesum Christum, Filium Dei unigenitum. Et ex Patre natum ante omnia saecula. Deum de Deo, lumen de lumine, Deum verum de Deo vero. Genitum, non factum, consubstantialem Patri: per quem omnia facta sunt. Qui propter nos homines, et propter nostram salutem descendit de coelis. Et incarnatus est de Spiritu Sancto ex Maria Virgine; et homo factus est. Crucifixus etiam pro nobis; sub Pontio Pilato passus, et sepultus est. Et resurrexit tertia die,

I believe in one God, the Father almighty, maker of heaven and earth, and of all things visible and invisible. And in one Lord Jesus Christ, the only-begotten Son of God. Born of the Father before all ages. God of God, light of light, true God of true God. Begotten, not made; of one substance with the Father: by whom all things were made. Who for us men, and for our salvation, came down from heaven. And was made flesh by the Holy Ghost of the Virgin Mary: and was made man. He was also crucified for us, suffered under Pontius Pilate, and was buried. And on the third day He rose

secundum Scripturas. Et ascendit in
coelum: sedet ad dexteram Patris. Et
iterum venturus est cum gloria, judicare
vivos et mortuos: cujus regni non erit
finis. Et in Spiritum Sanctum, Dominum
et vivificantem: qui ex Patre Filioque
procedit. Qui cum Patre et Filio simul
adoratur, et conglorificatur; qui locutus
est per prophetas. Et unam sanctam
catholicam et apostolicam Ecclesiam.
Confiteor unum baptisma in remissionem
peccatorum. Et expecto resurrectionem
mortuorum. Et vitam venturi saeculi.
Amen.

again, according to the Scriptures. And
ascended into heaven: He sitteth at the
right hand of the Father. And He shall
come again with glory to judge the living
and the dead; and of His Kingdom there
shall be no end. And in the Holy Ghost,
the Lord and Giver of life, who pro-
ceedeth from the Father and the Son.
Who together with the Father and the
Son is adored and glorified: who spoke
by the prophets. And in one holy, catholic and apostolic Church. I confess one
baptism for the remission of sins. And I
expect the resurrection of the dead. And
the life of the world to come. Amen.

Sanctus

Sanctus, Sanctus, Sanctus Dominus Deus
Sabaoth. Pleni sunt coeli et terra gloria
tua. Osanna in excelsis.

Holy, Holy, Holy Lord God of hosts.
Heaven and earth are filled with Thy
glory. Hosanna in the highest.

Benedictus

Benedictus qui venit in nomine Domini.
Osanna in excelsis.

Blessed is He that cometh in the name
of the Lord. Hosanna in the highest.

Agnus Dei

Agnus Dei, qui tollis peccata mundi,
miserere nobis. Agnus Dei, qui tollis
peccata mundi, miserere nobis. Agnus
Dei, qui tollis peccata mundi, dona nobis
pacem.

Lamb of God, who taketh away the sins
of the world, have mercy upon us. Lamb
of God, who taketh away the sins of the
world, have mercy upon us. Lamb of
God, who taketh away the sins of the
world, grant us peace.

Appendix 2b

Missa pro defunctis (Requiem Mass)

Introit

Requiem aeternam dona eis, Domine: et lux perpetua luceat eis. Te decet hymnus Deus in Sion, et tibi reddetur votum in Jerusalem: exaudi orationem meam: ad te omnis caro veniet. Requiem.

Eternal rest give unto them, O Lord: and let perpetual light shine upon them. A hymn, O God, becometh Thee in Sion; and a vow shall be paid to Thee in Jerusalem. O hear my prayer: all flesh shall come to Thee. Eternal rest.

Kyrie eleison

Kyrie eleison. Christe eleison. Kyrie eleison.

Lord, have mercy upon us. Christ, have mercy upon us. Lord, have mercy upon us.

Gradual

Requiem aeternam dona eis, Domine: et lux perpetua luceat eis. In memoria aeterna erit justus: ab auditione mala non timebit.

Eternal rest give to them, O Lord: and let perpetual light shine upon them. The just shall be in everlasting remembrance: he shall not fear the evil hearing.

Sequence

1. Dies irae, dies illa,
   Solvet saeclum in favilla:
   Teste David cum Sibylla.

   Day of wrath, O day of mourning,
   See fulfilled the prophets' warning;
   Heav'n and earth in ashes burning.

2. Quantus tremor est futurus,
   Quando judex est venturus,
   Cuncta stricte discussurus!

   Oh, what fear man's bosom rendeth
   When from heaven the Judge descendeth,
   On whose sentence all dependeth!

3. Tuba mirum spargens sonum
   Per sepulcra regionum,
   Coget omnes ante thronum.

   Wondrous sound the trumpet flingeth,
   Through earth's sepulchers it ringeth,
   All before the throne it bringeth.

4. Mors stupebit et natura,
   Cum resurget creatura,
   Judicanti responsura.

   Death is struck, and nature quaking,
   All creation is awaking,
   To its Judge an answer making.

5. Liber scriptus proferetur,
   In quo totum continetur,
   Unde mundus judicetur.

   Lo! the book exactly worded,
   Wherein all hath been recorded:
   Thence shall judgment be awarded.

6. Judex ergo cum sedebit,
   Quidquid latet apparebit:
   Nil inultum remanebit.

   When the Judge His seat attaineth,
   And each hidden deed arraigneth,
   Nothing unavenged remaineth.

7. Quid sum miser tunc dicturus?
   Quem patronum rogaturus,
   Cum vix justus sit securus?

   What shall I, frail man, be pleading?
   Who for me be interceding,
   When the just are mercy needing?

8. Rex tremendae majestatis,
   Qui salvandos salvas gratis,
   Salva me, fons pietatis.

   King of majesty tremendous,
   Who dost free salvation send us,
   Fount of pity, then befriend us!

9. Recordare, Jesu pie,
   Quod sum causa tuae viae:
   Ne me perdas illa die.

   Think, good Jesu, my salvation
   Caused Thy wondrous Incarnation.
   Leave me not to reprobation.

10. Quarens me, sedisti lassus:
    Redemisti crucem passus:
    Tantus labor non sit cassus.

    Faint and weary Thou hast sought me,
    On the cross of suffering bought me;
    Shall such grace be vainly brought me?

11. Juste judex ultionis,
    Donum fac remissionis,
    Ante diem rationis.

    Righteous Judge! for sin's pollution
    Grant Thy gift of absolution,
    Ere that day of retribution.

12. Ingemisco, tamquam reus:
    Culpa rubet vultus meus:
    Supplicanti parce, Deus.

    Guilty, now I pour my moaning,
    All my shame with anguish owning;
    Spare, O God, Thy supplicant groaning.

13. Qui Mariam absolvisti,
    Et latronem exaudisti,
    Mihi quoque spem dedisti.

    Thou the sinful woman savedst;
    Thou the dying thief forgavest;
    And to me a hope vouchsafest.

14. Preces meae non sunt dignae:
    Sed tu bonus fac benigne,
    Ne perenni cremer igne.

    Worthless are my prayers and sighing;
    Yet, good Lord, in grace complying,
    Rescue me from fires undying.

15. Inter oves locum praesta,
    Et ab haedis me sequestra,
    Statuens in parte dextra.

    With Thy favored sheep O place me,
    Nor among the goats abase me,
    But to Thy right hand upraise me.

16. Confutatis maledictis,
    Flammis acribus addictis,
    Voca me cum benedictis.

    While the wicked are confounded,
    Doomed to flames of woe unbounded,
    Call me with Thy saints surrounded.

17. Oro supplex et acclinis,
    Cor contritum quasi cinis:
    Gere curam mei finis.

    Low I kneel, with heart-submission,
    See, like ashes, my contrition;
    Help me in my last condition.

18. Lacrimosa dies illa,
    Qua resurget ex favilla

    Ah, that day of tears and mourning!
    From the dust of earth returning

19. Judicandus homo reus:
    Huic ergo parce Deus.

    Man from judgment must prepare him.
    Spare, O God, in mercy spare him!

20. Pie Jesu Domine, dona eis
    requiem. Amen.

    Lord, all pitying, Jesu blest, grant
    them Thine eternal rest. Amen.

Offertory

Domine Jesu Christe, Rex gloriae, libera
animas omnium fidelium defunctorum de

O Lord, Jesus Christ, King of Glory, deliver the souls of all the faithful departed

poenis inferni, et de profundo lacu: libera eas de ore leonis, ne absorbeat eas tartarus, ne cadant in obscurum: sed signifer sanctus Michael, repraesentet eas in lucem sanctam: Quam olim Abrahae promisisti, et semini ejus.

Hostias et preces tibi, Domine, laudis offerimus: tu suscipe pro animabus illis, quarum hodie memoriam facimus: fac eas, Domine, de morte transire ad vitam: Quam olim Abrahae promisisti, et semini ejus.

from the pains of hell and from the deep pit: deliver them from the lion's mouth, that hell may not swallow them up, and may they not fall into darkness; but may Thy holy standard-bearer, Michael, lead them into the holy light; which Thou didst promise to Abraham and to his seed.

We offer to Thee, O Lord, sacrifices and prayers: do Thou receive them in behalf of those souls whom we commemorate this day. Grant them, O Lord, to pass from death unto life; which Thou didst promise to Abraham and to his seed.

Sanctus

Sanctus, Sanctus, Sanctus Dominus Deus Sabaoth. Pleni sunt coeli et terra gloria tua. Osanna in excelsis.

Holy, Holy, Holy Lord God of Sabaoth. Heaven and earth are filled with Thy glory. Hosanna in the highest.

Benedictus

Benedictus qui venit in nomine Domini. Osanna in excelsis.

Blessed is He who cometh in the name of the Lord. Hosanna in the highest.

Agnus Dei

Agnus Dei, qui tollis peccata mundi, dona eis requiem. Agnus Dei, qui tollis peccata mundi, dona eis requiem. Agnus Dei, qui tollis peccata mundi, dona eis requiem aeternam.

Lamb of God, who takest away the sins of the world, grant them rest. Lamb of God, who takest away the sins of the world, grant them rest. Lamb of God, who takest away the sins of the world, grant them eternal rest.

Communion

Lux aeterna luceat eis, Domine: cum sanctis tuis in aeternum, quia pius es. Requiem aeternam dona eis, Domine, et lux perpetua luceat eis. Cum sanctis tuis in aeternum, quia pius es.

May light eternal shine on them, O Lord. With Thy saints forever, for Thou art merciful. Eternal rest give to them, O Lord: and let perpetual light shine upon them. With Thy saints forever, for Thou art merciful.

Responsory After Absolution

Libera me, Domine, de morte aeterna, in die illa tremenda: quando coeli movendi sunt et terra: Dum veneris judicare saeculum per ignem. Tremens factus sum ego, et timeo, dum discussio venerit, atque ventura ira. Quando coeli movendi sunt et terra.

Deliver me, O Lord, from eternal death in that awful day: when the heavens and the earth shall be moved: when Thou shalt come to judge the world by fire. Dread and trembling have laid hold on me, and I fear exceedingly because of the judgment and the wrath to come. When

Dies illa, dies irae, calamitatis et miseriae, dies magna et amara valde. Dum veneris judicare saeculum per ignem. Requiem aeternam dona eis Domine: et lux perpetua luceat eis. (The Responsory is then repeated up to "Tremens.")

the heavens and the earth shall be shaken.

O that day, that day of wrath, of sore distress and of all wretchedness, that great and exceeding bitter day. When Thou shalt come to judge the world by fire. Eternal rest grant to them, O Lord, and let perpetual light shine upon them. (The Responsory is then repeated up to "Dread.")

Appendix 2c

Te Deum

1. Te Deum laudamus: te Dominum confitemur.

We praise Thee, O God: we acknowledge Thee to be the Lord.

2. Te aeternum Patrem omnis terra veneratur.

All the earth doth worship Thee, the Father everlasting.

3. Tibi omnes Angeli, tibi Coeli et universae Potestates:

To Thee all Angels cry aloud, the Heavens, and all the Powers therein:

4. Tibi Cherubim et Seraphim incessabili voce proclamant:

To Thee Cherubim and Seraphim continually do cry:

5. Sanctus, Sanctus, Sanctus, Dominus Deus Sabaoth.

Holy, holy, holy, Lord God of Sabaoth.

6. Pleni sunt coeli et terra majestatis gloriae tuae.

Heaven and earth are full of the majesty of Thy glory.

7. Te gloriosus Apostolorum chorus:

The glorious company of the Apostles praise Thee:

8. Te Prophetarum laudabilis numerus:

The goodly fellowship of the Prophets praise Thee:

9. Te Martyrum candidatus laudat exercitus.

The noble army of Martyrs praise Thee.

10. Te per orbem terrarum sancta confitetur Ecclesia:

The holy Church throughout all the world doth acknowledge Thee:

11. Patrem immensae majestatis:

The Father, of an infinite majesty:

12. Venerandum tuum verum, et unicum Filium:

Thine honorable, true, and only Son:

13. Sanctum quoque Paraclitum Spiritum.

Also the Holy Ghost, the Comforter.

14. Tu Rex gloriae, Christe.

Thou art the King of Glory, O Christ.

15. Tu Patris sempiternus es Filius.

Thou art the everlasting Son of the Father.

16. Tu ad liberandum suscepturus hominem, non horruisti Virginis uterum.

When Thou tookest upon Thee to deliver man, Thou didst not abhor the womb of a Virgin.

17. Tu devicto mortis aculeo, aperuisti credentibus regna coelorum.

When Thou hadst overcome the sharpness of death, Thou didst open the kingdom of Heaven to all believers.

18. Tu ad dexteram Dei sedes, in gloria Patris.

Thou sittest at the right hand of God, in the glory of the Father.

19. Judex crederis esse venturus.

We believe that Thou shalt come to be our Judge.

20. Te ergo quaesumus, tuis famulis subveni, quos pretioso sanguine redemisti.

We therefore pray Thee, help Thy servants, whom Thou hast redeemed with Thy precious blood.

21. Aeterna fac cum Sanctis tuis in gloria numerari.

Make them to be numbered with Thy Saints in glory everlasting.

22. Salvum fac populum tuum Domine, et benedic haereditati tuae.

O Lord, save Thy people, and bless Thine heritage.

23. Et rege eos, et extolle illos usque in aeternum.

Govern them, and lift them up forever.

24. Per singulos dies, benedicimus te.

Day by day, we magnify Thee.

25. Et laudamus nomen tuum in saeculum, et in saeculum saeculi.

And we worship Thy name ever, world without end.

26. Dignare Domine die isto sine peccato nos custodire.

Vouchsafe, O Lord, to keep us this day without sin.

27. Miserere nostri Domine, miserere nostri.

O Lord, have mercy upon us, have mercy upon us.

28. Fiat misericordia tua Domine super nos, quemadmodum speravimus in te.

Let Thy mercy be upon us, as our trust is in Thee.

29. In te Domine speravi: non confundar in aeternum.

In Thee, O Lord, have I trusted: let me never be confounded.

Appendix 2d

Sequence: *Stabat Mater*

1. Stabat Mater dolorosa
   Juxta crucem lacrimosa
   Dum pendebat Filius.

   At the cross her station keeping
   Stood the mournful Mother weeping,
   Close to Jesus at the last.

2. Cujus animam gementem
   Contristatam et dolentem
   Pertransivit gladius.

   Through her heart, His sorrow sharing,
   All His bitter anguish bearing,
   Now at length the sword has passed.

3. O quam tristis et afflicta
   Fuit illa benedicta
   Mater Unigeniti.

   Oh, how sad and sore distressed
   Was that Mother, highly blest,
   Of the sole-begotten One.

4. Quae maerebat et dolebat,
   Pia Mater, dum videbat
   Nati poenas inclyti.

   Christ above in torment hangs;
   She beneath beholds the pangs
   Of her dying glorious Son.

5. Quis est homo qui non fleret,
   Matrem Christi si videret
   In tanto supplicio?

   Is there one who would not weep,
   Whelmed in miseries so deep,
   Christ's dear Mother to behold?

6. Quis non posset contristari,
   Christi Matrem contemplari
   Dolentem cum Filio?

   Can the human heart refrain
   From partaking in her pain,
   In that Mother's pain untold?

7. Pro preccatis suae gentis
   Vidit Jesum in tormentis,
   Et flagellis subditum.

   Bruis'd, derided, curs'd, defil'd,
   She beheld her tender Child:
   All with bloody scourges rent.

8. Vidit suum dulcem natum
   Moriendo desolatum,
   Dum emisit spiritum.

   For the sins of His own nation,
   Saw Him hang in desolation
   Till His spirit forth He sent.

9. Eia Mater, fons amoris,
   Me sentire vim doloris
   Fac, ut tecum lugeam.

   O thou Mother, fount of love!
   Touch my spirit from above;
   Make my heart with thine accord.

10. Fac ut ardeat cor meum,
    In amando Christum Deum,
    Ut sibi complaceam.

    Make me feel as thou hast felt,
    Make my soul to glow and melt
    With the love of Christ our Lord.

11. Sancta Mater, istud agas,
    Crucifixi fige plagas
    Cordi meo valide.

    Holy Mother, pierce me through,
    In my heart each wound renew
    Of my Saviour crucified.

12. Tui nati vulnerati,
    Tam dignati pro me pati,
    Poenas mecum divide.

    Let me share with thee His pain,
    Who for all my sins was slain,
    Who for me in torments died.

13. Fac me tecum pie flere,
    Crucifixo condolere,
    Donec ego vixero.

    Let me mingle tears with thee,
    Mourning Him who mourned for me,
    All the days that I may live.

14. Juxta crucem tecum stare,
    Et me tibi sociare
    In planctu desidero.

    By the cross with thee to stay,
    There with thee to weep and pray,
    Is all I ask of thee to give.

15. Virgo virginum praeclara,
    Mihi jam non sis amara:
    Fac me tecum plangere.

    Virgin of all virgins best,
    Listen to my fond request:
    Let me share thy grief divine.

16. Fac ut portem Christi mortem,
    Passionis fac consortem,
    Et plagas recolere.

    Let me, to my latest breath,
    In my body bear the death
    Of that dying Son of thine.

17. Fac me plagis vulnerari,
    Fac me cruce inebriari,
    Et cruore Filii.

    Wounded with his every wound,
    Steep my soul till it hath swoon'd
    In His very blood away.

18. Flammis ne urar succensus,
    Per te Virgo, sim defensus
    In die judicii.

    Be to me, O Virgin, nigh,
    Lest in flames I burn and die
    In His awful Judgment day.

19. Christe, cum sit hinc exire,
    De per Matrem me venire
    Ad palmam victoriae.

    Christ, when Thou shalt call me hence,
    Be Thy Mother my defense,
    Be Thy cross my victory.

20. Quando corpus morietur,
    Fac ut animae donetur
    Paradisi gloria.

    While my body here decays
    May my soul Thy goodness praise,
    Safe in Paradise with Thee.

    Amen. Alleluia.

    Amen. Alleluia.

Appendix 2e

Magnificat

1. Magnificat anima mea Dominum.

My soul magnifies the Lord.

2. Et exultavit spiritus meus in Deo salutari meo.

And my spirit rejoices in God my Savior.

3. Quia respexit humilitatem ancillae suae: ecce enim ex hoc beatam me dicent omnes generationes.

For he has regarded the low estate of his handmaiden: for behold, henceforth all generations will call me blessed.

4. Quia fecit mihi magna qui potens est: et sanctum nomen ejus.

For he who is mighty has done great things for me: and holy is his name.

5. Et misericordia ejus a progenie in progenies timentibus eum.

And his mercy is on those who fear him from generation to generation.

6. Fecit potentiam in brachio suo: dispersit superbos mente cordis sui.

He has shown strength with his arm, he has scattered the proud in the imagination of their hearts.

7. Desposuit potentes de sede, et exaltavit humiles.

He has put down the mighty from their thrones, and exalted those of low degree.

8. Esurientes implevit bonis: et divites dimisit inanes.

He has filled the hungry with good things, and the rich he has sent empty away.

9. Suscepit Israel puerum suum, recordatus misericordiae suae.

He has helped his servant Israel, in remembrance of his mercy.

10. Sicut locutus est ad patres nostros, Abraham et semini ejus in saecula.

As he spoke to our fathers, to Abraham, and to his posterity forever.

11. Gloria Patri, et Filio, et Spiritui Sancto.

Glory be to the Father, and to the Son, and to the Holy Spirit.

12. Sicut erat in principio, et nunc, et semper, et in saecula saeculorum, Amen.

As it was in the beginning is now and ever shall be; world without end, Amen.

(Luke 46–55)

A Selected Bibliography

This bibliography includes primarily books that have been referred to in the text, books that may lead the reader to a wider understanding of some of the points discussed, and the most important general reference works. The choral music scores mentioned or analyzed in the text can be found in the collected works of the respective composers, in the various sets of musical monuments, or in individual publications. In all three cases, the Heyer and Valentin items mentioned below will supply the necessary information about availability.

Adler, Guido, ed., *Handbuch der Musikgeschichte*, 2d ed., 2 vols., Keller, Berlin-Wilmersdorf, 1930.

Apel, Willi, *Gregorian Chant*, University of Indiana Press, Bloomington, 1958.

————, *Harvard Dictionary of Music*, 2d ed., Harvard University Press, Cambridge, 1969.

Austin, William, *Music in the Twentieth Century*, Norton, New York, 1966.

Baker's Biographical Dictionary of Musicians, 6th rev. ed. by Nicolas Slonimsky, G. Schirmer, New York, 1971.

Barzun, Jacques, *Berlioz and the Romantic Century*, 3d ed., 2 vols., Columbia University Press, New York, 1969.

Blume, Friedrich, *Geschichte der evangelischen Kirchenmusik*, Bärenreiter, Cassel, 1966.

Boetticher, Wolfgang, *Orlando di Lasso und seine Zeit*, 2 vols., Bärenreiter, Cassel, 1958.

Bücken, Ernst, ed., *Handbuch der Musikwissenschaft*, 13 vols., Athenaion, Potsdam, 1928–32.

Bukofzer, Manfred, *Music in the Baroque Era*, Norton, New York, 1947.

————, *Studies in Medieval and Renaissance Music*, Norton, New York, 1950.

Chase, Gilbert, *America's Music*, McGraw-Hill, New York, 1955.

Clapham, John, *Antonín Dvořák*, St. Martin's Press, New York, 1966.

Dean, Winton, *Handel's Dramatic Oratorios and Masques*, Oxford University Press, New York, 1959.

Deutsch, Otto E., and Donald R. Wakeling, eds., *Schubert Thematic Catalogue*, Norton, New York, 1951.

Einstein, Alfred, *The Italian Madrigal*, tr. by Alexander H. Krappe *et al.*, 3 vols., Princeton University Press, Princeton, N.J., 1949.

————, *Mozart: His Character, His Work*, tr. by Arthur Mendel and Nathan Broder, Oxford University Press, New York, 1945.

————, *Music in the Romantic Era*, Norton, New York, 1947.

Fellowes, Edmund H., *The English Madrigal Composers*, 2d rev. ed., Oxford University Press, New York, 1949.

Foss, Hubert, *Ralph Vaughan Williams: A Study*, Oxford University Press, London, 1950.

Geiringer, Karl, *Brahms: His Life and Works*, 2d rev. ed., Oxford University Press, New York, 1947.

————, *Haydn, A Creative Life in Music*, 2d rev. and enl. ed., University of California Press, Berkeley, 1968.

_____, *Johann Sebastian Bach*, Oxford University Press, New York, 1966.

Grout, Donald J., *A History of Western Music*, Norton, New York, 1960.

Grove's Dictionary of Music and Musicians, 5th ed. by Eric Blom, 9 vols., 1 suppl. vol., Macmillan, London; St. Martin's Press, New York, 1954, 1960.

Heyer, Anna H., *Historical Sets, Collected Editions, and Monuments of Music: A Guide to Their Contents*, 2d ed., American Library Association, Chicago, 1969.

Historical Anthology of Music, Archibald T. Davison and Willi Apel, eds., 2 vols., Harvard University Press, Cambridge, 1949, 1950. Abbr.: *HAM*.

Hörner, Hans, *G. P. Telemanns Passionsmusik*, Breitkopf & Härtel, Leipzig, 1933.

Jacobs, Arthur, ed., *Choral Music*, Pelican Books, Baltimore, 1963.

Jeppesen, Knud, *The Style of Palestrina and the Dissonance*, tr. by Margaret Hamerik, 2d rev. ed., Oxford University Press, London, 1946.

Journal, American Musicological Society, Boston, from 1948.

Kinsky, Georg, and Hans Halm, *Das Werk Beethovens: Verzeichnis seiner sämtlichen vollendeten Kompositionen*, Henle, Munich, 1955.

Koechel, Ludwig Ritter von, *Chronologisch-systematisches Verzeichnis sämtlicher Tonwerke Wolfgang Amade Mozarts*, 5th rev. ed. by Ernst Reichert, Breitkopf & Härtel, Wiesbaden, 1960.

Kretzschmar, Hermann, *Führer durch den Konzertsaal*, 2 vols., A. G. Liebeskind, Leipzig. Vol. I, "Kirchliche Werke," 5th ed., 1921; Vol. II, "Oratorien und weltliche Chorwerke," 5th ed., 1939.

Lang, Paul Henry, *George Frideric Handel*, Norton, New York, 1966.

_____, *Music in Western Civilization*, Norton, New York, 1941.

Lefebure, Dom Gaspar, ed., *St. Andrew Daily Missal*, Lohmann, St. Paul, Minn., 1945.

Leichtentritt, Hugo, *Geschichte der Motette*, reprint ed., G. Olms, Hildesheim, 1967.

Liber usualis, ed. by the Benedictines of Solesmes, Desclée, Tournai, 1950.

Moser, Hans Joachim, *Geschichte der deutschen Musik*, 5th ed., 3 vols., Cotta, Stuttgart, 1930.

_____, *Heinrich Schütz: His Life and Works*, tr. by Carl Pfatteicher, Concordia, St. Louis, Mo., 1959.

Music and Letters, London, from 1920.

Music Review, Cambridge, England, from 1940.

Musical Quarterly, The, G. Schirmer, New York, from 1945.

Musik in Geschichte und Gegenwart, Die, Friedrich Blume, ed., 14 vols., Bärenreiter, Cassel, 1949–68.

New Oxford History of Music, The, Egon Wellesz *et al.*, eds., 4 vols. to date, other vols. in preparation, Oxford University Press, London, 1957, 1968.

Parrish, Carl, ed., *A Treasury of Early Music*, Norton, New York, 1958. Abbr.: *TEM*.

_____, and John T. Ohl, eds., *Masterpieces of Music before 1750*, Norton, New York, 1951. Abbr.: *MM*.

Prentice-Hall History of Music Series, H. Wiley Hitchcock, ed., 9 vols., Prentice-Hall, Englewood Cliffs, N.J., 1965–67.

Reese, Gustave, *Music in the Renaissance*, rev. ed., Norton, New York, 1954.

_____, *Music of the Middle Ages*, Norton, New York, 1940.

Riemann, Hugo, *Musiklexikon*, 12th ed. by Willibald Gurlitt, 2 vols. biography, 1 vol. general reference, Schott, Mainz, 1959–67.

Schering, Hans, ed., *Geschichte der Musik in Beispielen*, Breitkopf & Härtel, Leipzig, 1931; reprinted, Broude Bros., New York, 1950.

_____, *Geschichte des Oratoriums*, Breitkopf & Härtel, Leipzig, 1911.

Schmieder, Wolfgang, ed., *Thematisch-systematisches Verzeichnis der musikalischen Werke von Johann Sebastian Bach*, Breitkopf & Härtel, Leipzig, 1950.

Slonimsky, Nicolas, *Music Since 1900*, 4th ed., Scribner's, New York, 1971.

Smallman, Basil, *The Background of Passion Music*, 2d ed., Dover, New York, 1970.

Spitta, Philip J., *J. S. Bach: His Work and Influence on the Music of Germany*, tr. by Clara Bell and J. A. Fuller-Maitland, 3 vols., Novello, London, 1899; reprinted, 2 vols., Dover, New York, 1951.

Strunk, Oliver, ed., *Source Readings in Music History*, Norton, New York, 1950.

Ulrich, Homer, *Music: A Design for Listening*, 3d ed., Harcourt Brace Jovanovich, New York, 1970.

——, and Paul A. Pisk, *A History of Music and Musical Style*, Harcourt Brace Jovanovich, New York, 1963.

Valentin, Erich, *Handbuch der Chormusik*, 2d ed., 2 vols., Gustav Bosse Verlag, Regensburg, 1968.

Wagner, Peter, *Geschichte der Messe*, 2 vols., reprint ed., G. Olms, Hildesheim, 1963.

Westrup, Jack A., and Frank L. Harrison, *The New College Encyclopedia of Music*, Norton, New York, 1960.

Young, Percy M., *The Choral Tradition*, Norton, New York, 1962.

Music Sources

The following list contains the principal sources of the choral compositions mentioned or discussed in this book and composed before about 1750. Abbreviations refer to the main collections in which the works are found, as follows:

CE   Collected editions, complete editions, *Gesamtausgaben*, etc., of the respective composer's works.

CMI   *I Classici della musica italiana* (Milan, 1918–21).

CW   *Das Chorwerk* (Friedrich Blume, ed., Wolfenbüttel and Zürich, from 1930).

DDT   *Denkmäler deutscher Tonkunst* (Leipzig, 1892–1931).

DP   *Documenta polyphoniae liturgicae sancte ecclesiae Romanae* (Rome, from 1947).

DTO   *Denkmäler der Tonkunst in Oesterreich* (Vienna, from 1894).

GMB   Arnold Schering, ed., *Geschichte der Musik in Beispielen* (Leipzig, 1931; reprint, New York, 1950).

HAM   Archibald T. Davison and Willi Apel, eds., *Historical Anthology of Music* (Cambridge, Mass., 1950).

MGB   Hugo Riemann, ed., *Musikgeschichte in Beispielen*, 4th ed. (Leipzig, 1929).

MM   Carl Parrish and John T. Ohl, eds., *Masterpieces of Music before 1750* (New York, 1951).

PAM   *Publicationen ältere Musik der deutschen Musikgesellschaft* (Wiesbaden, from 1926).

TCM   *Tudor Church Music* (London, 1923–29).

TEM   Carl Parrish, ed., *A Treasury of Early Music* (New York, 1958).

Adlgasser, Anton. SACRED MUSIC: DTO 80.

Arcadelt, Jacob. CHANSONS: Smith College Archives (Northampton, Mass.); MADRIGALS: CW 58.

Bach, Johann Sebastian. CANTATAS: CE 1, 2, 5, 7, 10, 12, 13, 16, 18, 20, 22–24, 26, 28–33, 35, 37, 41, 65 (Leipzig, 1851–1900; reprinted, Ann Arbor, 1947); MAGNIFICAT: CE 1; MASSES: CE 6, 8; MOTETS: CE 39; PASSIONS: CE 4, 12, 45; WEINACHTSORATO-RIUM: CE 5; MISCELLANEOUS: CE 11.

Beber, Ambrosius. PASSION: CW 66.

Benevoli, Orazio. MASS: DTO 20.

Biber, Heinrich. MASS: DTO 49; REQUIEM: DTO 59.

Binchois, Gilles. CHANSONS: MM, *Musikalische Denkmäler 2* (Mainz, from 1955); COM-PLETE WORKS: DP 5; SECULAR WORKS: CW 22.

Bourgeois, Loys. PSALMS: HAM, TEM, Sir Richard R. Terry, *Calvin's First Psalter* (London, 1932).

Buxtehude, Dietrich. CANTATAS: DDT 14; MOTETS AND OTHER WORKS: *Organum, series 1* (Leipzig, from 1924).

Byrd, William. ANTHEM: HAM; MASSES: TCM 2, 7, 9; MOTETS: MM, *Musical Antiquarian Society 6.* (London, c. 1840–48).

Caldara, Antonio. MADRIGAL: CW 25; MASS: DTO 26; ORATORIO: DTO 91.

Carissimi, Giacomo. ORATORIOS: CMI 5; WORKS: *Istituto italiano per la storia della musica* (Rome, from 1941); OTHERS: MM, TEM.

Cavalieri, Emilio del. LA RAPPRESENTAZIONE DI ANIMA E DI CORPO: CMI 10; FRAGMENT: TEM.

Charpentier, Marc-Antoine. SACRED WORKS: *Musique d'Église des XVIIe et XVIIIe siècles*, Series A of *Répertoire classique de musique réligieuse et spirituelle* (Paris, from 1913).

Clemens non Papa, Jacobus. MOTETS: CW 72; VOX IN RAMA: HAM; COMPLETE WORKS: *Corpus mensurabilis musicae 4* (Rome, from 1947).

Demantius, Christoph. PASSION: CW 27.

Dufay, Guillaume. KYRIE: MM; COMPLETE WORKS: *Corpus mensurabilis musicae 1–6* (Rome, from 1947); MISCELLANEOUS WORKS: CW 19.

Dumont, Henri. MOTETS: *Musique d'Église des XVIIe et XVIIIe siècles*, Series A of *Répertoire classique de musique réligieuse et spirituelle* (Paris, from 1913).

Dunstable, John. ISORHYTHMIC MOTET: TEM; COMPLETE WORKS: *Musica brittanica 8* (London, from 1951).

Eberlin, Johann Ernst. SACRED MUSIC: DTO 80.

Festa, Costanzo. MADRIGAL: HAM.

Fux, Johann Joseph. MASS: DTO 1.

Gabrieli, Andrea. MOTETS: CW 96, *L'Arte musicale in Italia 2, 3* (Rome, 1897–1908; reprinted, 1958); COMPLETE WORKS: American Institute of Musicology (Rome, from 1947).

Gabrieli, Giovanni. MOTETS: CW 10, 67; COMPLETE WORKS: *Corpus mensurabilis musicae 12* (Rome, from 1947).

Gastoldi, Giovanni. MADRIGAL: HAM, Hänssler Verlag (Stuttgart-Plieningen, n.d.).

Gesualdo, Carlo. MADRIGALS: HAM, MGB, MM, TEM, *Istituto italiano per la storia della musica, monumenti 1* (Rome, from 1941).

Gibbons, Orlando. MADRIGALS: *Musical Antiquarian Society 3* (London, c. 1840–48).

Gombert, Nicolas. CHANSON: HAM; COMPLETE WORKS: *Trésor musicale* (Brussels, 1865–93).

Goudimel, Claude. MASSES. *Monuments de la musique française au temps de la renaissance 9* (Paris, 1924–29); PSALMS: HAM, TEM, *Les Maîtres musiciens de la renaissance française 2, 4, 6* (Paris, 1894–1908).

Grandi, Alessandro. MOTETS: CW 40.

Graun, Karl Heinrich. ORATORIO: Peters Verlag (Frankfurt, 1931).

Handel, Georg Frideric. ANTHEMS: CE 34, 35 (Leipzig, 1858–94); ORATORIOS: CE (various); PASSIONS: CE (various); TE DEUMS: CE 25, 31, 37.

Hasse, Johann Adolph. MASSES, REQUIEM: DDT 29, 30; ORATORIO: DDT 20.

Hassler, Hans Leo. CHORALE CONCERTATO: TEM; MOTETS: DDT 2, HAM, MM, TEM; SACRI CONCENTUS: DDT 24/25; MISCELLANEOUS WORKS: DDT 7.

Isaac, Heinrich. CHORALIS CONSTANTINUS: DTO 10, 32.

Janequin, Clément. CHANSONS: CW 73, HAM.

Josquin des Prez. MOTET: MM; MISCELLANEOUS WORKS: CW 1, 3, 18, 20, 23, 33, 42, 57, 64.

Kerll, Johann Kaspar. MASSES: DTO 49; REQUIEM: DTO 59.

Krieger, Johann Philipp. CANTATAS: *Organum 1*.

Lalande, Michel-Richard de. MOTETS AND PSALMS: Huegel (Paris, 1950).

Landi, Stefano. ORATORIO: *L'Arte musicale in Italia 5* (Rome, reprint, c. 1958).

La Rue, Pierre de. MASS: DP 1b; MOTETS: CW 11, 91; REQUIEM: CW 11.

Lasso, Orlando di. CHANSONS: Möseler Verlag (Wolfenbüttel, 1905); PENITENTIAL PSALMS: Breitkopf & Härtel (Leipzig, 1905). MISCELLANEOUS WORKS: CW 13, 14, 34, 37, 41, 48.

Legrant, Guillaume. CREDO: HAM.

Lotti, Antonio. MASS, REQUIEM: DDT 60.

Lully, Jean-Baptiste. MOTETS, TE DEUM: CE (Paris, 1930–39).

Machaut, Guillaume. MASS, MOTETS: *Polyphonic Music of the Fourteenth Century* (Leo Schrade, ed., Monaco, from 1956).

Marenzio, Luca. MADRIGALS: GMB, HAM, MM, TEM, PAM 4i, 6.

Merulo, Claudio. MASS: HAM; MOTET: GMB.

Monte, Philippe de. MADRIGALS: DTO 41, CE 21 (Düsseldorf, 1927–39).

Monteverdi, Claudio. MADRIGALS, MAGNIFICAT, MASSES, VESPERS: CE (Asolo, 1926–42).

Morales, Cristóbal de. MASSES: *Hispaniae schola musica sacra 1* (Barcelona, 1894–98); MOTET: HAM.

Morley, Thomas. MADRIGALS: *The English Madrigalists* (London, from 1958).

Obrecht, Jacob. MASSES: CE (Amsterdam, 1908–21); MOTETS: CE, HAM.

Okeghem, Johannes. MASSES: CW 4, GMB, HAM, CE (Leipzig, from 1927).

Palestrina, Giovanni Pierluigi da. MADRIGALS: CE 2, 9, 22, 23 (Rome, from 1939); MAGNIFICATS: CE 16; MASSES: CE 1, 4, 6, 10, 15, 18, 19, 21; MOTETS: CE 3, 5, 7, 8, 11, 12; STABAT MATER: CE 20; TE DEUM: CE 14.

Purcell, Henry. ANTHEMS, MAGNIFICATS, ODES, TE DEUM: CE (London, from 1878).

Reutter, Johann Adam. MASSES: DTO 88.

Rore, Cipriano de. MADRIGALS: CW 5, HAM; Alfred Einstein, *The Italian Madrigal 3* (Princeton, 1949).

Rossi, Michel Angelo. ORATORIO: CMI 26.

Scandello, Antonio. PASSION: *Handbuch der deutschen evangelischen Kirchenmusik 1* (Göttingen, 1937); RESURRECTION HISTORY: Hanssler (Stuttgart, 1960).

Schein, Johann Hermann. MAGNIFICAT: CE 7 (Leipzig, 1901–23); MOTETS: CE 4, CW 12; CHORALE CONCERTATO: TEM.

Schmelzer, Johann Heinrich. MASS: DTO 49.

Schütz, Heinrich. AUFERSTEHUNGSHISTORIE: CE 1 (Leipzig, 1885–1927); CANTIONES SACRAE: CE 4; GEISTLICHE CHORMUSIK: CE 8; KLEINE GEISTLICHE KONZERTE: CE 6; PASSIONEN: CE 1; PSALMEN: CE 2, 3, 16; SIEBEN WORTE: CE 1; SYMPHONIAE SACRAE: CE 5, 7, 10, 11.

Sermisy, Claude. CHANSONS: *Les Maîtres musiciens de la renaissance française* (Paris, 1894–1908).

Steffani, Agostino. STABAT MATER: Möseler Verlag (Wolfenbüttel, 1956).

Strauss, Christoph. REQUIEM: DTO 59.

Tallis, Thomas. ANTHEM: TEM; MASSES, MOTETS: TCM 6; RESPONSORIUM: HAM.

Taverner, John. MASSES: TCM 1, 3.

Telemann, Georg Philipp. MOTETS: CW 104; PASSION: Barocco Verlag (Vaduz, Liechtenstein, 1964); WORKS: CE (Kassel, from 1950).

Tomkins, Thomas. ANTHEM: HAM; ANTHEMS AND SERVICES: TCM 7.

Tunder, Franz. CANTATAS: DDT 3.

Tye, Christopher. MASSES: *The Old English Edition 10* (London, 1889–1902; reprinted, 1965).

Vaet, Jacobus. MOTETS: CW 2.

Verdelot, Philippe. MADRIGALS: *Trésor musicale* (Brussels, 1865–93).

Viadana, Lodovico da. CENTO CONCERTI ECCLESIASTICI: M. Schneider, *Die Anfänge des Basso continuo* (Leipzig, 1918).

Victoria, Tomás Luis de. MASSES: CE, *Monumento de la musica española 25, 26* (Barcelona, from 1941); MOTETS: HAM.

Vitry, Philippe de. MOTETS: Leo Schrade, ed., *Polyphonic Music of the Fourteenth Century 3* (Monaco, from 1956).

Vivaldi, Antonio. ORATORIOS: CE (Milan, from 1947).

Walter, Johann. CHORALE: TEM; PASSION: O. Kade, *Die ältere Passionsmusik* (Güterloh, 1893); WITTEMBERGISCH GEISTLICH GESANGBUCH: *Publicationen ältere praktische und theoretische Musikwerke 7* (Leipzig, 1873–1905).

Weelkes, Thomas. ANTHEMS: *Musica Brittanica 23* (London, from 1951); MADRIGALS: *The English Madrigalists 9–13* (London, from 1958).

Wilbye, John. MADRIGALS: *The English Madrigalists 6, 7* (London, from 1958).

Willaert, Adrian. MOTETS: CW 59, HAM; COMPLETE WORKS: PAM 9.

Zachow, Friedrich Wilhelm. CANTATAS: DDT 21, 22.

Index

Page numbers in italics refer to musical examples.

Abendmusiken, 90
Abraham and Isaac (oratorio, Carissimi), 81
Acis and Galatea (oratorio, Handel), 113
Adlgasser, Anton, 118
Agostino, Paolo, 71–72
Aiblinger, Johann, 150
Alexander Balus (oratorio, Handel), 115
Alexander Nevsky (cantata, Prokofiev), 203
Allegro, L' (oratorio, Handel), 113
American music: Barber, 208; Foss, 203; Hanson, 210; Parker, 176; Persichetti, 193; Pinkham, 195; Romantic (late), 176
Americana (Thompson), 211, *212*
Anerio, Felice, 34–35, 70, 79
anthem: Baroque (late), 98–100; Byrd, 54–55, *54;* full, 52, 98; Gibbons, 55–56; Handel, 99–100, *100;* Purcell, 98–99, *98;* Tallis, 53–54; Tomkins, *55;* Tye, 38, 53; verse, 52, 98
antiphonal style, 2, 10, 45, 54, 67
Apostles, The (oratorio, Elgar), 176
Arcadelt, Jacob, 61
aria, 81, 101–02
arioso, 81
Ariosto, Lodovico, 62
Arise, O Lord (anthem, Byrd), 54
ars antiqua, 4
ars nova, 4; Machaut, 4–7, 9, 10
Ascension Oratorio (Bach), 113
Asola, Giovanni, 136
Athalia (oratorio, Handel), 114–15
Attaingnant, Pierre, 59
Audivi vocem (motet, Tallis), 47
Auferstehungs-Historie (Resurrection History, Schütz), 84, *84,* 85
Augenlicht, Das (cantata, Webern), 204
Austrian music. *See* German music
Ave Christe immolate (motet, Josquin), 27
Ave regina coelorum (motet, Grandi), 74
Ave verum corpus (motet, Mozart), 140–41
Avodath Hakodesh (Bloch), 193

Bach, Johann Sebastian, 51, 90, 117, 124, 176; chorale cantatas, 101–02, 112–13; Magnificat, 97; Masses, 103–07, *104, 106,* 165; motets, 91–93, *92;* Passions, 108–10, *111*

ballades, 9
ballata, 5, 15
balletti, 62, 64
Barber, Samuel, 208
Bardi, Giovanni, 67
Baroque music, early (1600–1675), 30, 51, 56, 66–87, 183; basso continuo, 67–68, 77; *bel canto,* 69, 81; Florentine Camerata, 67, 68; Gabrieli (G.), 46, 47, 67; Lully, 73, 77; madrigal, 86–87; Mass, 71–73; melody-bass polarity, 68; Monteverdi, 67, 69–71, 75, 76, 83, 86–87; motet, 73–77; opera, beginnings of, 68, 73; oratorio, 80–81; Passion, 81–83, 85–86; recitative style, 56, 68–69, 74, 81; "Resurrection History," 83–85; Schütz, 74–77, 84–86; sources, 66–67
Baroque music, late (1675–1750), 88–117, 134; anthem, 98–100; Bach, 90–93, 97, 101–10, 112–13; Buxtehude, 90; Carissimi, 110–11; Charpentier, 93, 110–11; chorale cantata, 100–02; Handel, 94–96, 99, 107–08, 113–16; Magnificat, 96–97; Mass, 102–07; motet, 88–93; oratorio, 110–16; Passion, 107–10; Purcell, 93–94, 96–99; Scarlatti, 112; Te Deum, 93–96; Telemann, 108; Vivaldi, 112
Bartók, Béla, 201–02
Bassani, Giovanni Battista, 132
basso continuo, 35, 67–68, 77, 118, 183; madrigal, 86–87
basso ostinato, 99, 100
Beatus vir (oratorio, Vivaldi), 112
Beber, Ambrosius, 82
Beethoven, Ludwig van, 118, 121, 147, 177; Masses, 122, 127–31, 145; oratorio, 139; *Symphony No. 9,* 142–44, *144,* 161, 181
Behold, O God (anthem, Byrd), 54
bel canto, 69, 81
Belshazzar (oratorio, Handel), 115
Belshazzar's Feast (oratorio, Walton), 197–98
Bembo, Pietro, 60
Benevoli, Orazio, 72
Berlioz, Hector: choral symphony, 161–63, 181; oratorio, 157–59, *159;* Requiem Mass, 151, 152–54, *154,* 170; Te Deum, 160–61
Bernstein, Leonard, 214

237